Transformative Learning and Teaching in Physical Education

Transformative Learning and Teaching in Physical Education explores how learning and teaching in physical education might be improved and how it might become a meaningful component of young people's lives. With its in-depth focus on physical education within contemporary schooling, the book presents a set of professional perspectives that are pivotal for realising high-quality learning and teaching for physical education.

With contributions from a range of international academics, chapters critically engage with vital issues within contemporary physical education. These include examples of complex learning principles in action, which are discussed as a method for bettering our understanding of various learning and teaching endeavours, and which often challenge hierarchical and behaviourist notions of learning that have long held a strong foothold in physical education. Authors also engage with social-ecological theories in order to help probe the complex circumstances and tensions that many teachers face in their everyday work environments, where they witness first-hand the contrast between discourses that espouse transformational change and the realities of their routine institutional arrangements.

This book enables readers to engage in a fuller way with transformative ideas and to consider their wider implications for contemporary physical education. Its set of professional perspectives will be of great interest to academics, policymakers, teacher educators and teachers in the fields of physical education, health and wellbeing. It will also be a useful resource for postgraduate students studying in these subject areas.

Malcolm Thorburn is a lecturer in Education and Physical Education at the Moray House School of Education, University of Edinburgh. He has taught extensively in secondary schools and occupied a number of curriculum development roles at local authority and national level. He has also published widely on aims and values, policy and professionalism and planning and practice issues in education and physical education.

Routledge Research in Education

Transformative Learning and Teaching in Physical Education

Edited by Malcolm Thorburn

Routledge
Taylor & Francis Group

LONDON AND NEW YORK

First published 2017
by Routledge
2 Park Square, Milton Park, Abingdon, Oxon OX14 4RN

and by Routledge
711 Third Avenue, New York, NY 10017

Routledge is an imprint of the Taylor & Francis Group, an informa business

2017 selection and editorial matter, Malcolm Thorburn; individual
chapters, the contributors

British Library Cataloguing-in-Publication Data
A catalogue record for this book is available from the British Library

Library of Congress Cataloging-in-Publication Data
A catalog record for this book has been requested

ISBN: 978-1-138-65018-3 (hbk)
ISBN: 978-1-315-62549-2 (ebk)

Typeset in Galliard
by Apex CoVantage, LLC

MIX
Paper from
responsible sources
FSC® C013056
www.fsc.org

Printed and bound in Great Britain by
TJ International Ltd, Padstow, Cornwall

Contents

Acknowledgements

Collectively, as authors we would like to thank a number of people for their help, encouragement and support during the preparation of this book; in particular the many learners and teachers in schools who have shaped and informed the development of our respective views and who have been so generous with their time. We are also extremely grateful to the educators, academics and policymakers how we shared dialogue with over many years and who have offered us constructive feedback on our various writings and presentations. Likewise, we wish as well to thank the student teachers at our respective universities with whom we have been able to discuss our various learning and teaching ideas over many years. Lastly, we would like to thank Thomas Storr and Heidi Lee from Routledge for their editorial assistance throughout.

Contributors

Editor and chapter author

Malcolm Thorburn is a lecturer in Education and Physical Education at the Moray House School of Education, University of Edinburgh. His main research interests are on professional change issues for teachers, especially in terms of conceptualising educational values, curriculum planning and enhancing pedagogical practices. He has published widely on aims and values, policy and professionalism and planning and practice issues in education and physical education. His publications cover a range of educational journals including as first author, recent articles in: *Journal of Curriculum Studies; Cambridge Journal of Education; Oxford Review of Education; Educational Review, Sport, Education and Society, Physical Education and Sport Pedagogy* and the *British Educational Research Journal*. He is the editor of *Wellbeing and Contemporary Schooling*. London: Routledge, 2017.

Chapter authors

Matthew Atencio has worked internationally as a lecturer and grant researcher at the University of Wollongong (Australia), University of Edinburgh (Scotland) and the National Institute of Education (Singapore). During his time in Scotland he worked on study aimed at improving Physical Education across the nation. Matthew was named the top early career education researcher in Scotland for his research. He is currently Assistant Professor in Sports and Physical Education at the California State University.

Nicola Carse is a lecturer in Primary Education at the University of Edinburgh whose main areas of research are currently in the areas of primary physical education and teacher education.

Shirley Gray is a lecturer in Physical Education at the Moray House School of Education, University of Edinburgh and is currently interested in: a critical analysis of the processes involved in the development of the physical education curriculum within the Curriculum for Excellence (Health and Wellbeing); self-determination theory, an investigation to understand pupil experience in physical education within the Health and Wellbeing curriculum; a longitudinal study investigating teachers' learning activities and learning as they engage with a new physical education curriculum; a comparative study investigating Canadian and Scottish student teachers' discourse concerning the curriculum, health and the body and an emotional intelligence study working with student teachers of physical education as they move through their four-year degree programme.

Andrew Horrell is a lecturer in Physical Education at the Moray House School of Education, University of Edinburgh whose current research interests include: physical education teachers' lives and careers; initial teacher education and curriculum policy, pedagogy and curriculum in physical education; aspects of teaching and learning, aesthetic perspectives through physical education; self-efficacy through physical education; using technology to support learning in physical education and teaching and learning approaches in gymnastics.

Mike Jess is a senior lecturer in Physical Education, co-deputy of the Institute and director of the Developmental Physical Education Group (DPEG) and Postgraduate Certificate in 3–14 Physical Education at the Moray House School of Education, University of Edinburgh. He is joint coordinator of the Scottish Primary Physical Education Project; a £5 million Scottish Government project that has been running since 2006. His academic and professional interests focus on how complexity thinking and ecological perspectives can inform future developments in curriculum, pedagogy and professional learning. He has written extensively on children's physical education, sport and physical activity.

Jeanne Keay has a background in teaching of physical education in schools and in Higher Education, in the areas of Education and Sport. She has held posts of Head of the Carnegie Centre for Physical Education at Leeds Metropolitan University as well as Head of Initial Teacher Training and Dean of Education at University of Roehampton. Jeanne is currently Vice-Principal and Pro Vice-Chancellor International at the University of the West of Scotland.

Paul McMillan is a senior teaching fellow at the Moray House School of Education, University of Edinburgh whose PhD research was a qualitative investigation of secondary physical education teachers' practice in Scotland. Guided by grounded theory and symbolic interactionism, the aim is to construct a theoretical framework to understand the key features of teachers' day-to-day practice. Investigating teachers' practice from a bottom-up perspective makes a contribution to knowledge in physical education by transcending some of the top-down and taken-for-granted ways teaching has been conceptualised in the physical education literature.

Justine MacLean is a lecturer in Physical Education at the Moray House School of Education, University of Edinburgh whose current research interests include the development of teacher confidence through identity, efficacy, esteem and agency; teacher engagement with and enactment of curriculum change; aesthetic experiences and engagement with physical education and teaching and sociocultural perspectives on physical education.

Fiona Mitchell is a Chancellor's Fellow at the University of Strathclyde. Her research interests are mainly focused on investigating behaviour change, particularly in hard-to-reach populations.

Kevin Morgan is a senior lecturer in Sport Pedagogy and Sport Coaching at the Cardiff Metropolitan University. Kevin is also Programme Director for the MSc in Sport Coaching and has published extensively on student learning and motivation in physical education and sports coaching contexts.

Rosemary Mulholland is a lecturer in Physical Education at the Moray House School of Education, University of Edinburgh whose main research interests are currently: teacher stress, wellbeing and coping; students teacher/NQTS stress, wellbeing and coping; curriculum change in physical education; teachers engagement with and enactment of curriculum change; professional learning partnerships associated with ITE; emotional intelligence, performance and wellbeing; aesthetic experience and engagement with physical education and teaching, the student teacher and aesthetic experience.

John Sproule is a professor of Physical Education at the Moray House School of Education, University of Edinburgh and was previously the Head of the Institute for Sport, Physical Education & Health Sciences. John's current research interests include a focus on: curriculum development; pedagogy; motivation in physical education and coach education – all areas in which he has published extensively.

Steven A. Stolz is a senior lecturer in Education at La Trobe University, Australia. Before becoming an academic, he taught for ten years as a secondary school teacher in the curriculum areas of mathematics, science, physical education, sport, and religious education. He is the past recipient of the Philosophy of Education Society of Australasia doctoral scholarship in 2011, and the Faculty of Education emerging researcher award in 2013. Currently, his primary areas of scholarship are educational philosophy and theory; however, due to his background in philosophy he also has a particular interest in the roots of MacIntyre's thought, application and future directions of his general project. He has published works in a diverse array of discipline areas across a range of international journals. His most recent book, *The Philosophy of Physical Education: A New Perspective*, was published by Routledge in 2014 and a forthcoming book that he is co-editing is titled, *Using Theory and Philosophy in Educational Research: Methodological Dialogues* (Routledge).

John Wang's areas of research include motivational and emotional aspects of physical activity and exercise. His recent publications have been on sport ability beliefs, achievement goals, intrinsic motivation, emotion, and self-esteem. He is an established researcher in the areas of achievement goal theory and self-determination theory. In addition, he has also written papers on outdoor education, project work and problem-based learning. John is currently a professor at the National Institute of Education, Singapore.

Ben Williamson is a lecturer on the Initial Teacher Education programme at the University of Stirling. Ben was previously a research fellow at the University of Exeter and a researcher at Futurelab, a non-profit educational organization, which explored the role of digital media and technology education.

Abbreviations

ACARA	Australian Curriculum, Assessment and Reporting Authority
AGT	Achievement Goal Theory
CLPL	Career-Long Professional Learning
CfE	Curriculum for Excellence
DPEG	Developmental Physical Education Group
GTCS	General Teaching Council of Scotland
HWB	health and wellbeing
LLPA	lifelong physical activity
MMA	mixed martial arts
MBP	models based practice
NAPLAN	National Assessment Programme – Literacy and Numeracy Programme
NCPE	National Curriculum of Physical Education
PISA	Programme for International Student Assessment
OECD	Organization for Economic Cooperation and Development
SSCP	School Sport Coordinator Programme
SDT	Self-Determination Theory
SRL	self-regulated learning
TARGET	Task, Authority, Recognition, Grouping, Evaluation and Time
TGFU	Teaching Games for Understanding
TPSR	Taking Personal and Social Responsibility
VCAA	Victorian Curriculum and Assessment Authority

Introduction

Rationale

This is a book about learning and teaching in physical education; how it might be improved; and the part physical education can play in being a meaningful component of young people's lives.

Through its in-depth focus on Physical Education in the context of contemporary schooling, the book invites interested academics, policymakers, teacher educators and teachers to critically engage with a set of professional perspectives that are pivotal for realising high quality learning and teaching and for achieving a vibrant future for physical education. Moreover, one of the many purposes of *Transformative Learning and Teaching in Physical Education* is to provide a resource for postgraduate students studying entire courses (or aspects) of Physical Education, School Sport and Health and Wellbeing. In addition, the book may have relevance for some students in the latter years of their undergraduate study, e.g. when working on chosen areas of investigation. As such, *Transformative Learning and Teaching in Physical Education* takes readers beyond an uncritical acceptance of bodies of knowledge and encourages critical reflection in ways that have the potential to challenge existing beliefs and attitudes as well as understandings.

We share Slavich and Zimbardo's (2012) view that transformational teaching contains many underlying characteristics that compliment approaches to learning such as active learning, collaborative learning, experiential learning and problem-based learning; all of which have evolved over the last 50 years. Therefore, we consider the term 'transformative' to be a useful summary term when reviewing the constructive benefits of critiquing physical education as a site for personal and social change. Thus, while there is need for a degree of measured caution when making claims for what physical education can realistically achieve, we do nevertheless write as authors who consider that an enhanced focus on critical pedagogy can lead to better quality learning experiences for learners and for physical education as a subject to become a more effective conduit for meeting (among other things) societal aspirations for increased physical activity and health awareness. This breadth of perspective is further enhanced by our focus on primary (3–11 years) and secondary school (12–18 years) sectors, and through recognising and understanding from the outset that teaching is a complex and demanding professional occupation, which benefits from teachers reviewing their practices and broader education mission throughout their careers.

In recognising that complexity principles, characterised by uncertainty and contradiction, have purchase in postmodern times, we use examples in various chapters of complex learning principles in action as a method for helping understand better various learning and teaching endeavours. These examples often challenge hierarchical and behaviourist notions of learning that have long had a strong foothold in the field of physical education. In this respect, many of the chapters in *Transformative Learning and Teaching in Physical Education* reflect Tinning's (2015, pp. 681–682) concern that the institutionalised expectations of there being a clear and relatively uncomplicated link between pedagogy and learning 'ignores the arguments of complexity thinking with its non-linear orientation to antecedents and events and its recognition that the pedagogical encounter . . . between task, teacher and learner is inherently complex and unpredictable'. As appropriate, various authors also engage with social–ecological theories in order to help probe more precisely the complex circumstances and tensions that many teachers face in their everyday work environments, where they witness first-hand the contrast between discourses that espouse transformational change and the realities of their routine institutional arrangements.

Collectively the approach taken forward in *Transformative Learning and Teaching in Physical Education* reflects the call from Evans and Davies (2011, p. 263) for greater transdisciplinary theorising that includes a focus on the 'complexity of embodied subjectivity . . . and communities we claim to serve'. Making progress on this basis involves a number of 'border crossings' (Evans & Davies, 2011, p. 263) that acknowledge and recognise that teachers' engagement with discourses in physical education need to be constructed with regard to societal expectations of physical education (societal perspective), the broader ethos and culture in schools (school perspective) and individual learners' interests (practice perspective). With this in mind, the chapter authors have set about analysing a diverse range of contemporary research in order to produce chapters that are highly valuable for a professional readership; framed as they often are by reviews of the links between academic theorising and school-based practice evidence. *Transformative Learning and Teaching in Physical Education* aims therefore to fulfil a key need in physical education through blending theory *and* practice and practice *with* theory.

Structure and context

The book is divided into four key transformative perspectives. These are

- a *societal perspective*, which engages with many of the main points of contestation surrounding physical education as part of contemporary schooling;
- a *theoretical perspective*, which presents a historical and contemporary-informed overview of the varied ways in which physical education can plausibly be conceptualised and supported;

- a *school perspective*, which helps identify and review many of the diverse ways in which physical education can be a key component in whole-school aims;
- a *practice perspective*, which critically analyses how teachers' pedagogical practices can enhance high quality learning in physical education.

Our perspectives-based approach enables readers to engage with the text in various ways: for example, through proceeding in a linear way from the general (societal) perspective to a review of learning and teaching (practice) considerations via a review of conceptual ways of analysing physical education (theoretical perspective) and through reviewing the constructive possibilities for physical education in realising whole-school aims (school perspective). However, if readers prefer they can begin with the practice perspective and proceed to the school, theoretical and societal perspectives in due course. Alternately the layout of the perspectives enables a more selective engagement with chapters that reflect particular areas of professional interest to take place. Across the chapters we draw on examples from the Anglophone world to support our findings; a process that is aided by the team of international academics who contribute to *Transformative Learning and Teaching in Physical Education*. In addition, in order to develop a depth of perspective on particular issues at particular times, we also use as appropriate the current Scottish context for exemplar purposes.

In each of the four perspectives, chapters use evidence-based research to critically analyse and discuss vital learning and teaching issues and points of contestation associated with present-day physical education. *Transformative Learning and Teaching in Physical Education* therefore seeks to connect with ongoing academic and professional debates about the nature and practice of physical education, and of how changes in practice might impact on future relationships between schools, unitary authorities and central government. It also engages with the extent to which teachers can be key drivers for increasing the quality of learners' learning experiences and expanding their accomplishments more widely. The combination of engaging teachers with a call to review and respond to a mix of external (beyond immediate subject boundaries) and internal (within the subject) challenges enhances the prospect of future learning and teaching practices benefitting physical education. The pursuit of these intentions is consistent with progressions in teacher agency – in short, from being an *effective* teacher through to being a *transformative* teacher (Sachs, 2003). On this basis, we urge educators to see it as part of their role and remit to question and critique practice and to further their professional learning through working in collaborative and collegiate ways with fellow professionals. This position supports the notion of teachers being enquiring professionals who engage in research into their practice and who critically review school statements, policy guidelines and societal aspirations in terms of their clarity and adequacy, in order to design the best programmes of physical education possible for the learners they teach. To help in this respect in two perspectives (theoretical and practice) chapters move from a broad focus (Chapters 3 and 8) to a more exemplar context (Chapters 4 and 9) in order to highlight in greater detail connections between theory and practice.

How the chapters are organised

Transformative Learning and Teaching in Physical Education aims to complement other texts in the broad area of physical education and to enable readers to broaden their practice through analysis, reflection and shared discussions in their professional communities. In providing an engagement point through four distinctive perspectives on physical education, *Transformative Learning and Teaching in Physical Education* is more than a toolkit-type book that advises teachers on what to teach and how to teach. Moreover, by incorporating and merging ideas from theory and practice, the book engages with a broad range of issues and concerns that are pertinent at various levels (societal, theoretical, school and practice) to the future of physical education, and that encourage professionals to critically explore the extended nature of their everyday professionalism. As the focus of each chapter is on research evidence and its relevance for *Transformational Learning and Teaching in Physical Education* each chapter will contain:

- *Abstract.* A short summary of the main arguments and findings of the chapter.
- *Introduction.* An outline of key arguments along with a summary of past recent developments.
- *Main findings.* A review of the main arguments that connect academic analysis with school-based practice.
- *Future directions.* Next steps where further research areas are needed to inform practice.
- *Summary of key findings.* Five bullet points that highlight essential points.
- *Reflective tasks.* Individual and group tasks that focus on essential issues.
- *Further readings.* Key suggested readings along with web links.
- *References.*

When descriptions are of school-based learning for learners between 3 and 18 years, we generally use the term 'physical education'. However, whenever discussion is on extended school-day sports-based participation or where physical education is being taught with particular regard for wider school objectives, we may make use of the terms such as 'school sport' and 'health and wellbeing' as appropriate. When discussing learning in schools, we usually use the term 'learners' rather than pupils or students.

The four perspectives unpacked

Societal perspective: The two chapters in this section critically engage with many of the main points of contestation surrounding physical education as part of contemporary schooling. Chapter 1 by Malcolm Thorburn focuses on 'Physical Education, economic liberalism and the free market' and analyses the changes in professionalism that might be ahead due to contrasting ideas on how the governance of physical education relates to the political economy of education. As such, arguments in these areas may shape future practice arrangements in areas such as: the outsourcing of teaching to private providers; access routes into teaching and the relationship between schools, universities and government at local and national level. It may also involve considering where physical education will be taking place, e.g. entirely in school contexts or in a mix of school and community settings. The chapter will also discuss the possibilities there are for emphasising the 'educational' in physical education and of labelling in neoliberal terms how school-based physical education should be considered as a 'premium product' that is worthy of investment and professional support during a period of sustained economic austerity.

In Chapter 2 Steven Stolz and Malcolm Thorburn consider 'Aims and values in physical education' and review specifically whether opposing traditions of physical education can ever be reconciled, and of whether in any event this would be helpful or not. Historically, physical education's concerns with aims and values have predominantly been an internal matter, of interest primarily to those teaching physical education. This has changed in recent decades; for not only have curriculum in schools expanded to include a full range of examination awards, but physical education has been markedly influenced by health, exercise science and sport-related perspectives as well as by a range of educational imperatives. This situation makes it unlikely that there will ever be a single agreed definition on what being physical educated means. With this in mind, the chapter focuses on analysing rival traditions, as this is pivotal for making sense of some of the contested claims for physical education and for developing a principled perspective on why it could reasonably be argued that physical education should continue to be a key component of learners' school education. The chapter concludes by offering an account of a prospective new tradition in physical education that might help advance such a claim.

Theoretical perspective: The two chapters in this section present an historical and contemporary-informed overview of the varied ways in which physical education can plausibly be conceptualised and supported. Chapter 3 by Mike Jess and Matthew Atencio considers how 'The transformational wind of theoretical change' might take place and begins by reviewing how physical educators have begun to question long-term connections with behaviourist practices, preferring instead to consider how postmodern thinking and constructivist learning perspectives could better inform physical education futures. On this basis, the knowledge and practices of physical education are not fixed entities; rather they are new approaches that can help learners negotiate the unpredictable and contradictory nature of their physical education-related learning experiences across their lifespan. Examples of such curriculum and pedagogy models in practice include: cooperative learning; outdoor and adventure activities; health-optimising physical education; Taking Personal and Social Responsibility and Physical Literacy. Collectively these various models present a more holistic vision of physical education possibilities, supported as they are by participative, interactive and authentic learning experiences. The chapter concludes by considering how two of these overarching curriculum frameworks, models-based practice and physical education as a connective specialism, may act as long-term catalysts to move the profession beyond using multi-activity approaches as the foundational basis for curriculum planning.

Following on from the breadth perspective adopted in Chapter 3, Chapter 4 by Mike Jess, Nicola Carse and Jeanne Keay references specifically primary school teachers' perspective on physical education through deploying an 'ecological framework and complexity principles as the basis for analysing teachers' professionalism'. The chapter proposes acknowledging the complex nature of the professional learning process due to the difficulties there are with low levels of teacher confidence and competence. As such, the chapter proposes that professional learning should seek to support teachers, individually and collectively, to develop the capacity to self-organise their practices in ways that can more effectively support learning. However, this approach to professional learning may well challenge many teachers as they need to move from using pre-prepared plans to using a more emerging pedagogy that focuses on the active role teachers play in creating and recreating learning experiences that support learners self-organising efforts over time.

School perspective: The three chapters in this section identify and review many of the diverse ways in which physical education can be a key component in realising whole-school aims. Chapter 5 by Mike Jess considers 'Starting young in physical education' and contemplates how learners' early movement experiences can integrate more coherently with other areas of the primary school curriculum. For this to happen it is suggested that much clearer connections with the educational agendas and practices that drive primary education are needed. Accordingly, the chapter discusses how primary teachers of physical education need to be supported in their attempts to develop more holistic and authentic learning experiences that act as a foundation for future learning. If successful, teachers will be able to create learning experiences that are developmentally appropriate, inclusive and connected with children's lives.

Chapter 6 by Justine MacLean further reviews the factors that enable teachers to initiate curriculum development and enact government-led policy in a way that schools are provided with greater autonomy, flexibility and responsibility and where 'Teachers are agents of policy and curriculum change'. The chapter begins by analysing the implications flexible policy frameworks can have on teachers' capacity to enact policy and enable learners to have educational experiences that reflect policy intentions. The chapter then connects more widely with international knowledge in the field of policy formation as a way of analysing teachers' capacity to embrace, translate and transform practice in physical education. Chapter 7 by Andrew Horrell and Rosie Mulholland analyses further 'The role professional learning communities play in school-based curriculum development'. It does this through exploring in detail how professional learning communities play an important role in building teachers' capacity for school-based curriculum development. The chapter reports on an interpretive study of nine schools where professional learning communities attempted to support teachers to reimagine and recast physical education. Analysis of data indicated that although government policy and curriculum frameworks produced organisational effects, these were subject to a complex process of reinterpretation when mapped onto local conditions.

Practice perspective: The four chapters in this section critically analyse how teachers' pedagogical practices can enhance learning in physical education. Chapter 8 by Shirley Gray, Fiona Mitchell and John Wang considers how to 'Create supportive learning environments' and begins by reviewing the strategies many governments have taken to promote physical education as part of health and wellbeing within the school and wider social context. In this light, health and wellbeing is considered as a broad and holistic way for incorporating physical health and wellbeing with mental, social and emotional health and wellbeing. The chapter then examines the ways in which a broader and more varied form of physical education might be enacted whereby learners' needs are firmly at the heart of the learning and teaching. Self-determination theory is presented as a useful framework to understand how this might be achieved; as this theory of personal growth and motivation highlights the relationship between the needs of learners and the ways in which the learning environment created by the teacher stimulates (or thwarts) learners' motivation, personal development and learning and wellbeing.

Chapter 9 by Shirley Gray, Kevin Morgan and John Sproule considers further how teachers' pedagogical practices might benefit learners 'Motivation, learning and development in physical education'. The chapter begins by framing teaching and learning in physical education as being complex, multifaceted and non-linear in nature as it requires a deep understanding of the factors that impact on learning and the pedagogical approaches that positively affect learning. The chapter then presents pedagogical ideas that have an holistic learning focus; encourage cognitive, social and affective development and support learners as they engage in personal mastery and self-regulated learning. The relationship between transformational teaching and physical activity levels are also reviewed.

Chapter 10 by Paul McMillan aims to 'Understand teachers' day-to-day practice' through reporting on an investigation of six secondary school teachers' practice and conceptions of pedagogy. Observational findings revealed variations in teachers' practice and semi-structured interviews showed that these variations were linked to three main areas: immediate and wider contextual influences; teacher–learner relationships and teachers' active negotiation of common and shared perspectives. Investigating teachers' practice in this way was found to transcend some of the top-down and taken-for-granted ways that teaching has been previously conceptualised in physical education. Chapter 11 by Ben Williamson considers 'The digitised future of physical education' as there is an increased expectation of increased use of technology in learning and teaching, especially as recent technological advancements in mobile technologies means that appliances and software can better benefit the subject. The chapter provides an analysis of the emergence of wearable and mobile activity trackers, biosensors and personal analytics apps in physical education, and argues that the algorithmic processes embedded in these devices and software has an increasingly powerful part to play in how people learn about their own bodies and health. These developments suggest the need for greater attention to how algorithmic systems can become embedded in emerging physical education technologies and pedagogical practices.

Taking all of the above into consideration, the final chapter (Chapter 12) by Steven Stolz considers 'Professional futures in physical education' and what the years ahead might hold for *Transformative Learning and Teaching in Physical Education*. The chapter reviews the challenges there might be for teachers to find spaces and opportunities to blend theory and practice and to experiment with pedagogical approaches that connect physical education with diverse school and societal goals. The chapter also casts a critical lens over how a career in physical education can continue to be considered as something that is a meaningful endeavour worthy of sustained commitment.

Summary

In conclusion, the book provides opportunities for readers to engage with:

- A research-informed focus on *Transformative Learning and Teaching in Physical Education*
- A *societal, theoretical, school and practice perspective* on learning and teaching that recognises that teaching is a complex and demanding professional occupation
- An activist view of teaching, where aiming to be a *transformative* teacher is seen as a key part of teacher agency
- A range of professional issues and concerns that are vital to engage with and critically explore if high quality *transformative learning and teaching* gains are to be realised.

References

Evans, J. & Davies, B. (2011). New directions, new questions? Social theory, education and embodiment, *Sport, Education and Society, 16*(3), 263–278.

Sachs, J. (2003). *The Activist Teaching Profession*. Buckingham: Open University Press.

Slavich, G.M. & Zimbardo, P.G. (2012). Transformational teaching: Theoretical underpinnings, basic principles and core methods, *Educational Psychology Review, 24*(4), 569–608.

Tinning, R. (2015). Commentary on research into learning in physical education: Towards a mature field of knowledge, *Sport, Education and Society, 20*(5), 676–690.

Part I
The societal perspective

1 Physical education, economic liberalism and the free market

Professional changes ahead?

Malcolm Thorburn

Introduction

As you read this chapter it may be that physical education is being taught in familiar ways that are a well-established part of public education. Classes will be grouped together in some way and the reassuring rhythm of lessons, intervals and bells will provide a comfortable backdrop against which time-honoured patterns of provision are rolled out. This familiar and traditional approach will bring order and stability to the lives of many learners and, of course, to the lives of many teachers as well (Thorburn, 2010). Such provision is likely to yield predictable if mixed results. Many learners will be thoroughly engaged in activity, grasp meaning from their movements and be buoyed by the well-run and sympathetically delivered programmes on offer. Other learners may find gains more modest; for some levels of enjoyment, motivation and learning may be conditional (e.g. activity and/or teacher dependent) while for others physical education may lack in meaning, choice and sociability (Tannehill, MacPhail, Walsh & Woods, 2015). However, as the chapter will highlight, these stable routines may be less enduring in the future than they have been in the past, as there is a 'growing tendency amongst governments world-wide to introduce forms of privatisation into public education and to move to privatise sections of public education' (Ball & Youdell, 2008, p. 9).

Neoliberal-based privatisation reforms are designed to achieve better outcomes and introduce greater choice in order to change traditional schooling. Thus, even though global concerns about obesity and physical inactivity have often seen a revival in the fortunes of physical education, these developments are taking place within a crowded and contested policy space where different public and private stakeholders are reviewing how various aims and performance targets can be achieved during a sustained period of economic austerity (Jess & Thorburn, 2016). These developments raise questions about the extent to which physical education can proactively engage with these priorities. For example, will neoliberal influences such as the outsourcing of teaching to private providers prove to be a help or a hindrance to the ways in which teachers negotiate curriculum spaces and organise their teaching? Gard (2015, p. 105) notes, that the tendency among most educationalists and physical educationalists to date has been one of a 'largely justified foreboding', based on the expectation that greater privatisation will lead to widening inequalities, with fewer opportunities being available to those from poorer backgrounds. Evans and Davies (2015a), for example, are concerned that pro-liberty arrangements may lead to a commodification of physical education, where 'buying' access to classes of choice becomes available for some, while others less fortunate make do with more modest provision. Under these arrangements, inequalities are accepted rather than challenged: physical education becomes an available choice (perhaps at a cost) rather than anything more akin to an educational entitlement. And, while Tozer (2012) provides an upbeat account of the joys and successes of teaching physical education and sport in independent (private) schools, other teachers may find certain aspects of neo-liberal education more perplexing.

Macdonald (2014, p. 496) rhetorically asks: 'If global neoliberalism is inevitable, is it a problem for Australian physical education? . . . [before equivocally answering] . . . "Yes", this is a problem as the ideology can . . . introduce curriculum solutions that are not suited to twenty-first century learners and learning . . . [and which] . . . limit universal access to physical education.' However, as Gard (2015, p. 115) notes, if we pre-judge this area 'then there really is no point spending time researching or discussing these phenomena'. Evidence of this happening is again provided by Macdonald (2014, p. 496), who, following on from citing the problems of economic liberalism, considers that to 'not engage with resources and services beyond the school, particularly given the richness of web-based resources and the personalised learning opportunities that they offer, is an anathema to education in the digital age'. This follows on from Macdonald's (2011) earlier view that in order to avoid de-professionalisation and to contribute more forthrightly to policy agendas, it would be prudent to engage with neo-liberal discourses. Given these varied and complex neoliberal influences that are orbiting around contemporary physical education, the chapter invites readers to critically reflect on how physical education might prosper as part of government ambitions for education, health and sport and/or as part of the increasing free market (neoliberal) arrangements that fund educational provision across much of the Anglophone (English-speaking) world. The chapter considers three theoretical sets of ideas for explaining the privatisation of education and educational futures prior to reviewing some of the main school-related, policy, partnership and professional challenges for physical education.

Main findings
Policy theorising

Endogenous and exogenous privatisation

In reviewing the privatisation of education, Ball and Youdell (2008) distinguish *endogenous* privatisation, which involves the importing of ideas and practices from the private sector and deploying these within the public sector in order to make efficiency gains, and *exogenous* privatisation, which involves the opening up of public education provision to private sector involvement on a profit-making basis. Very often endogenous privatisation provides the policy basis towards greater forms of exogenous privatisation; in effect, an eventual privatisation of education. Currently a myriad of endogenous and exogenous issues exist in physical education. These impact on student teachers' and teachers' professional identities and daily lives in terms of: the professional education of teachers (Pope, 2014); evaluating the worthiness of educational resources (Macdonald, 2015); reviewing the quality of pupils' learning experiences (Penney, Petrie & Fellows, 2015); reconsidering levels of teacher expertise (Powell, 2015); thinking through whether social inequalities are rising (Evans & Davies, 2015b); examining the role of policy entrepreneurs in shaping policy discussions (Thorburn, 2009) as well as analysing the country-specific contextual factors that influence the rise in outsourcing physical education to the private sector (Williams & Macdonald, 2015). More generically Gard (2015) considers that the part *choice* and *freedom* plays in new governance arrangements relative to the professional influences of *control, decision making* and *autonomy* is also a useful construct for reviewing privatisation influences. Collectively ,there is some urgency in reviewing these highlighted issues, for as Ball and Youdell (2008, p. 10) note, there is as yet 'no clear-cut research based evidence demonstrating the benefits of programmes of school choice [endogenous privatisation] or the contracting out of schools [exogenous privatisation] in terms of raising students' achievement.'

Reschooling and de-schooling

Key to considering how transformative futures for physical education might flourish is reviewing the extent to which reforms should take place as part of reschooling (i.e. where reform agendas confront the paradox that a better future is predicated on continuing with the public education arrangements that have largely prevailed in the past), or through de-schooling (i.e. where education takes place among a looser network of new learning communities), or through a mix of reschooling and de-schooling influences. Porter (1999) considers that market ideologies limit the capacity of schools to be independent and democratic and to fulfil the wider social and community functions that have typified their historical role. To remedy this, schools should be set broad objectives and thereafter have the freedom and decision-making autonomy to pursue them. Wrigley, Lingard and Thomson (2012) concur and argue that schools need to engage with new and wider educational networks in order to rebuild and sustain supportive systems of public education.

At face value, this is largely the situation that exists in Scotland, where physical education is thriving as part of enhanced government provision (reschooling), as physical education has succeeded in arguing for more curriculum time (i.e. two hours per week for all learners between 3 and 18 years) and an increase in teacher supply. These targets were based on arguing that it is vital to recognise physical education's contribution to a balanced education and for its potential for bringing about the cultural change of attitude towards healthy living that is required (Jess & Thorburn, 2016). The sense of renewal is reflected in teacher age demographics: the average physical education teacher is 36 years old compared to the all subject average of 42 years, with less than one-fifth of teachers (19.0%) over 50 years old (Scottish Government, 2014). However, as Kirk's (2010) futures thinking has highlighted, radical reform rather than more of the same is needed in order for physical education to thrive. Therefore, in Scotland, a dynamic future is likely to be dependent for the present on further changes *within* physical education, and through arguing that current levels of funding is money well spent. This analysis is consistent with Sinnema's (2016, p. 966) view that Scotland (unlike England and Australia) is one of the leading examples of where schools 'are asked to address the challenges inherent in designing and implementing a local curriculum in a manner that also ensures they give effect to a national curriculum'.

The three horizon framework

Leicester, Bloomer, Stewart and Ewing (2009) contrast how educational horizons that merely sustain, improve or adjust the present system differ from transformative innovations that signpost that something very different is taking place. The authors define three horizons. The first (H1) is based on improving matters from within present policy contexts. The second transition horizon (H2) happens when innovations are noted as working better than the original system. This is a confusing place, however, as there is a tension 'between the power of the first horizon and the attraction of the third' (Leicester et al., 2009, p. 28). Furthermore, it is difficult to introduce new ideas at the same time as familiar patterns of schooling are continuing, as teachers can be torn between trying to protect what they already have or invest in innovations that look set to replace it. The third horizon (H3) is the long-term successor to the first 'business as usual' horizon and advocates a completely new way of doing things. At any one time, all three horizons can be present and contesting their influence. For example, the first horizon's (H1) instinct for survival can lead to H2 innovations being mainstreamed 'in order to prolong the life of the existing system against the grain of the changing world' (Leicester et al., 2009, p. 12). The challenge if advocating visionary change is to introduce innovations that over time become coherent with H3 ideals. However, as Leicester et al. (2009) notes, the drive for system-wide improvement in schools has tended to coalesce around a global fixation with improving standards relative to international measures of educational attainment. Such standards-based reform opens up the possibility of neoliberal influences on education arguing for change (perhaps even radical change) but where the outcome is likely to be more of the same (H1) and *possibly* better (H2).

Physical education might need to be wary of this situation. For example, Kirk (2013) has recently advocated that a more fulsome engagement with sport education and physical literacy models may lead to a greater sense of purpose allied to better quality learning and teaching in physical education. However, the possibility exists, following Leicester et al. (2009) that the full six stages of H3 transition reform: compelling vision; encouragement for early adopters; realistic view of policy landscape; strategic exemplification and systems of support and evaluation are not fully engaged with. If this happens the future vision could become denuded and morph over time into something very similar to the ongoing reproduction of ineffective physical education-as-sport techniques programmes, which are cited as being a big part of the 'business as usual' malaise that is limiting the contribution of physical education programmes (Kirk, 2010). More broadly though in terms of health and physical education, McCuaig et al. (2016) considers that there *has* been a subtle erosion of shared social justice agendas in favour of an approach to participatory citizenship, which is founded on personal responsibility as the driver for improving society. Within this challenging context, McCuaig et al. (2016, p. 12) considers that teachers should be vigilant about the 'proliferation of market-based partnerships and the relations between the public and the private that are playing out in their schools and the discourses that are used to mobilise responsible citizenship'.

Physical education in the Anglophone world: A brief review of free market-related challenges

Types of schools and their implications for professionalism

As Evans and Davies (2015a) highlight, reviewing free market-related professional and practice challenges is complex, as circumstances vary *within* and *between* countries. This makes reviewing country-specific assessments of constraints and opportunities available worthwhile. In England increasing choice through expanding the number and range of school types is a key part of a neoliberal policy agenda for raising educational standards (Mortimore, 2013). Schools can differ according to: legal status; curriculum focus; pupil selection and types of academy. This diversification has been ongoing for 30 years and reflects a shared political consensus, as the earlier emphasis on comprehensive schooling and fairness has 'shifted to derisory depictions of bog-standard comprehensives as the economy faltered and policy makers' confidence in the capacity of any polity waned' (Courtney, 2015, p. 2). Effectively the proliferation of different types of secondary schools, e.g. academies, faith schools, has led to schools functioning as individual corporations rather than as part of a network of schools under local democratic (local authority) control (Evans & Davies, 2014). In 2016, the Conservative Government were so besotted with academy schools that they planned to go even further along the free market route by making *all* schools of academy status, before pressure from many quarters (including their own party members) led to cessation of this intention.

In this increasingly fragmented landscape, the ambitions of neoliberalism often need to co-exist alongside neoconservatism, which typically has a focus on the promotion of national interest and identity. Accordingly, schools need to balance being sufficiently distinctive in order to be successful in the market place (neoliberalism) but sufficiently similar to fulfil curriculum obligations considered valuable and that enable comparisons with other schools to take place (Courtney,

2015). Penney and Evans (1999) attest to the difficulties of achieving this balance. The authors found in England that there was a less than fulsome engagement with the progressivist possibilities that existed in new national curriculum arrangements. Instead, physical education was considered to have more to offer in terms of increasing the school profile through offering greater school sport opportunities, as this brought greater recognition to the school. On this basis, physical education and school sport could contribute to arguing that schools were both *similar* to other schools (neoconservative influences) but also *different and better* than these schools (neoliberalism influences).

While in England, 'comprehensive is the type [of school] that dare not speak its name' (Courtney, 2015, p. 16) in Scotland market models of education 'run against the grain . . . [as] . . . democratic values, comprehensive schools, equality of access and positive discrimination have long been distinguishing hallmarks of national and local authority policies' (MacBeath, 2013, p. 1014). There is very little school diversification in Scotland, e.g. according to legal status; curriculum focus or pupil selection, and the independent (private school) sector is also small (less than 5% of pupils). Therefore, the policy status quo (H1) is likely to remain, as the first 50 years of comprehensive schooling (1965–2015) has shown 'that the concept of comprehensive education, especially when linked to underlying values of liberty, equality and fraternity, is still a valuable concept for analysing, inspiring and guiding education systems and for exploring their possible future directions' (Murphy, Croxford, Howieson & Raffe, 2015a, p. 205). Collectively, the intention is that these three interlocking values of democracy (liberty, equality and fraternity) can complement each other as in comprehensive schools, 'the diversity of the community is more fully represented than in more homogenous schools where there is an element of selection by faith, ability to pay, or through some form of academic test' (Murphy et al., 2015b, p. 46). In terms of implications for professionalism in physical education the diverse and/or settled influences informing school provision in the United Kingdom highlight the need for teachers to understand their school in terms of to whom are they accountable and what are the values of the school they are teaching in (or aspire to teach in). For example, physical educators in Scotland should consider how their teaching dovetails with the underpinning values of comprehensive education? By contrast, teachers in England might be wise to understand and review the precise schooling status arrangements that apply in the schools they are teaching in.

For teachers teaching under diverse neoliberal arrangements the challenges are equally tricky to navigate. In Aotearoa New Zealand, Petrie, Penney and Fellows (2014) found, when analysing the impact of health and physical education arrangements on subject values, learning and teaching and structural considerations such as funding, working relationships and patterns of employment, that the market was saturated with open market providers. However, Petrie et al. (2014) also found continuing neoconservative influences at work as, even though over four-fifths of primary schools (86.3%) received privatised programme support, it was government providers (e.g. the Ministry for Health and Sport New Zealand) that provided just under three-fifths (57.3%) of the funding.

In addition, despite the breath of structural change evident, Petrie et al. (2014) found little evidence of curriculum change. More duplication and 'business as usual' rather than diversity was evident with new providers providing little specificity on how national curriculum learning outcomes were going to be realised. Furthermore, Pope (2014, p. 501) highlights that there was public support for business-as-usual education as prospective treasury-informed government plans to cut teacher numbers and increase class sizes were met with 'a massive disapprobation from multiple education bodies and a vehement outcry from parents'. This led to a reduction in intended plans, even though new charter schools, which would operate in similar ways to academy and free schools in England i.e. as independent state-funded schools with more freedom than local authority state schools over finance, the curriculum, and teachers' pay and conditions, remain.

In a further sign of complexity, Williams and Macdonald (2015) found when collecting data on the reasons why in Australia both primary and secondary schools used outsourcing arrangements, that teachers and school principals considered outsourcing to be of *educational* as well as *organisational* worth. This is despite (as with Petrie et al., 2014) weaknesses with the extent to which outsourced provision mapped onto curriculum outcomes. Moreover, Williams and Macdonald (2015) uncovered, as with Griggs (2010) in England, that expertise was most often considered to be in the hands of providers rather than school teachers, with this being particularly evident in the range of choices providers could offer. These difficulties are particularly acute in primary schools where an increase in private agencies delivering parts of physical education programmes is evident (see Chapter 3). Powell (2015) also noted, in an in-depth study of outsourcing in two Aotearoa New Zealand primary schools, that privatisation reinforced the notion of the teacher being inexpert and the providers being expert. This led to curriculum convergence and, as a consequence, physical education being framed as simply 'sport'. Williams and Macdonald (2015) also found that new neoliberal policies allowed schools to act as if they were businesses (endogenous influence) with private providers then assuming educational responsibilities in order to generate income and profit (exogenous influence). Questions about expertise and choice raise issues about teachers' future role with Macdonald (2011, p. 43) considering whether physical education teachers will 'become knowledge brokers, skilled at appraising resources, managing and interpreting data sets and monitoring the contribution of various PE suppliers and services' in years to come. On this basis, teachers in the future might need to review whether having an enhanced quality assurance type remit (and perhaps less of a subject teaching remit) articulates clearly with the 'making a difference' type reasoning that often underpins the professional identity of many physical education teachers (Flintoff, 2003). Furthermore, within the broad area of expertise and choice, Gard (2015, p. 119) finds it 'distressing' that many teachers appear to find it unproblematic to accept that they are less expert than new providers, even though there continues to be very little evidence that this is the case. This suggests that teacher confidence and resilience may not necessarily be thriving (as most reasonably minded people would wish) under outsourced arrangements.

Policy enactment and curriculum engagement

Gard (2015, p. 113) considers it 'axiomatic that the more resources and services parents and teachers have to choose from when constituting the HPE (health and physical education) experiences of students, the less relevant detailed and centrally developed curricular become'. This begs the question of whether national curriculum arrangements will be as influential in the future as they have in the recent past in terms of detailing subject aims and defining teachers' roles and responsibilities. If this is the case, new governance practices in education will need to be viewed afresh and not via a nostalgic approach that recalls times when teachers had a greater policy say in curriculum planning and pedagogical practices. Evans (2014, p. 548) considers this to be necessary and notes that 'it is beginning to seem rather quaint and just a little archaic' to even consider that other possibilities exist. Indeed, even in countries where the 'pulse of democracy' (Macdonald, 2014, p. 498) still thrives, such as Scotland, Gray, Mulholland and Maclean (2012) uncovered evidence of government control of the policy-making process. This was noticeable through the extent to which members of the national policy-making group (e.g. selected teachers and representatives from curriculum stakeholder groups) considered that their contribution was relatively modest in shaping the eventual national framework presented. These findings reflect Petrie et al. (2014) evidence that stakeholders in health and sport in Aotearoa New Zealand now shape the nature of learners' learning experiences to a much greater extent than previously. Thus, an ongoing challenge for physical education at the macro policy level is in communicating aims and purposes relative to the wider goals of education, health and sport. In these respects, the 'resigned passivity' Pope (2014, p. 509) notes, when it comes to contributing to and challenging reforms, is unhelpful. Furthermore, the diminished role of teacher education programmes and the closer link being established between learners' achievements and measures of teachers' performance are contributing towards teachers' loss of control and autonomy in their professional role at school level. Therefore, even though physical education remains as part of national curriculum arrangements, the increasingly decentralised professional development arrangements poorly supports teachers and leads to them lacking in expertise and the ability to make the most of the pedagogical opportunities that exist. Therefore, physical education in Aotearoa New Zealand runs the risks of mirroring Kirk's (2010) concerns re shallow learning and more of the same in physical education; albeit at a time where provision is provided by a mix of public *and* private providers, and where many of the private providers do not employ registered teachers.

School and community partnerships

In the United States of America, McCullick (2014) considers that there is a gap between the relatively high levels of public and wider political support for physical education and low levels of support at national, state and local government level. This comment broadly mirrors Ball and Youdell's (2008, p. 104) view that the United States tends 'to be staunchly anti-government and pro-liberty and . . . generally antagonistic towards public run services'. Furthermore, McCullick (2014) believes that the curriculum emphasis on high-stakes testing in a narrow range of academic subjects exacerbates the plight of physical education where the subject's marginal profile is reflected in weak policy guidance – especially in the way that multi-various terms, e.g. physical activity, physical training – are used relative to physical education. This can lead to problems in communicating what the benefits of being physically educated are and to parental confusion on the links between physical education, health improvement and academic success. Therefore, while most school communities think quite kindly of physical education, it is not to the point of investing in it sufficiently to make it pivotal to education and schooling. When it comes to addressing this challenge, McCullick (2014, p. 542) considers that physical education 'should unilaterally be promoting and doing what it is supposed to have been doing since it became a subject over a century ago' rather than chasing a clutch of wider educational goals, e.g. contributing to making learners smarter, raising test scores etc. Ennis (2006) largely concurs with McCullick's (2014) reasoning about the challenges physical education faces but is exhausted by the prospect of improving matters within existing school structures. Ennis (2006, p. 53) notes that:

> I have been hopeful over the last 25+ years that by developing quality programs taught by skilled physical educators, physical education might *earn* a place of value in school programs. But we have countless examples of excellent physical educators who run quality programs who must fight every day to retain control over facilities and instructional time and compete for miniscule amounts of resources. I don't believe the respect argument works very well in these contexts.

The detail of Ennis's (2006) proposal that physical education should consider moving out of school and take place in community centres, in order to create a highly needed service within a high-demand environment, is very brief, but the expectation is that children from poor or disadvantaged backgrounds would not be excluded. As many would probably share this ambition, a key question becomes one of how physical education might seek to work more productively across school and community settings in ways that help avoid undue fragmentation of purpose (McCuaig et al., 2016).

Since the new millennium many schools across the United Kingdom have been involved in School Sport Coordinator Programmes (SSCP), which aim to create more socially inclusive opportunities for young people to be physically active and involved in sport in their local environments (Flintoff, 2003). Typically, physical education teachers have been freed up from their normal teaching duties to cultivate better school–community partnerships and to organise and promote SSCP. From the outset certain issues adversely affected programmes, e.g. the annual monitoring and evaluation evidence collected was very basic and relied on uncorroborated participation figures (Coalter & Thorburn, 2003) with the lack of more probing contextualised questions on how to sustain improvements continuing to be a weakness of policy and practice (Smith & Leech, 2010). This is unfortunate, as for programmes to be socially inclusive, they are likely to require reflective review on the pedagogical strategies chosen for increasing participation (e.g. targeted planning) as well as examining the activities offered. Flintoff (2008) found, for example, that despite new participation opportunities being available there was still a reliance on male competitive activities and a rather simplistic 'open door' conception of how equity and opportunity were provided. This calls into question the coherence of pupils' physical education and wider school sport experiences in ways that reflect Pope's (2011) concern that teachers need to keep abreast of young peoples' sporting interests and present them with experiences that enable them to connect physical education with sport in ways that strengthen connections to the culture they live in. Failure to achieve such coherence could lead to physical education 'being pulled ever downward by greater education and political forces, creating a maelstrom and plunging towards eminent peril only to become a curriculum anomaly' (Pope, 2011, p. 282).

Most school and community partnerships programmes (whether stated explicitly or not) are underpinned by ideas on how sport-related participation in and beyond school can build social cohesion and increase human capital, e.g. helping people to become lifelong active citizens (Coalter, 2007). However, achieving such aspirations are not without their challenges; e.g. Flintoff (2003) found that school sport coordinators were reluctant to give up their physical education teaching role and Coalter and Thorburn (2003) noted that many young teachers were not particularly keen to become involved in the SSCP as they were unclear about how it would benefit their career plans and employment prospects. This is understandable, as the financing of many extended school day sport programmes has often been beset by relatively short-term funding cycles, which are prone to changing political influences. In this respect, it was encouraging that in 2010 the United Kingdom government performed a major U-turn by agreeing to continue funding for 450 school sport partnerships across England after previously pledging to scrap funding. The momentum for the U-turn was led by headteachers, Olympic sportspeople, young people and certain sections of the media. Nevertheless, evidence of political interventions continue to influence debates on the value of physical education and school sport for, as Thorburn (2014) notes, surrounding the competition, celebration and theatre of the London 2012 Olympic Games was associated discussion on how the games could provide lasting legacy benefits for the host nation. This led to the Prime Minister (David Cameron) venturing that certain types of activities, specifically Indian dance, were not substantive enough, relative to competitive team sports, to count towards achieving national curriculum activity time targets for active participation in secondary school age programmes. This intervention, along with Flintoff's (2008) findings that competitive sport continues to dominate many of the out-of-school hours learning opportunities available, emphasises some of the complex *within* and *beyond* challenges physical education continues to face. In addition, Phillpots and Grix (2014) highlight how the new horizontal rather than hierarchical governance arrangements that were expected to apply across school communities in the United Kingdom from 2002 onwards failed to materialise and have been replaced by more centralised decision making, tighter fiscal control and a policy emphasis that is biased towards competitive school sport.

Future directions

For physical education teachers approaching retirement age their initial school appointment may have become 'a job for life'. There have been, of course, economic upheavals along the way and physical education has been more or less in vogue at certain times but employment is likely to have been secure and stable. Now it seems quite certain that such settled arrangements are unlikely to continue and probably already sound anachronistic to many readers. In many respects, this transfer from 'the way it was' to 'the way it is' is well underway and reflects, in part, the effects of economic liberalism and the free market on physical education. Therefore, it might be that teachers in the future have a number of roles and remits, some in the public sector and some in the private sector, some on a longer-term basis, some dependent on new funding streams or payments by parents and some involving greater partnership working with staff from a range of health, sport and education backgrounds. All of this might be considered as part of the general paraphernalia of privatisation: it takes settled schooling arrangements, disrupts them, throws them up in the air and anticipates they will land in a better shape. Time will tell if this is the case or not.

However, as this chapter has highlighted, structural changes to types of school, while important as part of analysing the conditions necessary for education change (Wrigley et al., 2012), is only one part of the complexity surrounding neoliberalism, as the diversity in school types can often camouflage the continuing influence of the state, whose role is 'becoming more, not less powerful' (Courtney, 2015, p. 17). Thus, 'the ebbs and flows of macropolitical ideology' (Gard, 2015, p. 111), and the complex relationships between neoliberalism and neoconservatism, means that greater choice and freedom for pupils and parents need not necessarily be equated with loss of professional control and autonomy for teachers. Therefore, as well as grappling with the multiple odds and ends of neoliberalism, tomorrow's physical education teachers need to be on their game when reviewing their: subject values and professional identity; role in policy enactment; contribution to greater networking; building links with community partners and contribution to realising wider societal goals. The forthcoming chapters in *Transformative Learning and Teaching in Physical Education* largely focus on such matters: e.g. how can physical education be conceived of in ways that contain a clear educational rationale (Chapter 2); analysis of teachers' professionalism (Chapter 4); assisting teachers in their efforts as agents of policy and curriculum change (Chapter 6); supporting teachers in their professional communities (Chapter 7); and helping teachers to create and thrive in more supportive learning environments (Chapter 8).

Summary of key findings

- Neoliberalism is a complex set of practices that aims to promote market-led ideas in education allied to a diminishing role for the public sector
- Neoliberal free market imperatives for choice and freedom raise professional-related concerns about control and autonomy and social concerns about increasing inequalities
- Neoliberalism often co-exists alongside neoconservatism, which typically has a focus on the promotion of national interest and identity
- Neoconservative influences remain evident in many countries, e.g. in terms of funding physical education provision and in terms of curriculum and assessment regulation
- Physical education careers will be more complex to navigate than previously. Reviewing school aims and considering how your teaching contribution articulates with these aims and with the wider school ethos is likely to become increasingly important.

Reflective tasks

- Review to what extent you consider physical education could thrive under neoliberalism-informed schooling arrangements.
- Do any of the three theoretical sets of ideas used for explaining the privatisation of education and educational futures help explain your current teaching (or future teaching) context?
- Can physical education produce programmes that are valued *within* school (i.e. in the curriculum) as *beyond* school (i.e. in the market place)?
- Can neoliberalism and equality of pupil opportunity be achieved?
- Under neoliberalism, how can the de-professionalisation of physical education teachers be avoided?
- Under neoliberalism, what futures do you consider exist for physical education to constructively contribute to social inclusion and civic renewal?
- Can greater choice and freedom for pupils and parents exist alongside high levels of professional control and autonomy for physical education teachers?

Further readings

Ball, S. (2007). *Education Plc: Understanding Private Sector Participation in Public Sector Education*. New York: Routledge.
Rizvi, F. & Lingard, B. (2010). *Globalizing Education Policy*. London: Routledge.

References

Ball, S. & Youdell, D. (2008). *Hidden Privatisation in Public Education*. Brussels: Education International. Retrieved from www.ei-ie.org.
Coalter, F. (2007). Sports clubs, social capital and social regeneration: Ill-defined interventions with hard to follow outcomes?, *Sport in Society, 10*(4), 537–559.

Coalter, F. & Thorburn, M. (2003). *An Evaluation of the School Sport Co-Ordinator Programme in Scotland: A Research Study for Sport Scotland.* Edinburgh: Sport Scotland.

Courtney, S.J. (2015). Mapping school types in England, Oxford review of education. Retrieved from http://www.tandfonline.com/doi/full/10.1080/03054985.2015.1121141.

Ennis, C. (2006). Curriculum: Forming and reshaping the vision of physical education in a high need, low demand world of schools, *Quest, 58*(1), 41–59.

Evans, J. (2014). Neoliberalism and the future for a socio-educative physical education, *Physical Education and Sport Pedagogy, 19*(5), 545–558.

Evans, J. & Davies, B. (2015a). Physical education, privatisation and social justice, *Sport, Education and Society, 20*(1), 1–9.

Evans, J. & Davies, B. (2015b). Neoliberalism, privatisation and the future of physical education [Special issue], *Sport, Education and Society, 20*(1), 1–9.

Flintoff, A. (2003). The school sport co-ordinator programme: Changing the role of the physical education teacher?, *Sport, Education and Society, 8*(3), 231–250.

Flintoff, A. (2008). Targeting Mr average: Participation, gender equity and school sport partnerships, *Sport, Education and Society, 13*(4), 393–411.

Gard, M. (2015). They know they're getting the best knowledge possible: Locating the academic in changing knowledge economies, *Sport, Education and Society, 20*(1), 1–9.

Gray, S., Mulholland, R., & MacLean, J. (2012). The ebb and flow of curriculum construction in physical education: A Scottish narrative, *Curriculum Journal, 23*(1), 59–78.

Griggs, G. (2010). For sale – primary school physical education: £20 per hour or nearest offer?, *Education 3–13, 38*(1), 39–46.

Jess, M. & Thorburn, M. (2016). 'Physical education.' In: D. Wyse, L. Hayward & J. Pandya (Eds.) *The Sage Handbook of Curriculum, Pedagogy and Assessment* (pp. 441–455). London: Sage.

Kirk, D. (2010). *Physical Education Futures.* London: Routledge.

Kirk, D. (2013). Educational value and models-based practice in physical education, *Educational Philosophy and Theory, 45*(9), 973–986.

Leicester, G., Bloomer, K., Stewart, D., & Ewing, J. (2009). *Transformative Innovation in Education: A Playbook for Pragmatic Visionaries.* Axminster: Triachy Press.

MacBeath, J. (2013). 'Scenarios for the future of schooling and education.' In: T.G.K. Bryce, W.H. Humes, D. Gillies & A. Kennedy (Eds.) *Scottish Education* (pp. 1012–1022). Edinburgh: University of Edinburgh Press.

Macdonald, D. (2011). Like a fish in water: Physical education policy and practice in the era of neoliberal globalization, *Quest, 63*(1), 36–45.

Macdonald, D. (2014). Is global neo-liberalism shaping the future of physical education?, *Physical Education and Sport Pedagogy, 19*(5), 494–499.

Macdonald, D. (2015). Teacher-as-knowledge-broker in a futures-orientated health and physical education, *Sport, Education and Society, 20*(1), 27–41.

McCuaig, L., Enright, E., Rossi, A., Macdonald, D., & Hansen, S. (2016). An eroding social justice agenda: The case of physical education and health edu-business in schools, *Research Quarterly for Exercise and Sport.* Retrieved from http://dx.doi.org/10.1080/02701367.2016.1163978.

McCullick, B.A. (2014). From the cheap seats: One consideration of school-based PE's position in contemporary American schools, *Physical Education and Sport Pedagogy, 19*(5), 533–544.

Mortimore, P. (2013). *Education Under Siege: Why There Is a Better Alternative.* Bristol: Policy Press.

Murphy, D., Croxford, L., Howieson, C., & Raffe, D. (2015a). 'The values of comprehensive schooling.' In: D. Murphy, L. Croxford, C. Howieson & D. Raffe (Eds.) *Everyone's Future: Lessons from Fifty Years of Scottish Comprehensive Schooling* (pp. 39–51). London: Trentham.

Murphy, D., Croxford, L., Howieson, C., & Raffe, D. (2015b). 'What have we learned from the Scottish experience?' In: D. Murphy, L. Croxford, C. Howieson & D. Raffe (Eds.) *Everyone's Future: Lessons from Fifty Years of Scottish Comprehensive Schooling* (pp. 196–205). London: Trentham.

Penney, D. & Evans, J. (1999). *Politics, Policy and Practice in Physical Education.* London: E. & F.N. Spon.

Penney, D., Petrie, K., & Fellows, S. (2015). HPE in Aotearoa New Zealand: The reconfiguration of policy and pedagogic relations and privatisation of curriculum and pedagogy, *Sport, Education and Society, 20*(1), 42–56.

Petrie, K., Penney, D., & Fellows, S. (2014). Health and physical education in Aotearoa New Zealand: An open market and open doors?, *Asia-Pacific Journal of Health, Sport and Physical Education, 5*(1), 19–38.

Phillpots, L. & Grix, J. (2014). New governance and physical education and school sport policy: A case study of school to club links, *Physical Education and Sport Pedagogy, 19*(1), 76–96.

Pope, C.C. (2011). The physical education and sport interface: Models, maxims and maelstrom, *European Physical Education Review, 17*(3), 273–286.

Pope, C.C. (2014). The jagged edge and the changing shape of health and physical education in Aotearoa New Zealand, *Physical Education and Sport Pedagogy, 19*(5), 500–511.

Porter, J. (1999). *Reschooling and the Global Future: Politics, Economics and the English Experience.* London: Symposium Books.

Powell, D. (2015). Assembling the privatisation of physical education and the 'inexpert' teacher, *Sport, Education and Society, 20*(1), 73–88.

Scottish Government. (2014). Teacher census results. Retrieved from http://www. gov.scot/Topics/Statistics/Browse/School-Education/PubTeacherCensus.

Sinnema, C. (2016). 'The ebb and flow of curricular autonomy: Balance between local freedom and national prescription in curricular.' In: D. Wyse, L. Hayward & J. Pandya (Eds.) *The Sage Handbook of Curriculum, Pedagogy and Assessment* (pp. 965–983). London: Sage.

Smith, A. & Leech, R. (2010). Evidence: What evidence?: Evidence-based policy making and school sport partnerships in North West England, *International Journal of Sport Policy, 2*(3), 327–345.

Tannehill, D., MacPhail, A., Walsh, J., & Woods, C. (2015). What young people say about physical activity: The Children's Sport Participation and Physical Activity (CSPPA) study, *Sport, Education and Society, 20*(4), 442–462.

Thorburn, M. (2009). Physical education, the policy entrepreneur and comprehensive schooling: Can they exist in harmony?, *Forum, 51*(1), 101–105.

Thorburn, M. (2010). 'What future for physical education.' In: M. Thorburn & S. Gray (Eds.) *Physical Education: Picking Up the Baton: Policy & Practice in Education No. 27* (pp. 68–77). Edinburgh: Dunedin Academic Press.

Thorburn, M. (2014). Values, autonomy and well-being: Implications for learning and teaching in physical education, *Educational Studies, 40*(4), 396–406.

Tozer, M. (Ed.). (2012). *Physical Education and Sport in Independent Schools.* Wood-bridge: John Catt.

Williams, B.J. & Macdonald, D. (2015). Explaining outsourcing in health, sport and physical education, *Sport, Education and Society, 20*(1), 57–72.

Wrigley, T., Lingard, B., & Thomson, P. (2012). Pedagogies of transformation: Keeping hope alive in troubled times, *Critical Studies in Education, 53*(1), 95–108.

2 Aims and values in physical education

Can rival traditions of physical education ever be resolved?

Steven A. Stolz and Malcolm Thorburn

Introduction

From an historical point of view, the aims and values of physical education are constantly changing due to internal (*within the subject*) rivalry over traditions of physical education and external (*beyond the subject*) influences vying for hegemonic control (Stolz, 2014). Nowhere is this more evident than contemporary school curricula, which have been significantly influenced by health, exercise and sport science and sport-related professionals. Similarly, educationalists have also shaped the extent to which physical education can enter the educational mainstream through, for example, confirming (or otherwise) the legitimacy of high-stakes examination awards in physical education. In addition, there is (as noted in Chapter 1) an increase in the outsourcing of physical education. This aligns with stakeholders' neoliberal interest in increasing the privatisation and profit-making potential of education as well as policy entrepreneurs seeking to influence particular aims and values within physical education. Therefore, while it is never likely (or desirable) that there is a single agreed definition on the point and purpose of physical education (Stolz, 2014), it is important due to the shift in meanings that have occurred over the years that teachers, academics, policy-makers continually revisit these aims and values in order to seek coherence and clarity. With this in mind, the chapter focuses on analysing a mix of internal and external claims as a means to make sense of some of the contested claims of physical education and to highlight those aims and values (or traditions) that should be a key component of school education in the future.

Our position is underpinned by Dewey's (1916) seminal work, *Democracy and Education*, which highlights how discussions of educational values cannot occur without revisiting educational aims. Dewey (1916, p. 231) states that:

> The specific-values usually discussed in educational theories coincide with aims which are usually urged. They are such things as utility, culture, information, preparation for social efficiency, mental discipline or power, and so . . . discussion of values has usually been centered about a consideration of the various ends subserved by specific subjects of the curriculum. It has been a part of the attempt to justify those subjects by pointing out the significant contributions to life accruing from their study.

Following Dewey, this means that discussions concerning educational aims and values at some point leads to a scenario where physical education is compared and judged against other subjects in the curriculum or other subjects being compared with physical education. According to Dewey (1916) this is most likely to occur when the 'direct experience' of being a learner in the subject is lacking and questions arise surrounding its alleged 'value' in the curriculum.

To some it may seem like we are overstating the situation and engaged in academic discourse that is unnecessarily 'theoretical' regarding something that does not directly affect physical education 'practice'. However, we would argue that such a view has created a false distinction between 'theory' and 'practice' that confuses the nature of knowledge (Stolz, 2013a, 2014). Furthermore, such a view has missed the point that the aims and values of physical education are embodied in the learning activities or 'experiences' of learners in physical education and therefore should be the concern of those involved in the subject. For the sake of clarity, we use the term 'aims' to suggest a range of activities intentionally selected to bring about a predetermined end; whereas the term 'values' leads to something being viewed as 'good' or 'bad' according to a predetermined criteria of ends. Although each are interrelated in some way, particularly in an educational context, we should not lose sight of the fact that physical education is located in an historical tradition that is constantly changing due to ongoing debate about what physical education *is* or what we *want* it to be (Kirk, 2010; Stolz, 2014; Stolz & Kirk, 2015a, 2015b). The sheer diversity of traditions found in physical education makes our task of revisiting subject aims and values even more important, particularly when there are noticeable points of contestation and conflict between rival traditions. This may either lead a tradition to divide into two or more warring parties with its respective adherents transformed into critics of each other's position, or the tradition fails to survive and becomes extinct.[1]

Given the above, we will be concerned with the critical discussion of three issues in this chapter:

- We revisit the debate surrounding the aims and values of physical education and provide a brief critique of the axiological debate engaged in during the latter part of the twentieth century.
- We answer our self-imposed question: Can rival traditions of physical education ever be resolved?
- We argue that if progress is to be made in physical education that is *transformative*, then the subject needs to be synthesised into a new tradition based around embodied learning and physical culture.

Main findings
A critique of the axiological debate: The aims and values of physical education revisited

Part of the problem surrounding the aims and values of physical education concerns how we understand the logical connection between aims and values and how to judge the value of each aim. Therefore, when we use value claims, such as 'X is good', we are referring to something that is non-instrumentally good due to its intrinsic properties and the *telos* of the good may be worth obtaining in order to achieve this relationship. Often the adages used to explain intrinsic value usually takes the form of learning or doing something 'for its own sake', which is a non-derivative good. Conversely, extrinsic value focuses on the instrumental properties of the proposed derived good, e.g. exercising could be an external good as it might help you lose weight.[2] As such, the initial aim or intention becomes important in ascertaining whether the *telos* of the activity is good or bad. Here we start to see how the different senses of the term 'good' can quickly complicate our understanding of value because not all relationships between internal and external goods are neatly applicable in a straightforward fashion.

Although this account of the distinction between intrinsic and extrinsic value is not exhaustive, for the purposes of this section it highlights the logical connection between educational aims and the value we assign to them. For instance, if the aim of a middle-school teacher of a compulsory co-educational physical education class was to develop certain virtues of character, then most reasonable people would agree that using mixed martial arts (MMA) in full contact form as seen in Ultimate Fighting Championship and Bellator MMA as a means to achieve such ends would be morally questionable as there are more effective means to develop character that is non-violent, not to mention fundamentally misunderstands what it means to educate the virtues. This is an extreme example to make our point that the means used to achieve the desired educational aim may be ruled out as being educationally questionable within the context of formal schooling. Carr (1998) makes the pertinent point that we normally anticipate the positive benefits associated with the teaching of certain subjects and this is why we rule some things 'in' and 'out'. We agree with Carr (2003) in his discussion of *intrinsic* and *extrinsic* value of subject matter in education that there is a 'kernel of truth' in the alleged connection between *educational value* of a subject and conditions of *being educated*. Carr goes on to argue that this does not mean that this makes it a *necessary* or *sufficient condition* that educational value of a subject is valued for its own sake, as certain activities may have no educational significance or a subject can be valued without being valued for its own sake. Of course, it would be odd to value something that does not fit neatly with the purposes and goals of education, as this is what it means to be an educated person. However, schools do have a range of plural aims that are, strictly speaking, not educational. This raises a number of awkward questions surrounding the plurality of aims found in physical education and, as a result, more needs to be said about whether there is only one value assigned to each educational aim in physical education or a range of values. Certainly, Carr (1997), Laker (2000), Reid (1997), and Stolz (2014) have argued that there are a plurality of aims and values in physical education that require being able to make so-called 'choices',[3] but these choices are impossible to make if some of the aims and values are incompatible with each other.

A response to Peters' conceptual account of 'worth-while' activities in education

The catalyst for many discussions about aims and values in physical education in the latter part of the twentieth century can be largely attributed to the work of R. S. Peters (1966) conceptual account of education, particularly in relation to what Peters deemed to be 'worth-while' activities in the curriculum. Although, Peters (1966) in *Ethics and Education* does not specifically refer to the subject 'physical education', it can be inferred from his critique that activities of a practical nature are considered of limited cognitive value as the skills of practical activities are a matter of 'knack' (or 'knowing how' rather than 'knowing that') and hence not worthy of extended curriculum time. Furthermore, and every bit as damaging, Peters (1966, p. 159) considered that 'what there is to know [i.e. about practical activities] throws very little light on much else'.[4] This is precarious ground for physical education in that what is being contested is that the skills of physical education owe little to cognition and that participation in the activities that typically shape the curriculum are of little wider benefit within education. In response to this influential account of education, we start to see quite sophisticated accounts on how physical education programmes might be adapted to either meet the liberal education paradigm associated with Peters' account of education (e.g. Carr, 1997; McNamee, 2005); or to argue that the liberal education paradigm is partially or completely flawed, and at the same time provide an alternative conception of physical education (Reid, 1996a, 1996b, 1997; Stolz, 2013a, 2014). These later authors were, in effect, arguing that physical education's response to Peters' (1966) conceptual account of education was incompatible with the historical traditions of physical education and an emphasis on practical knowledge. It is also worth noting that Carr (1997) argues that Peters' liberal education paradigm makes the distinction between educational and non-educational activities in the wrong place and, as a result, confusion exists about the 'intrinsic' and 'extrinsic' value of subjects, the demarcation of knowledge into 'theory' and 'practice', and 'instrumental' and 'non-instrumental' accounts of education. We agree with Carr (1997) on this point and, as a result, we intend to revisit this debate in order to contextualise our discussion and provide conceptual clarity for what follows.

Four aims (physical (or psychomotor), cognitive, affective and socio-moral) of physical education discussed

Debates surrounding the aims and values of physical education are a perennial issue within the literature (see, e.g., McNamee, 2005; Laker, 2000; Reid, 1997; Whitehead, 2013). It is important to note that the debate is essentially axiological in nature, particularly surrounding the 'intrinsic' and 'extrinsic' notion of activities utilised in the name of physical education. Indeed, a precursory survey of associated literature and curricula documents across the Anglophone (English-speaking) world (e.g. Australian Curriculum, Assessment and Reporting Authority, 2012; Department of Education, 2013; Learning and Teaching

Scotland, 2009) highlights a preoccupation with four general aims. These are: the physical or psychomotor; the cognitive; the affective; and the socio-moral.[5] When it comes a range of plural aims such as these, there is often a perception that physical education can 'do it all', even though there is insufficient evidence to verify that physical education can do everything it claims (Laker, 2000). Part of the problem concerns the physical education discipline area and a profession that advocates promoting a broad range of plural aims with little prior thought given to systems of assessment and reporting on the predetermined ends of each aim. Compared to other subjects in the curriculum with well-established systems of assessment and reporting, such as mathematics, science, English and so on, it could be argued that physical education has much ground to 'make up' if it wishes to verify the claims it makes in relation to aims. Whether physical education can in fact 'do it all' therefore is an open question and worthy of further discussion and debate concerning the plural aims professed.

Unsurprisingly, the first aim (physical or psychomotor) has a long history in physical education with authors (e.g. Capel, 2000) outlining the nuances between sport and physical education, as well as a large body of literature to support game-centred teaching approaches to teaching in physical education (Stolz & Pill, 2014). Although there are quite distinct differences between sport and physical education, professional views in this area are relatively resistant to change, as evident by claims that physical education teachers have not changed the way that they teach (see, e.g., Kirk, 2010). It could be argued that physical education teachers are not concerned with these subtle nuances as their main focus is on the '*interpretative pragmatics*' of how to understand and interpret knowledge in their teaching practice (Stolz & Pill, 2016a, 2016b). This is why Kirk's (2010) argument that the dominant practice of physical education in schools – 'physical education-as-sport techniques' – has some traction due to the disproportionate amount of time and emphasis placed upon certain pedagogical approaches that are dedicated to skill acquisition and motor development of sport-specific skills in 'multi-activity' programmes. Whether the physical or psychomotor aim of physical education is educational in the strict sense is therefore an open question and worthy of further discussion and rigorous debate. The reason why this aim of physical education should be scrutinised on a regular basis is due to some of the questionable practices that take place in the name of this aim. For instance, the 'drill' method found in traditional instruction of physical education utilises repetition of practice in order for learners to gain familiarity and expertise of specific sports-specific motor skills. The problem is that this method misinterprets skill acquisition and motor development theory and isolates the learning of specific sports-related motor skills from its usage and, hence, decontextualises the skill and renders learning of little benefit to learners. Unfortunately, this continues to be practised in various guises and is a common occurrence in multi-activity programmes. It is important to point out at this juncture that the multi-activity programme simply does not allow enough time for learners to transition linearly from beginner to master in the acquisition of skill, and even if the multi-activity programme did not exist in schools, it is doubtful whether there is enough time in physical education programmes to master one skill to the level of expert, particularly when there are a range of other skills requiring attention. Furthermore, and maybe more importantly, it is questionable how the non-instrumental and/or instrumental claims of the physical or psychomotor can connect with transformative accounts of education that are possible. Additionally, whether anyone can function *without* this aim (most would agree that we cannot function in contemporary society without numeracy and literacy) is open to doubt. If the skill learned was of instrumental benefit, say for vocational purposes, then maybe; but physical education mostly exists within the confines of the school. Likewise, only a small percentage of the population becomes professional sportsmen and sportswomen and even then careers are relatively short and the sports-specific motor skills learned are largely developed outside of physical education. So the idea that this aim can fulfil an instrumental role in the form of developing vocational skills is tenuous at best. It is possible, however, to have an *educational appreciation* of an activity if it is related to meaningful engagement with those parts of our cultural heritage that are valued, particularly in relation to understanding who we are or might aspire to be.

For the second aim (cognitive), much work has been undertaken to find practical ways to connect the learning activities that are unique to physical education with traditional methods of measuring and assessing knowledge (e.g. high-stakes examination awards) in order to justify physical education's place in the curriculum as an academic study. Thorburn and Collins (2003, 2006a, 2006b) researched teachers' curriculum and pedagogical decision-making, the quality of learners' learning experiences and the effectiveness of contrasting assessment instruments and found that it proved very difficult for many teachers to make learning and assessment gains through the practical experiential learning approaches expected. Accordingly, the 'academicisation' of physical education has quite rightly been criticised for reinforcing mind/body dualisms whereby the practice of physical education through practical learning, which takes place in games hall, gymnasium and the like, are separated out from the academic learning that takes place in classrooms. Not only is this problematic because it creates a false dualism, it neglects the importance of engaging in professional enquiry about how learner-centred experiential-based narratives can be generated from practical experiences and integrated with associated knowledge of skill, fitness and sport-orientated decision-making strategies. As Thorburn (2007, p. 179) has highlighted, in many high-stakes examination awards, 'physical education is being studied but only rarely experienced'. This situation reflects how the academic study of physical education has often become deflected from more overarching physical education concerns such as the development of the whole person and the role of embodiment and physical culture in learning (Reid, 1996a, 1996b, 1997; Stolz, 2013b, 2014, 2015a; Thorburn, 2008; Thorburn & Stolz, 2015).

The third aim (affective) is arguably not really well understood for a range of complex reasons. In the Anglophone world of physical education, Arnold's (1979, 1988) conceptual account of education 'about', 'through' and 'in' movement has been highly influential in curriculum design, particularly in Australia.

At this time, it is the education *in* movement that is of interest as it is often connected with the affective domain in physical education. Part of the problem with the affective aim of physical education revolves around the notion of subjectivity or subjective consciousness, and the difficulty of measuring how people make sense of their world. Due to the diversity of ways that we understand and make sense of our world as agents, a range of interpretations that are personally meaningful and that could be used in an educational context are available. Indeed, a recent critique by Stolz and Thorburn (2015) of Arnold's (1979, 1988) conceptual account of meaning in movement, sport and physical education highlights some of the difficulties that have tended to be overlooked or not rigorously scrutinised as a means to open up and refocus the debate concerning this aim. Certainly, we would argue that the affective aim has considerable potential within physical education, particularly when it is connected with concepts such as Dewey's notion of experiential learning, knowing and inquiry. That said, this aim will always be at odds with educational systems that want to assess learner understanding through traditional assessment methods and instruments due to its emphasis upon subjectivity.

In the last aim, it could be argued that even less is known about the rich historical legacy of the socio-moral domain in physical education.[6] Sometimes it is inferred or assumed that playing certain games and sports will develop learners' social and moral character deemed to be virtuous dispositions that are considered to be 'good'. Usually, such views find their expression in terms such as 'sportsmanship', 'fairness', 'fair play' and so on as values that are aspirational. There is, however, a significant difference between espousing these terms and inculcating them in learners so they become stable and long-term dispositions of virtue. Likewise, to overstate the significance of games and sports in physical education and its alleged connection with socio-moral development is a fallacy (Carr, 1998; Stolz, 2014). This does not in any way exclude the possibility that this may happen, but to infer that there is causal-type relationship between games/sports and socio-moral development is simply misguided. In order to connect physical education with socio-moral development is no easy undertaking, as it requires a systematic approach from various moral habitats (e.g. family, extended family and friends, primary and secondary schools and so on) to aid and support learners. Likewise, it requires learners to have the cognitive capacity to be independent reasoners and learn by example while being critically supervised in practice (see MacIntyre, 1999). It also requires pedagogical skills from the teacher, values modelled and exemplified in action by the teacher, and a whole-school approach towards socio-moral development that is consistent with other moral habitats. Taking into consideration the complexities of socio-moral development, it seems rather odd to advocate that physical education is the only place (the 'uniqueness fallacy') where this could occur. Of course, there is the possibility that physical education could support such development, but then so could many other subjects in the school curriculum. Therefore, we need to be cautious not to overstate what we are claiming for in physical education in this respect.

A brief critique of 'pleasure' as an aim and value

As highlighted earlier, whatever mix of aims are taken forward in the name of physical education, we need to judge the merits of each aim, especially when it comes to determining whether associated values contribute primarily as a non-instrumental good or as an instrumental good. For example, there is a long line of advocacy arguing that pleasure (a non-instrumental good) represents some form of distinctive curriculum claim (Pringle, 2010; Reid, 1997). However, following Dewey (1913/1969), we consider it is important to recognise that *interest* is different from *pleasure*. For, as Jonas (2011) notes, Dewey wished to extend learners' interests in the widest possible sense and not in narrower terms e.g. when considering whether participation in learning was pleasurable or not. Consequently, this involves engaging in experiences that are not always immediately aligned with learners' perceived interests. This is necessary if learners' personal growth – the cornerstone of Deweyan educational philosophy – is to become an extended feature of learning environments. If school programmes are confused on this key point, it 'can easily degenerate into bad pedagogy' (Jonas, 2011, p. 127), as capturing learners' initial attention can end up taking precedence over realising more substantive learning gains. As Kirk (2010) and numerous other writers have highlighted, there is considerable evidence of this happening in secondary school physical education, where the multi-activity approach is annually rolled out in an attempt to hold learners' attention and to chance upon activities that might become of interest to learners. However, as Kirk (2010) is quick to mention, there is very little merit in supporting this form of planning, and continuing with it is likely to lead to further subject demise and possible extinction. So, the challenge for physical educators is to think of how learning can support learners' interests in physical activity and to do so in ways that highlight how learners' personal growth can be measured (i.e. against national standards if required).

Can rival traditions of physical education ever be resolved?

We recognise that to some extent certain contemporary debates on aims and values in physical education are unlikely to ever be resolved. For example, physical educationalists are likely to remain divided on whether they perceive rugby union to be an acceptable curriculum activity. At one end of the continuum, some may consider it as a brutish and overly physical activity that leaves participants prone to injury, anxiety and embarrassment. However, at the other end of the continuum, some may consider that if effectively taught, rugby union has the potential to develop courage, discipline, self-esteem and confidence. While it is important to understand that there will always be competing views about aims and educational value, the larger issue is whether physical educationalists consider that reviewing traditions in physical education is a good idea or not. Stolz and Kirk (2015a, 2015b) provide an interesting discussion on these matters and, in terms of where this chapter positions itself, we support the case for having lively discussions on aims and values as it reflects a conceptual vibrancy in physical education that is vital for robust professional learning and engagement with new ideas. As such, we consider that reviewing traditions in physical education represents a viable way of evaluating popular practices alongside assessing advocacy calls for greater (internal and/or external) change.

MacIntyre on rival traditions of enquiry

A central tenet of Alasdair MacIntyre's (1988, 1999, 1981/2007) multidisciplinary theorising on philosophy, virtue and ethics is that rival traditions are very often in a state of flux and riven with internal conflicts and tensions: for example, in a physical education context, arguments for or against the relative importance attached to examination (academic) programmes for some learners compared to the importance attached to programmes of what is often referred to as 'core' physical education for the vast majority of learners. Such comparisons are not necessarily counterproductive to consider, for as Stolz (2014, p. 153) notes, continuous conflict 'is a normal part of what it means to be a tradition of practices'. As such, MacIntyre's (1999, 1981/2007) works, which have had a wide-ranging influence on contemporary moral, social and political philosophy, can reasonably be extended to include transformative physical education. For as MacIntyre (1981/2007, p. 223) notes, not only can the benefits of practice sustain individual lives in ways that an 'individual may seek out his or her good as the good of his or her life, but also in sustaining those traditions which provide both practices and individual lives with their necessary historical context'. However, while we might be inclined to proceed on this basis, we also recognise following our review of physical education that many of the aims and values discussed are incompatible; fractured as they are by various levels of incoherence between intrinsic and external purposes and through confused health-related, sporting and educational claims. For this reason, we consider that the task before us is to argue for a new tradition that avoids an 'epistemological crisis' in physical education and where the eventual outcome is likely to be more profound than more of the same (Kirk, 2010). This line of thinking is consistent with MacIntyre, who recognises that existing traditions, if they are incompatible, will eventually splinter or form a new tradition (Stolz, 2015b). Thus, it is better to recognise (rather than ignore) existing traditions when planning a new tradition.

A new tradition of physical education: Embodied learning and physical culture

To make transformative progress, there is a need to recognise that engagement in physical education needs to be synthesised with regard to both individual learners' interests and in relation to the broader ethos and culture in schools, where there is an increased expectation of shared participation and interaction with others. To address these various challenges, we draw upon aspects of phenomenology to provide a theoretically sound basis for arguing that embodied learning should be the foundational basis of physical education programmes (Stolz, 2014; Thorburn & Stolz, 2015). Stolz (2013b, 2014, 2015a) and Thorburn (2008) writings on phenomenology draw extensively on the work of Merleau-Ponty (1962, 1963, 1968) to critically explore the implications of the phenomenal body and what it means to come to know the world through embodied learning experiences. Merleau-Ponty (1968) was among the founding fathers of phenomenology (i.e. along with Husserl, Heidegger, Sartre) and explored in most detail how the experiences and movements of the body can play a key role in our perception of the world. Merleau-Ponty asserts that lived-body experiences should not be separated from cognitive learning; rather the holistic nature of the 'body-subject' provides a way of perceiving relations between the body and the world, which avoids over-privileging the role of abstraction and cognition (concepts and rules) and under-representing the centrality of the body in human experience. Moreover, rather than being bound by the false dualisms of reason/emotion and mind/body, Merleau-Ponty communicated a concept of lived space, where the body-subject's experience is referenced through movement and language. Consequently, knowledge is not something to be understood in a detached way, but is founded upon integrated perceptual experiences that reveal ever more of the world as we live and experience it (Merleau-Ponty, 1962).

In assessing the physical education possibilities for more engrossing forms of embodied-type learning experiences, Kretchmar (2006) considers that challenging and situated learning environments need to be generated where meaning can emerge from solving problems, and where activity-based habits and successes can be referenced against clear standards of achievement and criteria for excellence (i.e. carefully establishing a relationship between the internal and external goods of practice). Kretchmar (2000, p. 269) reviewed how this might be achieved and concluded that the three most frequently used strategies – the prudential, the intellectual and the affective – were all of limited benefit as they became limited in teaching through either an 'exercise-as-useful', 'movement-as-understood' or 'activity-as-enjoyed' approach being rolled out, with all three failing to equip learners with suitably meaningful experiences. Thorburn and MacAllister (2013) believe that one contributory value missing has been an adequate appeal to the achievement of a type of movement-of-personal-value criterion, which recognises that there is educational merit 'in exploring how movements are experienced, performed and evaluated from an accurate phenomenological perspective' (Stolz, 2014, p. 64).

Thorburn (2008) attempted to articulate (with particular reference to swimming) how this might be possible through utilising a Merleau-Pontian phenomenology of physical education that was based on integrating learners' lived-body performance experiences with the acquisition of an increasingly detailed subject knowledge in the context of a high stakes examination award. Thorburn (2008) outlined how learners through integrating the triadic relationship framed by the body-subject, the nature (form) of activities and associated subject knowledge could develop the capacity to improve their practical ability and critical thinking at pre-tertiary level. If successful, learning gains would connect the *internal* benefits of learning being of interest to the learner with the external benefits of learning being measured against national standards of achievement. Furthermore, as Peters (1973, p. 240) argued that an educated person should be able to 'connect up these different ways of interpreting his experience so that he achieves some form of cognitive perspective', so it should be in a physical education examination award context, that learners can merge a narrative focus on performance experiences that dovetails with an increasingly detailed focus on associated subject knowledge.

Embodied learning, physical culture and school planning

Encouraging as the Thorburn (2008) review might be, the larger issue is how embodied learning and physical culture can link to whole-school aims. As such, our next task is to tease out key arguments on how learners' embodied learning experiences in physical education can be constructively developed and enriched in a context that is loosely bound by Deweyan notions of democratic education and MacIntyre's views on the internal goods of practice. From this position, we extend our thinking on how these goods can be shared more widely through emphasising the relational possibilities for physical education to build coherent bridges with the diverse aims and ethos in different schools, for as noted in Chapter 1, schools are in many cases becoming ever more distinct in their aims.

Following the young learners' journey through their school years we recognise that embodied learning approaches can become challenging as learners' interests become ever more specific. This can make it problematic to accommodate learners' interests in a whole class context. Furthermore, such an insular focus is unhelpful within a concept of physical education that is informed by personal growth *and* social and moral aspirations. As MacIntyre (1999) notes, to overly ascribe moral agency to the individual is problematic as it values the subjective person over social cohesion and under-acknowledges the importance of community decision making. On this basis, physical educators need to creatively consider how learners can come to appreciate that as education progresses, so does is the expectation of sharing participation and interaction with others, and adopting a perspective on learning that 'has to do with the universal–personal, not the particular–personal' (Martinkova & Parry, 2011, p. 194).

We believe that progress on this basis would help physical education meet the two conditions Carr (1998) requires for physical education to be of value to curriculum, i.e. that it is widely endorsed as being morally beneficial in society and that it can effectively operate within the context of formal schooling. Furthermore, we consider that these two conditions can be achieved through following MacIntyre's (1981/2007) holistic vision that it is from inside practices that learners and teachers can recognise and appreciate how the goods of practice are informed by personal narrative, the virtues that derive from our social and moral life and through developing good habits. Moreover, through practice learners can become increasingly adept at cultivating stable values that display practical wisdom e.g. as evident through learners focusing on achieving excellences of character. To help learners achieve these goals requires teachers to facilitate discussion and help learners to critically engage with their experiences, recognise available choices and discern viable ways forward (Dewey, 1938) – in brief, to follow standard Aristotelian-informed plans for teaching where there is a threefold emphasis on: the requirement for practice; the need for teachers to exemplify the virtues and through extended opportunities for learners to exercise reflection and deliberation (Arthur & Carr, 2013). Progress in this way is largely consistent with Kretchmar's (2006) view that physical education can be a genuine turning point in learners' lives with challenging and situated learning environments creating opportunities for learners to reference their activity-based habits against the achievement of clear standards of success. This enables learners to make greater sense of their individual and whole-school world, with their doubts and intuitions informing the establishment of more rounded physical culture understandings that are accurate (objective) and relevant to their lives (i.e. having an internal value).[7]

Future directions

In this chapter we have tried to add to the conceptual vibrancy associated with the historic traditions of physical education by providing a brief outline of how the social and moral claims of physical education as part of whole-school physical culture might constructively be advanced. We do this after having earlier in the chapter revisited the debate surrounding the various contested aims and values of physical education and having provided a brief critique of the axiological debate that physical education was required to respond to during the latter part of the twentieth century. We then progressed to answer our self-imposed question: Can rival traditions of physical education ever be resolved? This led to the development of our argument that for physical education to be transformative, the subject needs to be synthesised into a new tradition based around embodied learning and physical culture. In advancing our view, we recognise there are other physical educationalists that view matters differently and who consider other aims and values deserve greater recognition. In this light we encourage other physical educationalists to add to the debate by developing their own critiques, as this is exactly what is required for the benefits of physical education to continue to flourish within contemporary schooling. For as MacIntyre (1999, p. 136) notes, 'we learn what our common good is, and indeed what are individual goods are, not primarily and never only by theoretical reflection, but in everyday shared activities and the evaluations of alternatives that those activities impose'.

Summary of key findings

- There is a close relationship between educational aims and those things we consider to be valuable in an educational sense.
- Often what we 'value' in education is connected with conditions of being educated or what we mean by our understanding of an educated person.
- The axiological debate in physical education is complex, but essentially revolves around an understanding of instrumental and non-instrumental goods and where to draw and demarcate these.

- Interest is different from pleasure as an educational aim.
- Quite how physical education aims connect with whole-school aims is key to transformative educational futures.
- We argue that embodied learning and physical culture should be a 'new' tradition in physical education due to its transformative potential.

Reflective tasks

- Why should teachers be interested in the aims and values of physical education?
- Why are plural aims in physical education claimed to be problematic?
- Physical education seems to be preoccupied with four general aims (physical or psychomotor, cognitive, affective and socio-moral). Can physical education claim to contribute to all these aims? If so, how? If not, why?
- How would you assess and report on each general aim?
- What learning experiences/activities would you 'include' or 'exclude' from the physical education curriculum? Justify your reasons for each.

Further readings

Arnold, P. (1997). *Sport, Ethics and Education*. London: Cassell.
Best, D. (1978). *Philosophy and Human Movement*. London: Allen & Unwin.
Carden, S.D. (2006). *Virtue Ethics: Dewey and MacIntyre*. London: Continuum.
Carr, D. (1991). *Educating the Virtues*. London: Routledge.
Dewey, J. (1902/1990). *School and Society: The Child and the Curriculum*. Chicago, IL: University of Chicago Press.
Dewey, J. (1938/1963). *Experience and Education*. New York, NY: Collier Books.
Jess, M., Keay, J., & Carse, N. (2016). Primary physical education: a complex learning journey for children and teachers, Sport, Education and Society, 21(7), 1018–1035.
Kretchmar, R.S. (2005). *Practical Philosophy of Sport and Physical Education Activity* (2nd ed.). Champaign, IL: Human Kinetics.
Lutz, C.S. (2012). *Reading Alasdair MacIntyre's after Virtue*. London: Continuum.
McNamee, M. & Bailey, R. (2010). 'Physical education.' In: R. Bailey, R. Barrow, D. Carr & C. McCarthy (Eds.) *The SAGE Handbook of Philosophy of Education* (pp. 467–480). London: Sage.
O'Loughlin, M. (2006). *Embodiment and Education: Exploring Creatural Existence*. Netherlands: Springer.
Sokolowski, R. (2000). *Introduction to Phenomenology*. Cambridge: Cambridge University Press.
Tinning, R. (2010). *Pedagogy and Human Movement: Theory, Practice, Research*. London: Routledge.

Notes

1 For an excellent critique that provides an historical analysis of how the tradition of 'physical education-as-gymnastics' became extinct in favour of 'physical education-as-sport-techniques', see the work of Kirk (1990, 1992, 2010).

2 Of course, it could be argued that people enjoy exercising for the sake of exercising. A good example is Murakami's (2008) book titled *What I Talk about When I Talk about Running*.
3 It is interesting to note that Kirk's (2010) conception of the 'idea of the idea' or id² of physical education is a type of immutable essence. Even though Kirk argues that his conceptual account of 'physical education-as-sport-techniques' is not an essence of physical education, his position could be argued to take the form of monism (one essence/substance or single reality). This of course has significant ramifications for physical education.
4 We recognise that R. S. Peters' views about practical pursuits in the curriculum 'softened' in later works; however, it could be argued that the damage had already been done.
5 Other aims worth noting can take various forms ranging from 'health literacy', 'health-related fitness', 'health-based physical education' and 'health-orientated physical education'. Another aim can be captured by the term 'life-long participation or activity' or what Stolz (2014) refers to as 'physical education as preparation for leisure'. In a sense, this is an extension of the health tradition, however, its aims and values are different and hence classified as a separate tradition of physical education. To list all the aims of physical education and their various iterations would be quite lengthy and provide an unnecessary distraction from the point and purpose of this section. For an overview, refer to Chapter 1 of Stolz's (2014) book titled *The Philosophy of Physical Education: A new perspective*.
6 For an historical overview of this literature, see Chapter 5 from Stolz (2014).
7 For a more extended discussion in this area, see Thorburn and Stolz (2015).

References

Arnold, P. (1979). *Meaning in Movement, Sport and Physical Education*. London: Heinemann.

Arnold, P. (1988). *Education, Movement and the Curriculum*. London: Falmer Press.

Arthur, J. & Carr, D. (2013). Character in learning for life: A virtue-ethical rationale for recent research on moral and values education, *Journal of Beliefs and Values, 34*(1), 26–35.

Australian Curriculum, Assessment and Reporting Authority (ACARA). (2012). *Shape of the Australian Curriculum: Health and Physical Education*. Sydney, NSW: Australian Curriculum, Assessment and Reporting Authority.

Capel, S. (2000). 'Physical education and sport.' In: S. Capel & S. Piotrowski (Eds.) *Issues in Physical Education* (pp. 131–143). London: Routledge.

Carr, D. (1997). Physical education and value diversity: A response to Andrew Reid, *European Physical Education Review, 3*(2), 195–205.

Carr, D. (1998). 'What moral educational significance has physical education? A question in need of disambiguation.' In: M. McNamee & J. Parry (Eds.) *Ethics and Sport* (pp. 119–133). London & New York: Routledge.

Carr, D. (2003). *Making Sense of Education: An Introduction to the Philosophy and Theory of Education and Teaching*. London & New York: Routledge.

Department of Education. (2013). National curriculum in England: Physical education programmes of study. Retrieved from https://www.gov.uk/government/publications/national-curriculum-in-england-physical-education-programmes-of-study/national-curriculum-in-england-physical-education-programmes-of-study.

Dewey, J. (1913/1969). *Interest and Effort in Education*. Bath: Cedric Chivers.

Dewey, J. (1916). *Democracy and Education*. New York, NY: The Free Press.

Dewey, J. (1938). *Experience and Education*. New York, NY: Macmillan.

Jonas, M.E. (2011). Dewey's conception of interest and its significance for teacher education, *Educational Philosophy and Theory, 43*(2), 112–129.

Kirk, D. (1988). *Physical Education and Curriculum Study: A Critical Introduction*. London: Croom Helm.

Kirk, D. (1990). 'Defining the subject: Gymnastics and gender in British physical education.' In: D. Kirk & R. Tinning (Eds.) *Physical Education, Curriculum and Culture: Critical Issues in the Contemporary Crisis* (pp. 43–66). London: Falmer Press.

Kirk, D. (1992). *Defining Physical Education: The Social Construction of a School Subject in Postwar Britain*. London: Falmer Press.

Kirk, D. (2010). *Physical Education Futures*. London: Routledge.

Kretchmar, R.S. (2000). Moving and being moved: Implications for practice, *Quest, 52*(3), 260–272.

Kretchmar, R.S. (2006). Life on easy street: The persistent need for embodied hopes and down-to-earth games, *Quest, 58*(4), 344–354.

Laker, A. (2000). *Beyond the Boundaries of Physical Education*. London: Falmer Press.

Learning and Teaching Scotland. (2009). Health and wellbeing outcomes. Retrieved from http://www.ltscotland.org.uk/curriculumforexcellence/healthandwellbeing/index.asp.

MacIntyre, A. (1988). *Whose Justice? Which Rationality?* London: Duckworth.

MacIntyre, A. (1999). *Dependent Rational Animals*. London: Duckworth.

MacIntyre, A. (1981/2007). *After Virtue: A Study in Moral Theory* (3rd ed.). London: Duckworth.

Martinkova, I. & Parry, J. (2011). An introduction to the phenomenological study of sport, *Sport, Ethics and Philosophy, 5*(3), 185–201.

McNamee, M. (2005). 'The nature and values of physical education.' In: K. Green & K. Hardman (Eds.) *Physical Education: Essential Issues* (pp. 1–20). London: Sage.

Merleau-Ponty, M. (1962). *The Phenomenology of Perception*. London: Routledge.

Merleau-Ponty, M. (1963). *The Structure of Behaviour*. (A.L. Fisher, Trans.). Pittsburgh, PA: Duquesne University Press.

Merleau-Ponty, M. (1968). *The Visible and the Invisible*. Evanston, IL: Northwestern University Press.

Murakami, H. (2008). *What I Talk about When I Talk about Running*. London: Harvill Secker.

Peters, R.S. (1966). *Ethics and Education*. London: George Allen & Unwin.

Peters, R.S. (1973). 'The justification of education.' In: R.S. Peters (Ed.) *The Philosophy of Education* (pp. 239–267). Oxford: Oxford University Press.

Pringle, R. (2010). Finding pleasure in physical education: A critical examination of the educative value of positive movement affects, *Quest, 62*(2), 119–134.

Reid, A. (1996a). The concept of physical education in current curriculum and assessment policy in Scotland, *European Physical Education Review, 2*(1), 7–18.

Reid, A. (1996b). Knowledge, practice and theory in physical education, *European Physical Education Review, 2*(2), 94–104.

Reid, A. (1997). Value pluralism and physical education, *European Physical Education Review, 3*(1), 6–20.

Stolz, S.A. (2013a). The philosophy of G. Ryle and its significance for physical education: Some thoughts and reflections, *European Physical Education Review, 19*(3), 381–396.

Stolz, S.A. (2013b). Phenomenology and physical education, *Educational Philosophy and Theory, 45*(9), 949–962.

Stolz, S.A. (2014). *The Philosophy of Physical Education: A New Perspective*. London & New York: Routledge.

Stolz, S.A. (2015a). Embodied learning, *Educational Philosophy and Theory, 47*(5), 474–487.

Stolz, S.A. (2015b). MacIntyre, rival traditions and education, *Discourse: Studies in the Cultural Politics of Education, 37*(3), 358–368.

Stolz, S.A. & Kirk, D. (2015a). David Kirk on physical education and sport pedagogy: In dialogue with Steven Stolz (part 1), *Asia-Pacific Journal of Health, Sport and Physical Education, 6*(1), 77–91.

Stolz, S.A. & Kirk, D. (2015b). David Kirk on physical education and sport pedagogy: In dialogue with Steven Stolz (part 2), *Asia-Pacific Journal of Health, Sport and Physical Education, 6*(2), 127–142.

Stolz, S.A. & Pill, S. (2014). Teaching games and sport for understanding: Exploring and reconsidering its relevance in physical education, *European Physical Education Review, 20*(1), 36–71.

Stolz, S. & Pill, S. (2016a). A narrative approach to exploring TGfU-GS. *Sport, Education and Society, 21*(2), 239–261.

Stolz, S. & Pill, S. (2016b). Telling physical education teacher education tales through pedagogical case studies. *Sport, Education and Society, 21*(6), 868–887.

Stolz, S.A. & Thorburn, M. (2015). A genealogical analysis of Peter Arnold's conceptual account of meaning in movement, sport and physical education, *Sport, Education and Society*. Retrieved from http://dx.doi.org/10.1080/13573322.2015.1032923.

Thorburn, M. (2007). Achieving conceptual and curriculum coherence in high-stakes school examinations in physical education, *Physical Education and Sport Pedagogy, 12*(2), 163–184.

Thorburn, M. (2008). Articulating a Merleau-Pontian phenomenology of physical education: The quest for active learner engagement and authentic assessment in high-stakes examination awards, *European Physical Education Review, 14*(2), 263–280.

Thorburn, M. & Collins, D. (2003). Integrated curriculum models and their effects on teachers' pedagogy practices, *European Physical Education Review, 9*(2), 187–211.

Thorburn, M. & Collins, D. (2006a). The effects of an integrated curriculum model on learner learning and attainment, *European Physical Education Review, 12*(1), 31–50.

Thorburn, M. & Collins, D. (2006b). Accuracy and authenticity of oral and written assessments in high-stakes school examinations, *Curriculum Journal, 17*(1), 3–25.

Thorburn, M. & MacAllister, J. (2013). Dewey, interest and well-being: Prospects for improving the educational value of physical education, *Quest, 65*(4), 458–468.

Thorburn, M. & Stolz, S.A. (2015). Embodied learning and school-based physical culture: Implications for professionalism and practice in physical education, *Sport, Education and Society*. Retrieved from http://www.tandfonline.com/doi/full/10.1080/13573322.2015.1063993.

Whitehead, M. (2013). 'What is the education in physical education?' In: S. Capel & M. Whitehead (Eds.) *Debates in Physical Education* (pp. 22–36). London: Routledge.

Part II
The theoretical perspective

3   The transformational wind of theoretical change

An historic and contemporary view of physical education

Mike Jess and Matthew Atencio

Introduction

While physical education has been a regular feature of the school curriculum around the world for over a hundred years, the subject area has typically been viewed as sport, games or play and has subsequently had a 'shadowy, marginal existence in education' (Ozoliņš & Stolz, 2013, p. 888). Since the turn of this century, however, there is some evidence of physical education experiencing a recovery in many Western countries as awareness of the lifelong benefits of physical activity and concerns about pediatric obesity and inactivity permeate public and political arenas (Jess & Thorburn, 2015). While we recognise that this revival may help secure physical education's mid-to-long term survival in the school curriculum, we also suggest that future developments are likely to be 'messy' as the subject finds itself increasingly located in congested, contested and largely neoliberal policy spaces. As sport, health and education stakeholders jockey to influence future curriculum trajectory (Petrie & Hunter, 2011), the complexity of this political landscape is likely to be a constant. In particular, with neoliberalism more commonplace globally, the outsourcing of physical education has become increasingly common, particularly in primary schools, with the result that the subject is increasingly being used to meet narrow instrumental goals that many believe will decrease the educational contribution physical education can make in the school setting (e.g. McCullick, 2014). Therefore, while the current state of affairs for physical education may appear to be encouraging, the future health of the subject in schools remains open to some conjecture.

Acknowledging this 'edgy' context, this chapter considers how the physical education profession is addressing the educational status issue in terms of the curriculum frameworks being developed to secure the subject's future position in schools. To do this, we first discuss how physical education has found itself in its current situation by reflecting on the non-linear evolution of the subject throughout the previous century and the accompanying lack of consensus about its main purpose in schools. In particular, we discuss the emergence of the one-size-fits-all, behavourist-inclined multi-activity approach that was to become the dominant curriculum approach in many countries (Kirk, 2010). However, as disquiet with the educational value of this approach grew, we also explore how the early part of the twenty first century revealed a noticeable theoretical shift as the physical education profession moved to develop curriculum approaches that acknowledged the more complex and holistic nature of the subject. Building on this, we conclude the chapter by proposing that the future of physical education may be best served by encompassing an overarching and complexity-informed curriculum approach that overtly positions physical education within a lifelong learning perspective. To do this we suggest a focus on the developmental integration of the connective and models-based approaches that have recently gained some traction in the contemporary physical education literature.

Physical education in the twentieth century

To place physical education in its current context, we first consider some key features of the subject's evolution throughout the late nineteenth and twentieth centuries. It was with the introduction of mass schooling in the late nineteenth century that physical education first appeared as a school subject in many countries. While other subjects may have been included in the curriculum on the basis of their perceived cognitive or intellectual value, the introduction of physical education was primarily founded on concerns about the poor physical fitness and health of the armed forces at the time (Kirk, 1992). From this instrumental beginning, physical education has consistently struggled to convince key stakeholders of its capacity to make a legitimate and valuable contribution to the *education* of children and young people. Consequently, physical education often finds itself positioned on the margins of the school curriculum.

These concerns about educational status were less evident in the early part of the twentieth century, mainly because the subject was viewed as a form of physical training dominated by Swedish or German gymnastics. However, following World War II, curriculum development in physical education emerged as a more contested area as influences from within and outside the physical education profession sought to extend the subject's focus beyond its drill and regimented heritage (Kirk, 2013). With secondary schooling now universal and male teachers entering the profession in significant numbers, attempts were made to reorient physical education along more educational lines. While limited government input offered physical educators the freedom to develop their own curriculum approaches, as an embryonic area of study lacking 'intellectual tradition' (Gard, 2008), the development process proved to be messy and often uncomfortable. As different groups set out to locate the subject in line with various, sometimes conflicting, interests, few overarching, coherent and robust curriculum visions materialised (Goodson, 1987) although a distinct schism between the male and female sectors of the profession appeared. While the females supported a more aesthetic and creative approach, the incoming male teachers favoured a more scientifically-informed movement skill model focused on games and sports. Tension between these 'gendered' viewpoints was to be apparent for many years, particularly as initial teacher education programmes were being developed and delivered in 'all-male' or 'all-female' institutions. However, with the more scientific movement approach linking to the positivist worldview of the time, this approach began to dominate the physical education landscape, particularly when it was extended beyond games and sports to become the multi-activity approach. Leaning towards behaviourist learning theory, this multi-activity approach consisted of short 6–8 week 'blocks' of different physical activities, primarily focused on the development of the technical movement skills involved in different activities and was initially considered to have some educational potential. This prominence was enhanced further when teacher education institutions were to become mixed-gender and increasingly focused on the secondary school years (Kirk, 2002).

As physical educators grappled to design an educationally worthwhile curriculum, two external events were to impact on developments. In the mid-1960s, the debate about the subject's educational status was revisited when two prominent educational philosophers raised concerns about physical education's place in the curriculum. Writing from the Platonic–Cartesian philosophical perspective that had long dominated Western education thinking, Hirst (1968) and Peters (1966) presented a view of the school curriculum that distinguished the mind from the body and, critically, privileged different intellectual enquiry modes. Most notably, Peters (1966) challenged physical education's place in the curriculum by proposing that games, the key component of the multi-activity approach, were morally unimportant, not serious, of limited cognitive content and easily mastered. While he later amended his views to acknowledge practical activities may be of some educational value (Peters, 1983), this initial writing impacted heavily on the physical education profession and has remained an ongoing topic of concern (e.g. Ozoliņš & Stolz, 2013).

In addition to the status debate, the 1980s, for the first time, began to see governments take a more prominent role in curriculum development and implementation. For many within physical education, and education in general, this interventionist role was to create tension, particularly because these new developments were often driven by neoliberal principles focused on economic, market-driven and performativity agendas. While the education profession remained largely wedded to a social justice agenda and increasingly supportive of constructivist, inclusive and critical approaches to learning, the raising of standards, increased teacher accountability and economic competitiveness all began to permeate school practices. On the margins, physical education proved to be of limited interest to policymakers and the subject increasingly took on a more instrumental role to support sport and health agendas. As the physical education profession continued its internal quarrels, it was to become an onlooker from the boundary of the crowded policy arena (Penney, 2006). In a short period of time, the subject had moved from being in 'a world of its own' (Thorburn & Horrell, 2011, p. 74) into a policy space it was to find particularly difficult to enter or influence.

It is also important to recognise that the second half of the twentieth century saw physical education increasingly focus on the secondary years of schooling and become less concerned about the primary years. While some primary school development activity was apparent in the 1980s, e.g. through a number of short-lived daily physical education programmes, concerns about the quality of primary physical education became a regular feature in the literature. The limited number of specialist teachers working in the primary sector, relatively low quality teaching by generalist class teachers and inadequate initial teacher education and professional development were all identified as key issues for the primary physical education sector.

As these internal and external issues took centre stage for the physical education profession, the 1980s saw the emergence of new curriculum thinking in physical education as scholars began to raise questions about the educational worth of the multi-activity approach. Sport Education (Siedentop, 1994) and Teaching Games for Understanding (TGfU) (Bunker & Thorpe, 1982) were introduced and have become the most prominent and long-lasting examples of this new thinking. While neither approach was designed as an overarching curriculum framework, they both introduced a more holistic way to view aspects of the physical education curriculum and were to instigate a move beyond the physical focus and behaviourist practices associated with the multi-activity approach. Progress towards these new curriculum approaches was, and continues to be, modest and it was soon apparent that existing curriculum models had become particularly 'resistant to change' (Penney, 2006). However, by the end of the century, concerns about the educational worthiness and thinking underlying the multi-activity approach had increased and there was a growing consensus of an urgent need to construct new curriculum approaches that were 'sufficiently defensible, rigorous, and relevant within contemporary school cultures to ensure that the subject [or learning area] is positioned as legitimate work' (Macdonald & Brooker, 1997, p. 155). However, with external agents now driving the direction of physical education in many countries, a worldwide survey specifically commissioned for a World Summit in Physical Education in Berlin in 1999 reported that the physical education profession was finding it difficult to make a significant impact on national developments within this new policy context and that it was 'suffering from decreasing curriculum time allocation, budgetary controls with inadequate financial, material and personnel resources, low subject status and esteem and is being even more marginalised and undervalued by authorities' (Hardman & Marshall, 2000, p. 34). While the twentieth century had seen physical education become a universal part of most curricula around the world, with a focus on the secondary years and connections more closely aligned to health or sport agendas, as we moved into a new century the future of physical education as a school subject seemed to be in some peril.

The early twenty-first century

As global concerns about obesity and physical inactivity came to the fore at the beginning of the new century, the seeds of a revival for physical education were soon apparent in many countries (Thorburn, Jess & Atencio, 2011). Although this is welcomed by many, the political landscape in which this revival has developed continues to be crowded and contested as stakeholders from education, health, sport and other sectors seek to influence the future direction of the subject. For example, physical education developments in countries like Scotland,

Australia and New Zealand are now firmly rooted within a health discourse, while sport and competition agendas remain the driver in England (Department for Education, 2013). As a consequence, while physical education may seem to now have a more secure positioning in many school curricula, the enduring concern for the physical education profession is that this elevated position has its basis in the subject's capacity to meet a range of non-educational and ever-changing imperatives. In particular, while physical education's heightened status has seen increased government funding, there has been a decline in the financial support from education stakeholders and an increased contribution from the sport and/or health sectors (Evans & Davies, 2014). As was highlighted in Chapter 1, as neoliberalism continues to dominate the political landscape, accountability measures linked to specific health and sport imperatives and an increase in the outsourcing of physical education teaching are beginning to change the nature of the physical education experience for many children. It is therefore conceivable that in some countries, while physical education may remain part of the school curriculum, its future contribution may be increasingly aligned to 'other' agendas and quickly return to the margins of the school curriculum.

While returning to the margins of the school curriculum may be one impending scenario, we take the view that a more positive picture may evolve if much of the contemporary academic and professional work currently being carried out by the physical education profession can be harnessed effectively in the years to come. Subsequently, in this next section, we briefly consider how contemporary developments represent a shift towards a more educational perspective on physical education before presenting an overarching framework that synthesises a number of contemporary developments that, we suggest, create a realistic and authentic educational vision for the future of physical education.

Contemporary educational developments in physical education

Around the turn of the century, there was evidence of the physical education profession beginning seriously to question its association with the positivist-leaning multi-activity curriculum approach. Although this activity approach may still dominate in many parts of the world, concerns about its educational value have become common as many now view it as simply a sampling mechanism to introduce learners to a range of fragmented activity experiences that have little connection with the deep learning that can act as the foundation for engagement in different learning activities across the lifespan. Accordingly, and in response to the emergence of ideas from postmodern thinking (e.g. Fernández-Balboa, 1997), a perceived need for learning experiences that were more relevant to learners' complex needs was increasingly voiced and there were moves towards a curriculum process aimed at supporting learners who could 'deal with the uncertainty of conflicting and changing knowledge' (Wright, 2004, p. 6). As principles from interpretive, critical, feminist, poststructuralist and complexity perspectives became regular features of the physical education literature, so the curriculum reform agenda has become increasingly informed by thinking from constructivist, situated, critical, ecological, dynamical systems and complexity perspectives on learning. As a result, this theoretical shift has acted as the catalyst for calls to introduce physical education curriculum and pedagogy that are more participative, interactive, meaningful and situated (e.g. Ovens, Hopper & Butler, 2013).

While Sport Education and TGfU were not initially designed as part of the postmodern shift, they have not had both created some traction within the physical education world and efforts were subsequently made to integrate them with these new conceptualisations of knowledge and learning. Both approaches thus became the precursors of a number of new curriculum and pedagogical models that include cooperative learning, place-based learning, critical pedagogy, health-based physical education, Taking Personal and Social Responsibility (TPSR), physical literacy and numerous others (see Tannehill et al., 2013). While these new models focus on different dimensions of the physical education experience, they are all connected with more contemporary thinking, present a more holistic vision of physical education and can offer more participative, interactive and authentic experiences. However, while these recent developments point towards a clear commitment to a contemporary educational agenda for physical education, curriculum cohesion and the robustness and flexibility of course descriptions have received renewed attention amid calls to create overarching curriculum frameworks that are more integrated, robust and flexible in nature.

Complexity thinking

With these contemporary approaches in mind, our own curriculum efforts over the last decade have focused on the robustness and flexibility just discussed as we have tried to integrate ideas from a range of perspectives to design an overarching physical education curriculum framework. From this perspective, we take the view that ideas from complexity thinking not only connect with many of the contemporary views on learning but also have the potential to create an overarching framework that can help unify many of these views. Consequently, before we present a summary of our current ideas on this overarching curriculum, we present a review of the key complexity thinking principles that inform our educationally-focused view of physical education.

For us, complexity thinking is best explained by focusing on how systems made up of many different interacting parts function, e.g. cars, watches and humans. While complicated systems like cars or watches work in a pre-programmed, closed loop and predictable manner, we suggest that humans are different because they are complex systems that are less predictable, more dynamic and adaptable. The flexibility within complex systems stems from the fact the different parts of the system self-organise as they interact with each other and with the wider external system. Complex systems therefore have the capacity to produce both predictable and unpredictable outcomes. Crucially, from the myriad of interactions that occur, complex systems are able to exhibit structure, order and predictability while also revealing an inherent unpredictability. Applying this self-organising principle to the education system, children, teachers, schools, local authorities and governments are all viewed as complex systems that are constantly interacting to function in ways that display a balance between order and structure and adaptability and uncertainty. As such, all these 'actors' within the education system self-organise and interact to produce emergent behaviours that have the co-existing potential to exhibit both predictability and unpredictability (Davis & Sumara, 2010).

The more we have been able to understand these key points, the more we have come to concentrate on working out how to support the self-organising, interactive and emergent nature of the learning process in physical education. For this, ideas from ecological and complexity thinking have helped us better understand the complex nature of the learning process and we have increasingly used the following principles to inform our approach to physical education: self-organisation and emergence, predictability and unpredictability, similarities and diversities, connectedness and nestedness, ambiguous bounding and edge of chaos and recursive elaboration. While most of the discussion that follows focuses on these complexity principles, we must highlight that key features of ecological thinking were initially helpful because, like complexity, they focus on the relational nature of behaviour as it emerges from the interaction between the individual, environment and tasks being undertaken (Rovegno, 2006). As our thinking about complexity evolved, therefore, we used this ecological interactionist view as the foundation from which we describe the relationship between the self-organising individual and the ever-changing boundaries created by environmental factors, the task and the individual themselves. The key here is that, while learners may be functioning within similar boundaries, they will interpret these changing boundaries in their own self-organising way based on their previous experiences, their current capacities and their personal interpretation of the different boundaries. As such, as learners self-organise they are constantly interpreting the boundaries in their own way, hence the term 'ambiguous'.

As these interactions continue over time a process of recursive elaboration takes place as tasks are revisited in ways that may be quite similar but will often be different; e.g., when you play a game of basketball each time you receive the ball it is likely you will be in a different position in the court and with a different configuration of players around you. This revisiting process is a key part of complex learning because it leads learners to respond to the ever-changing boundaries (or constraints) in different ways, sometimes responding inside, other times around and maybe even beyond the parameters of the boundaries. Critically, these different responses around the 'edge of chaos' result in a wide range of outcomes from learners that include making errors, being creative, consolidating behaviours and also challenging themselves as part of a complex learning process. As this recursive elaboration process unfolds the complex learning process becomes 'dynamic, self-renewing and creative' and brings forth 'new knowledges and ways of being' (Osberg, Doll & Trueit, 2009, p. 225). Simply repeating the same drill-like tasks is unlikely to help support this elaborate type of complex learning.

As our work with complexity thinking evolved, we further explored how three complexity principles help bring coherence to the learning process: *connectedness, similarity* and *diversity*. Given the relational nature of humans as complex systems, making appropriate connections is central to the learning process because 'new properties and behaviours emerge not only from the elements that constitute a system, but from the myriad connections among them' (Mason, 2008, p. 48). However, while there is the potential for connections to exist between people and/or knowledge, these connections can be limited or even non-existent and, as a result, lead to the disconnection associated with weaker forms of learning. Conversely, stronger connections have the potential to support the coherence needed to apply and transfer learning across different contexts. We would suggest that it is this weak type of connectivity that is the problem with the multi-activity approach because the 'sampling' of physical activities limits the internal connections within the subject and makes it difficult to develop the shared understanding that bring coherence to the learning experience. As a consequence, we have increasingly worked to develop an approach towards physical education that is based on connected experiences that seek to integrate learning across learners' schooling and lives (Penney & Jess, 2004).

Most recently, we have been persuaded that this connectivity and coherence can be best supported by focusing on the co-existing complexity principles of similarity and diversity. On the one hand, similarities are the inward-looking, more common features of physical education that bring order and coherence to the learning process. These similarities help create the 'sameness' that contributes to the coherence of experiences by enabling interactions between different internal parts and externally with the broader nested system. By highlighting similarities, we believe that physical education is likely to become a more coherent experience as it will help learners engage in experiences that help them recognise and share similarities across different contexts, e.g. generic attacking and defending principles in TGfU that transfer across different games. However, the diversities within and between complex systems are the outward-looking aspects that support adaptable and creative actions in response to the dynamics across a range of contexts. In physical education these differences highlight how learners 'require diverse and unexpected responses in terms of physical movement, cognitive reasoning and social interaction' (Chow & Atencio, 2012, p. 2). As we discussed above, this diversity is critical because learners rarely respond to situations in exactly the same way, so need diverse behaviours to help them be adaptable and creative across contexts.

However, while similarities and diversities may be contrasting aspects of complex systems, they also act as harmonising features by operating reciprocally to preserve the effective working and coherence of the system. While too much similarity leads to the 'sameness' and impacts on the system's ability to be adaptable in different contexts, too much diversity results in limited coherence between the system's parts and also limits efficiency and adaptability. Subsequently, if physical education experiences need to be connected and coherent, we have increasingly argued that ideas from complexity thinking highlight the need to design a mix of learning experiences that focus concurrently on the similarities that bring order and structure and the diversities that support adaptable and creative behaviours across different contexts.

As we have grappled with, and shared, these complexity thinking principles, we have gradually built a vision of an educationally-oriented physical education curriculum around the following beliefs:

- Children and young people are complex *self-organising, interactive and emergent* learners.
- Teachers use their own self-organising professional judgement to design and deliver learning tasks that are focussed on:
  - a long-term recursive elaboration process
  - experiences that are connected and coherent
  - a mix of learning tasks that are based on similarities and diversities
  - amending task and environmental boundaries so that learners can consolidate, be challenged and be creative.

While we acknowledge that these considerations have significant implications for teachers' pedagogy, particularly in relation to the amending of tasks and environmental boundaries, in this chapter we concentrate on how these considerations have influenced our view on the curriculum process in physical education. Accordingly, we will finish the chapter by discussing key drivers for an overarching complexity-informed physical education framework.

An overarching complexity-informed physical education framework

Developmental, lifelong and lifewide drivers

From this complexity perspective, we first propose that a key goal of physical education is to support learners' abilities to effectively self-organise their engagement in different forms of physical activity across their lives. This represents an approach to physical education that actively seeks to connect school-based learning with the learning that takes place in the physical activity contexts beyond schooling. It also mirrors contemporary moves towards an education system acknowledging that learning not only takes place in schools but in other sites and at different times (e.g. Scottish Executive, 2004). We stress, therefore, that in this self-organising way the role of physical education is to support the learning that effectively connects with 'lifewide as well as lifelong' learning (West, 2004, p. 141).

As a starting point for this lifelong and lifewide driver, curriculum physical education, extra-curricular activities and community experiences have key roles in helping learners connect and sustain their participation in an assortment of physical activity pursuits throughout their lives *for whatever reasons they choose.* These reasons could be for personal health, lifestyle, enjoyment, social interests and, for some, to improve or excel in a specific activity. Significantly, these reasons relate to a life of complex learning and not one that is solely about engagement in physical activity. Over a decade ago, Penney and Jess (2004) conceptualised lifelong physical activity (LLPA) holistically as having four dimensions:

- functional physical activity, in response to demands of everyday work and home life;
- recreational physical activity, as a leisure pursuit, which, for many, is a socially-orientated activity;
- health-related physical activity, concerned with fitness, wellbeing and/or rehabilitation;
- performance-related physical activity, concerned with self-improvement and/or success in performance environments.

As learners move through their school years and beyond, these LLPA dimensions involve a self-organising web of decision making as each individual recognises the demands of different activities and acknowledges their own needs, abilities and interests at different times in their lives. The key point here is the purpose each individual puts on an activity at a given time in their lives. Activities therefore are not inherently associated with a single LLPA dimension; rather these associations fluctuate as learners self-organise to engage in particular activities for different reasons.

While the Penney and Jess (2004) paper continues to have some traction within the physical education literature, there do not appear to be any examples of serious engagement with this lifelong approach. This is particularly evident within the primary school context where physical education is still either seen as a break from the 'real work' of the classroom or used to 'fit into' secondary school agendas. However, we take the view that this connected lifelong and life-wide approach would enable physical education to have a more educational and developmental focus and could inform and represent a focal point for curriculum development in schools from the preschool to the senior secondary years and beyond.

Deep and cumulative learning

Focusing on this lifelong and lifewide agenda, the recursive elaboration principle discussed previously becomes another key driver for school physical education. Revisiting tasks is particularly important because, without this, it is almost impossible to develop the deep and cumulative learning that organises our knowledge into a cohesive framework that can be applied and transferred across different contexts (Bransford, Brown & Cocking, 2000). To achieve this deep and cumulative learning, learners need to engage in deliberate practice in relation to learning goals so that learning 'unfolds recursively by constantly invoking and elaborating established associations' (Davis & Sumara, 2010, p. 201). Therefore, within the context of contemporary thinking about physical education, this deep learning not only suggests the acquisition of adaptive and creative movement competence over time but also the concurrent developing of the cognitive, social and emotional learning that will support engagement in a wide range of lifelong and lifewide physical activity contexts (Jess, Atencio & Thorburn, 2011).

Unfortunately, developing the deep and cumulative learning that supports a connected and cohesive physical education experience will not happen if the curriculum continues to be conceptualised and organised in ways that are 'destined to have partial and short-lived relevance to many people's lives' (Penney & Jess, 2004, p. 275). As we have noted numerous times in this chapter, the traditional multi-activity approach with its superficial and fragmented sampling experiences is unlikely to develop deep and cumulative learning that enables application and transfer across different contexts. With this deep and cumulative learning in mind, we have been attracted by two recent developments that set out to present an overarching view of the physical education curriculum, i.e. physical education as a 'connective specialism' (Penney, 2008) and 'models based practice' (MBP) (Kirk, 2013).

Integrating the 'connective specialism' and 'models-based practice' approaches

The idea of physical education as a 'connective specialism' resonates with much of what has been written above because it proposes that learning tasks should focus on the core knowledge and skills that act as the catalyst to support participation in physical activity across a range of contexts (MacDonald, 2014). Physical education is therefore seen as the 'hub' to integrate school learning with the learning experiences in 'real-life' contexts (Rovegno, 2006). This not only aligns with ideas from situated learning and social constructivism, but also highlights the importance of collaboration in local settings and across the different sectors of the school and community systems. Situating learning in this self-organising way captures the lived experiences of young people and shows how, as learners, they integrate and co-construct school knowledge with their lives. This idea of a 'connective specialism' is apparent in much of our own work with the primary physical education curriculum, where we have been particularly attracted to core learning as being the connective catalyst (Jess, Keay & Carse, 2016).

Taking a slightly different view towards an overarching curriculum, MBP is based on the belief that physical education has a number of different forms (Casey, 2012). It proposes that a range of new contemporary curriculum models (discussed earlier), and others still to be developed, can be used collectively to construct an overarching curriculum framework that seeks to achieve a range of holistic educational outcomes. While MBP may appear to have similarities with the multi-activity approach, its attraction is in the belief that these different forms of physical education have the potential to contribute to a wide range of educational outcomes (Kirk, 2013). Teachers and schools therefore need to have the autonomy to choose appropriate curriculum models based on the attributes of the learners, the local context and the learning aspirations of the teachers and/

or school. While there are few examples of this approach being used in secondary schools yet, Quay and Peters (2008) in Australia have explored the possibilities of the framework by focussing on primary school children's skill and fitness, personal and social development and physical activity learning by integrating a physical education programme to include fundamental motor skills, creative games making, TGfU, sport education and TPSR. In our own work, we have termed this diverse range of models as applications and, as we now discuss, integrate them with our ideas on core learning (Jess et al., 2016).

From a complexity perspective, therefore, we recommend integrating these two overarching approaches to produce a unifying framework that presents core learning as the similarities to bring overarching order and structure to the curriculum experience while MBP offers a diverse range of models that can help consolidate, apply, transfer and extend core learning across a range of different physical activity contexts. In addition, we have recently been discussing how physical education may benefit from broadening the range of these physical activity contexts to move beyond the traditional focus on more formal physical activities, particularly team games, and include the more informal physical activities that have become popular in many local communities, e.g. skateboarding, cycling and walking. As such, this integrated, broader approach not only offers a mix of similar and diverse learning experiences but considerable self-organising and recursive potential for *all* learners. In addition, and we believe critically, it also presents teachers with the opportunity to become curriculum architects who, in their own context, can design connected and coherent lifelong and lifewide programmes focused on clear educational aims.

Future directions

Acknowledging that this chapter has largely been a conceptual exploration of the changing face of physical education over the last hundred years, we finish by considering how the complexity-informed ideas we have presented as an overarching framework may unfold in the future. In context, we recognise that much of what we have written stems from our applied efforts in primary physical education with the Developmental Physical Education Group (DPEG) at the University of Edinburgh over the last 15 years. During this time, as we have worked with our ideas for Basic Moves, Early Moves, Core Learning and different applications, much of our work has involved an ongoing grappling with the theory that informs these curriculum approaches (see Jess et al., 2016). In a similar vein to points made earlier about Sport Education and TGfU, we stress that our starting point for these curriculum ideas was not complexity thinking, but more a concern with the existing early childhood physical education curriculum we saw in schools. Consequently, we were trying out something different and, while we were to some extent successful in our initial efforts, the last decade has seen us focused on efforts to collectively work with the theory while concurrently trying to apply our ideas in practice: recursive elaboration in practice. In addition, given that our work has been focused in preschool and primary settings, we are conscious that the continued focus of the physical education profession on the secondary years has meant that the impact of our work on any wider curriculum development has been limited to date. This chapter, therefore, represents our first significant attempt to take our ideas, developmentally, beyond the primary years. The next step is to share the content with our undergraduate and postgraduate students, primary and secondary teachers and, in journal articles, with the academic community. It is also our intention to apply the ideas presented with the primary teachers we work with within the local community. Progress may still be relatively modest but, if the last 15 years are anything to go by, the next 15 should be interesting.

Summary of key findings

- The historical development of physical education over the last hundred years has had a significant impact on the way the subject areas is viewed within the educational arena today.
- The future of physical education will be influenced by a wide range of key stakeholders across a number of domains.
- Complexity thinking is presented as a useful way to view learners within the physical education context.
- Developmental, lifelong and lifewide drivers have the potential to more clearly position physical education as a subject area of educational value.
- Integrating ideas from physical education as a 'connective specialism' and 'models-based practice' may offer a more robust educational view of physical education for the future.

Reflective tasks

- Discuss the benefits of having a good understanding of the historical development of physical education over the last century.
- Why is it beneficial for physical education to be viewed as an educational subject area?
- Discuss your views on yourself (or others) as a self-organising and interactive complex system.
- Review whether it is important to identify the similarities and diversities that make up physical education.
- Review whether the integration of physical education as a 'connective specialism' and 'models-based practice' can create a physical education approach that is more connected and cohesive.

Further readings

Jess, M. & Gray, S. (2016). 'Curriculum reform and policy cohesion in physical education.' In: C. Ennis (Ed.) *Routledge Handbook of Physical Education Pedagogy* (pp. 143–156). London: Routledge.

Kirk, D. (1992). *Defining Physical Education: The Social Construction of a School Subject in Postwar Britain*. London: Falmer Press.
Ovens, A., Hopper, T., & Butler, J. (Eds.). (2013). *Complexity Thinking in Physical Education: Reframing Curriculum, Pedagogy and Research*. London: Routledge.

References

Bransford, J., Brown, A., & Cocking, R. (2000). *How People Learn: Brain, Mind, and Experience & School*. Washington, DC: National Academy Press.
Bunker, D. & Thorpe, R. (1982). A model for the teaching of games in secondary schools, *Bulletin of Physical Education, 18*(1), 5–8.
Casey, A. (2012). Models-based practice: Great white hope or white elephant?, *Physical Education and Sport Pedagogy, 19*(1), 18–34.
Chow, J. & Atencio, M. (2012). Complex and nonlinear pedagogy and the implications for physical education, *Sport, Education and Society, 19*(8), 1034–1054.
Davis, B. & Sumara, D. (2010). 'Enabling constraints: Using complexity research to structure collective learning.' In: J. Butler & L. Griffin (Eds.) *More Teaching Games for Understanding: Moving Globally* (pp. 105–120). Champaign, IL: Human Kinetics.
Department for Education. (2013). *The National Curriculum: Framework Document*. London: Department for Education.
Evans, J. & Davies, B. (Ed.). (2014). Neoliberalism, privatisation and the future of physical education [Special issue], *Sport, Education and Society, 20*(1), 1–9.
Fernãndez-Balboa, J. (Ed.). (1997). *Critical Post-Modernism in Human Movement, Physical Education and Sport*. Albany: University of New York Press.
Gard, M. (2008). Producing little decision makers and goal setters in the age of the obesity crisis, *Quest, 60*(4), 488–502.
Goodson, I. (1987). *School Subjects and Curriculum Change*. London: Falmer Press.
Hardman, K. & Marshall, J. (2000). *World-Wide Survey of the State and Status of School Physical Education, Final Report*. Manchester: University of Manchester.
Hirst, P. (1968). 'Liberal education and the nature of knowledge.' In: R. Archambault (Ed.) *Philosophical Analysis and Education* (pp. 113–138). London: Routledge & Kegan Paul.
Jess, M., Atencio, M., & Carse, N. (2016). Integrating complexity thinking with teacher education practices: A collective yet unpredictable endeavour in physical education?, *Sport, Education & Society*. Retrieved from http://www.tandfonline.com/doi/full/10.1080/13573322.2016.1225195.
Jess, M., Atencio, M., & Thorburn, M. (2011). Complexity Theory: Supporting Curriculum and Pedagogy Developments in Scottish Physical Education. *Sport Education and Society, 16*(1), 179–199.
Jess, M., Keay, J., & Carse, N. (2016). The primary physical education curriculum process: More complex than you might think!!, *Education 3–13: International Journal of Primary Elementary and Early Years Education*. Retrieved from http://www.tandfonline.com/doi/full/10.1080/03004279.2016.1169482.
Jess, M. & Thorburn, M. (2015). 'Physical education.' In: D. Wyse, L. Hayward & J. Pandya (Eds.) *The Sage Handbook of Curriculum, Pedagogy and Assessment* (pp. 441–455). London: Sage.
Kirk, D. (1992). *Defining Physical Education: The Social Construction of a School Subject in Postwar Britain*. London: Falmer Press.

Kirk, D. (2002). 'Physical education: A gendered history.' In: D. Penney (Ed.) *Gender and Physical Education* (pp. 24–38). London: Routledge.

Kirk, D. (2010). *Physical Education Futures*. London: Routledge.

Kirk, D., (2013). Educational Value and Models-Based Practice in Physical Education, *Educational Philosophy and Theory, 45*(9), 973–986,

Macdonald, D. (2014). Is global neo-liberalism shaping the future of physical education?, *Physical Education and Sport Pedagogy, 19*(5), 494–499.

Macdonald, D. & Brooker, R. (1997). Assessment issues in a performance-based subject: A case study of physical education, *Studies in Educational Evaluation, 23*(1), 83–102.

Mason, M. (2008). What is complexity theory and what are its implications for educational change?, *Education Philosophy and Theory, 40*(1), 135–149.

McCullick, B. (2014). From the cheap seats: One consideration of school-based PE's position in contemporary American schools, *Physical Education and Sport Pedagogy, 19*(5), 533–544.

Osberg, D., Doll, W., & Trueit, D. (2009). Editorial: Limiting complexity, *Complicity: An International Journal of Complexity & Education, 6*(2), iii–x.

Ovens, A., Hopper, T., & Butler, J. (2013). *Complexity Thinking in Physical Education: Reframing Curriculum, Pedagogy and Research*. London: Routledge.

Ozoliņš, J. & Stolz, S. (2013). The place of physical education and sport in education, *Educational Philosophy and Theory, 45*(9), 887–891.

Penney, D. (2006). 'Curriculum construction and change.' In: D. Kirk, D. Macdonald & M. O'Sullivan (Eds.) *The Handbook of Physical Education* (pp. 565–579). London: Sage.

Penney, D. (2008). Playing a political game and playing for position: Policy and curriculum development in health and physical education, *European Physical Education Review, 14*(1), 33–50.

Penney, D. & Jess, M. (2004). Physical education and physically active lives: A lifelong approach to curriculum development, *Sport, Education and Society, 9*(2), 269–287.

Peters, R.S. (1966). *Ethics and Education*. London: Allen & Unwin.

Peters, R.S. (1983). 'Philosophy of education.' In: P. Hirst (Ed.) *Educational Theory and Its Foundational Disciplines* (pp. 30–61). London: Routledge & Kegan Paul.

Petrie, K. & Hunter, L. (2011). Primary teachers, policy, and physical education, *European Physical Education Review, 17*(3), 325–339.

Quay, J. & Peters, J. (2008). Skills, strategies, sport, and social responsibility: Reconnecting physical education, *Journal of Curriculum Studies, 40*(5), 601–626.

Rovegno, I. (2006). 'Situated perspectives on learning.' In: D. Kirk, D. Macdonald & M. O'Sullivan (Eds.) *The Handbook of Physical Education* (pp. 262–274). London: Sage.

Scottish Executive. (2004). *A Curriculum for Excellence: The Curriculum Review Group*. Edinburgh: The Scottish Executive.

Siedentop, D. (1994). *Sport Education*. Champaign, IL: Human Kinetics.

Tannehill, D., van der Mars, H., & MacPhail, A. (2014). Building effective physical education programs. Burlington: MA: Jones and Bartlett.

Thorburn, M. & Horrell, A. (2011). Power, control and professional influence: The curious case of physical education in Scotland, *Scottish Educational Review, 43*(2), 71–83.

Thorburn, M., Jess, M., & Atencio, M. (2011). Thinking differently about curriculum: Analysing the potential contribution of physical education as part of 'health and wellbeing' during a time of revised curriculum ambitions in Scotland, *Physical Education & Sport Pedagogy, 16*(4), 383–398.

West, L. (2004). 'The trouble with lifelong learning.' In: D. Hayes (Ed.) *Key Debates in Education* (pp. 138–142). London: Routledge Falmer.

Wright, J. (2004). 'Critical inquiry and problem-solving in physical education.' In: J. Wright, D. Macdonald & L. Burrows (Eds.) *Critical Inquiry and Problem-Solving in Physical Education* (pp. 19–31). London: Routledge.

4 The primary school teacher perspective

Using an ecological framework and complexity principles as the basis for analysing teachers' professionalism

Mike Jess, Nicola Carse and Jeanne Keay

Introduction

In recent years, professional learning has been recognised as a key feature of teacher education and increasingly as a career-long endeavour (Scottish Government, 2011). The traditional linear conception of professional learning, in which short continuing professional development, or CPD, 'courses' are delivered *to* teachers via one-off isolated sessions by 'experts', is now viewed as overly simplistic (Fleet & Patterson, 2001) as it 'contradict(s) everything we know about the ways in which people are most likely to learn' (Armour, 2006, p. 204). Contemporary approaches towards professional learning are subsequently being presented as a much more complex and dynamic phenomenon involving a wide range of activities concerned with increasing teachers' knowledge bases, skill sets and attitudes (Sheridan, Pope Edwards, Marvin & Knoche, 2009, p. 385). To explore the complexity of the professional learning process, this chapter engages in a reflective critique of the non-linear and 'messy' trajectory of the professional learning efforts of the Developmental Physical Education Group's (DPEG) at the University of Edinburgh. Stemming from more than 15 years' work, this longitudinal project offers an insight into the complex, unpredictable and transformative nature of the professional learning process from both the perspective of the group itself and the teachers it has worked with over this time. As such, the chapter discusses the DPEG's theoretical shift towards complexity thinking, how this impacted on the group's own professional learning and the way it now approaches the professional learning of students and teachers in a more transformative manner.

Main findings

To explore the move towards complexity-informed professional learning approaches, the chapter is split into four related sections.

- The Developmental Physical Education Group (DPEG)
- Initial professional learning efforts
- Complexity thinking and professional learning
- The DPEG, complexity and professional learning.

The Developmental Physical Education Group (DPEG)

The DPEG is a group of teachers, lecturers and researchers in the Institute of Sport, Physical Education and Health Sciences at the University of Edinburgh whose goal is to design an innovative and integrated theory/practice approach to primary physical education (Jess, Keay & Carse, 2016). The group came together in 2001 following a successful grant application to the main Scottish sport agency, Sportscotland, from which they developed Basic Moves: a developmental movement approach for children aged between 5 and 7 years. Originally consisting of a lecturer, a seconded primary physical education teacher and a part-time research assistant, the group expanded considerably after 2006 when it was awarded a larger grant by the Scottish Executive[1] to develop and deliver a postgraduate physical education programme for primary teachers. Between 2006 and 2013, the group delivered this masters-level programme to over 500 generalist primary teachers across 16 local authorities in Scotland, during which time the group increased in size to include two lecturers, a postdoctoral researcher, three full-time PhD students, three teaching fellows/associates, an administrator and a number of associate members. Since then, while the group remains based at the University of Edinburgh, some group members have moved to lecturing, teaching and management posts across Scotland, England and the USA. As such, the group's primary physical education efforts have evolved to include a series of curriculum, pedagogy, professional learning and advocacy projects in a range of venues.

Initial professional learning efforts

As the development of Basic Moves gained momentum, the DPEG soon became engaged in professional learning activities aimed at disseminating its ideas to teachers working in primary physical education. In the immediate and local context, these professional learning activities focused on the collaborative efforts of a small group of lecturers and teachers who met regularly to develop and introduce Basic Moves into local schools. This was a period of intense discussion and negotiation as the group worked to develop a shared vision and approach for the project. However, these efforts proved to be extremely 'messy'. There were numerous uncomfortable meetings as individuals' traditional views of primary physical education was challenged and group members attempted to cope with new ideas, different roles, successes and failures. Some of these initial group members were to remain heavily involved in the project and create the foundation for the group's long-term work, while others quickly decided to leave the project at this early stage. Furthermore, at the local authority and national levels, the group's professional learning efforts were becoming more wayward and unpredictable.

Coinciding with a renewed interest in physical education at the Scottish policy level, the ideas from Basic Moves received exposure in various national publications (Scottish Executive, 2003) and the DPEG was presented with the opportunity of extending the scope of its professional learning activities beyond its initial small-scale efforts. A national conference in 2003 attracted in excess of 200 delegates and was followed by the introduction of a national training programme for teachers in March 2004. This programme consisted of two-day professional development courses at two related levels and attempted to move beyond the 'tips for teachers' and pre-prepared lesson plans that had become a common feature of primary physical education professional learning courses. However, while these university-based courses attracted high teacher numbers in the first year of the programme, and received positive evaluations from most primary teachers, it was soon apparent that too much reliance was being placed on the traditional top-down and off-site delivery approach. As teachers returned to their primary schools with little ongoing support, some were well received by colleagues; but others met resistance from school management and colleagues, while others stopped teaching Basic Moves as they were isolated as the sole practitioner using this approach in their settings (Atencio, Jess & Dewar, 2012). A further problem emerged for the group as in its enthusiasm to disseminate Basic Moves it had unwittingly treated course delegates as 'empty vessels' who were in need of this new knowledge. This approach led to many more experienced professionals, particularly primary physical education specialist teachers, becoming unhappy about their passive and limited role in the professional learning experience. It has taken the DPEG many years to repair the damage caused by these early ill-informed professional learning attempts.

By the end of 2005, the DPEG was conscious that it needed to reconsider its approach to its professional learning activities, particularly when it identified how educational writers were highlighting that 'traditional' approaches to teachers' professional learning were no longer appropriate (e.g. Deglau & O'Sullivan, 2006). As the group had learned to its own discomfort, this view stemmed from the fact that teachers were being treated as passive recipients of new knowledge and were rarely offered the opportunity to revisit and engage more deeply with the content presented at the courses (e.g. MacNaughton, 2005). The group became increasingly aware that successful professional learning needed to be designed *for* and *with* teachers and should be relevant to their everyday practice in context (Helterbran & Fennimore, 2004). In addition, from a social constructivist perspective, the role of collaboration as a key feature of teachers' professional learning was also being stressed. While some writers proposed the importance of developing teacher networks (e.g. Fleet & Patterson, 2001), others emphasised the potential that communities of practice offered to focus on issues, problems and successes experienced in practice (Wenger, 1998). This contemporary literature helped the DPEG recognise that teachers were not technicians (Lingard, Hayes & Mills, 2003), but professionals who, individually and collectively, should play a more significant role in their own continuing professional learning.

Towards the end of 2006, the DPEG was given the opportunity to amend its approach towards professional learning and embrace activities that were theoretically-informed, accredited and incorporated 'more participative, situated, collaborative and supportive activities' with a specific view to build teacher capacity in primary physical education (Jess & McEvilly, 2013, p. 9). In response to the recommendations from the first national Physical Education Review Group (Scottish Executive, 2004), and in conjunction with the University of Glasgow, the DPEG was commissioned by the Scottish Executive to develop, deliver and evaluate the impact of postgraduate certificates in physical education specifically aimed at primary teachers. At the University of Edinburgh, this part-time qualification was developed as the Postgraduate Certificate in 3–14 Physical Education and, for a number of years, was delivered at three sites across eastern Scotland (Edinburgh, Perth and Aberdeen). Enrolment to the programme was free to all registered teachers and, between 2006 and 2012, resulted in over 500 primary teachers taking part in the programme. Studied over a two-year period, the PgCert was to be the catalyst for the DPEG to reorient its professional learning efforts and, as we discuss in more detail later in the chapter, the programme offered the group the opportunity not only to study primary physical education in more depth but also to develop an approach to professional learning informed by principles from complexity thinking.

Complexity thinking and professional learning

When the DPEG began the process of reorienting its approach to professional learning, it concurrently started to explore and grapple with a range of contemporary theoretical perspectives in order to conceptually underpin the work. Initially, ideas from ecological theory, dynamical systems, social constructivism and situated learning all proved helpful in making better sense of the group's efforts to reconceptualise primary physical education, although these ideas also led to some disconnect as the different perspectives influenced different elements of the group's work in curriculum, pedagogy and professional learning. For example, while ideas from ecology were more apparent in early years movement activities, situated perspectives appeared more relevant to the group's work with undergraduate students and teachers. While parts of the primary physical education puzzle made more sense, the overall picture remained messy and often disconnected. However, as members of the group began to work with ideas from complexity thinking, a number of key principles gradually began to act as an overarching frame for much of this group's work (Jess, Atencio & Thorburn, 2011). Consequently, as in Chapter 3 where complexity principles were employed to inform the curriculum development ideas presented, this chapter explores how, in an overarching manner, complexity thinking gradually began to influence the DPEG's professional learning efforts.

Complexity thinking

By viewing the key stakeholders within the education system as complex systems, e.g. the children, teachers, classes, schools, communities and policy actors, complexity principles have increasingly influenced the DPEG's view of professional learning. Unlike complicated systems made up of pre-programmed parts that interact in a consistent manner to perform tasks with some degree of certainty, e.g. a watch or a car, the different parts of a complex system self-organise as they interact with the different boundaries created by their own structure and the external environment in which they function (Prigogine, 1976). While this self-organising ability supports a degree of order and predictability within the system, the 'rich interactions' (Cilliers, 1998) between the different parts also help the system to be unpredictable and adaptable as it interacts with ever-changing environmental demands outside the system (Morrison, 2003). Humans, as complex systems, therefore have the potential to be unstable and open-ended while also being structured and ordered. The focus of complexity is subsequently not only on the complex system itself but also on the interactions that take place between the different elements (Ovens, Hopper & Butler, 2013). Complexity thinking therefore views the stakeholders within the education system as active agents engaging in a development or learning process that is self-organising, interactive, non-linear and uncertain. This complexity can be captured by considering how government policies are enacted in schools. While many policymakers may envisage the linear implementation of their policies, Ball, Maguire and Braun (2012, p. 144) highlight how schools are 'far more differentiated and loosely assembled than is often thought to be the case'. As such, this complex makeup of schools means that these 'policies are intimately shaped and influenced by school-specific factors which act as constraints, pressures and enablers of policy enactments' (Ball et al., 2012, p. 19). Schools, therefore, function as complex self-organising systems as they interact with a myriad of ever-changing internal and external influencing factors.

Complex professional learning: The starting point

In line with this complexity view, ecological theory has been a useful starting point for the DPEG's thinking about professional learning, because it also considers human behaviour to be a relational phenomenon that emerges from the interaction between the learner, environment and tasks being attempted (Rovegno, 2006). Taking the view that teachers meet many new starting points over their professional careers, each of these new opportunities engages teachers, as self-organisers, in an interaction with the different boundaries set by the new tasks/ knowledge, the children they teach, the environment in which they work and also themselves. For example, in a traditional professional learning sense, a group of newly-qualified teachers attend a short, off-site course focussed on a specific physical education topic, e.g. Basic Moves, and return to their schools with the intention of including this new knowledge or skill in their practice. On returning to their schools, each teacher then takes part in a self-organising process as their initial efforts see them interact with the new knowledge or content (the task), their previous experience and initial responses of the children they teach (individuals), the facilities, equipment, response of colleagues, school ethos and national policy influences (environment) and also their personal strengths and weaknesses in terms of their own knowledge, pedagogy, motivation etc. As such, as each teacher interprets and negotiates these different 'situated' boundaries, they will adapt to the situation in their own self-organising way; hence the 'ambiguous' nature of the different boundaries. From a professional learning perspective, this example highlights how each different teacher will have significantly different starting points on the basis of their previous experiences, current capacity to engage with the new knowledge and also their personal cognitive and emotional response to the contextual boundaries that impact on their initial engagement with the new task. At this starting point for new professional learning, a complexity thinking view raises important questions about the appropriateness and value of the short, off-site courses that are delivered to passive recipients who are expected to learn in the same way. As such, we now explore in more depth how professional learning experiences based on complexity thinking principles could be more participative, collective and contextually situated.

From this complexity perspective, and building on the ecological starting point, a range of complexity principles, most notably self-organisation emergence, connectedness, nestedness, ambiguous bounding, 'edge of chaos' and recursive elaboration, can help develop a better understanding of the professional learning process as it unfolds. At the heart of this process, professional learning evolves in a recursive and iterative manner as teachers revisit the new knowledge and skills over a period of time. The nature of this revisiting process is critical as it has the potential to support the deep professional learning that organises teachers' knowledge and practice into a conceptual framework that can be applied and transferred across different contexts (Bransford, Brown & Cocking, 2000). This focus on deep learning resonates with more contemporary notions of professional learning where learning is promoted through a continuous process of collaborative inquiry rather than the traditional transmission of set knowledges by 'experts' (Drew, Priestley & Michael, 2016).

To support this recursive elaboration process, the complexity concepts of connectedness and nestedness have important implications for the way in which deep learning develops. Given the relational nature of teachers as complex systems, developing appropriate connections between key elements is central to the learning process because 'new properties and behaviours emerge not only from the elements that constitute a system, but from the myriad connections among them' (Mason, 2008, p. 48). However, while many of these connections will 'naturally' exist, they do not necessarily support the deep and coherent learning that can be applied and transferred across contexts. For example, while some strong connections may help support links between teachers' thinking and practice, weaker connections can lead to the isolation associated with more surface and segmented learning. This weak connectivity would seem to be the main problem with the traditional 'quick fix', short course approach to professional learning because it is often difficult for teachers to integrate new knowledge with existing knowledge and practice and also develop shared understandings with colleagues. Subsequently, taking a complexity thinking approach would suggest there is a need to explore how teachers can be supported to engage in a more connected professional learning approach that creates coherent, connected and situated experiences that can integrate the learning across individual and collective thinking and practice.

Alongside these local connections, there is also a need to acknowledge the influence of the nested school and policy contexts on teachers' practice. With complex systems embedded within nested systems that are 'simultaneously a unity, a collection of unities and a component of a greater unity' (Davis & Sumara, 2001, p. 85), teachers' professional learning will be influenced by the ever-changing school-wide, local authority and national policy trajectories (see Chapter 1 for more about the diverse arrangements that now cover how schools are governed). The relationship between these different nested layers, however, is not straightforward and linear, but creates a 'ripple effect' as the smaller systems feed into the larger system, which in turn exerts influence back into the smaller parts of the system (Morrison, 2003). Accordingly, while policymakers may view the implementation of education policy as a relatively straightforward and simple process, the reality is more complex as policies are viewed differently in different contexts and subsequently enacted in different ways and also to different degrees (Ball et al., 2012). The expectation that traditional professional learning approaches will effectively support developments within these complex local scenarios would seem to be unrealistic and, as noted earlier, overly simplistic.

As the recursive elaboration process unfolds over time and teachers' deeper professional learning develops, their behaviours will oscillate around the edges of the different boundaries they meet. However, while some behaviours remain inside the boundaries, others move around boundaries and others extend beyond the different task, individual and environmental boundaries within their professional context. Over time, therefore, these different 'edge of chaos' behaviours result in teachers' consolidating, challenging and being creative with their behaviour or potentially stagnating, becoming disrupted and even making clear errors and mistakes. Deep, coherent and cumulative professional learning is therefore not the result of a straightforward, time-limited transmission process but one that involves a messy recursive process involving periods of consolidation, stagnation, challenge, disruption, creativity and errors. From a complexity perspective, as teachers engage with a complexity-informed professional learning process they not only acknowledge different starting points but, as the process unfolds, engage in a complex learning process that is self-organising, iterative, connected, bounded and subsequently non-linear. With this background in mind, a complex-informed view of professional learning connects with much of the contemporary literature on professional learning and has presented the DPEG with a useful lens to support the way it now approaches the ongoing development of its professional learning efforts. As such, we now explore how the DPEG have attempted to use these complexity principles to inform its professional learning efforts in recent years.

The DPEG, complexity and professional learning

As ideas from complexity thinking gradually began to inform and frame the DPEG's work, the group members have spent much of the last decade not only grappling to build their own understanding of complexity principles but sharing their thinking with each other and concurrently applying complexity principles in their teaching and professional learning work. Consequently, while the DPEG's early collaborative experiences around 2001 proved to be a significant professional learning experience for the development of the group, it is important to acknowledge that this last decade has been an equally important collective professional learning experience for the group. Therefore, before considering how complexity thinking has gradually come to inform the group's professional learning efforts with students and teachers, the chapter discusses how the group's own engagement with complexity thinking has become a key component of professional learning from both a personal and a collective perspective.

In the initial period of working with complexity thinking, two members of the group spent time negotiating the complexity literature in education and integrated complexity principles with the ecological frame (see Jess et al., 2011). As this development work evolved, the group was regularly engaged in informal conversations about complexity in relation to research and teaching. By 2012, these informal conversations led to a decision being made to undertake a more formal collaborative self-study to track how complexity thinking was shaping the group's professional knowledge and practice (Jess, Atencio & Carse, 2016). This self-study project (see LaBoskey, 2004) has taken the form of a series of focus group and individual interviews involving seven members of the group and has revealed important findings that have not only helped focus the group's ongoing discussions about complexity thinking but, more importantly, have informed the group's professional learning work with students and teachers.

As the self-study evolved, a key finding highlighted how complexity principles have not simply been 'taken off the shelf' and applied by group members in their work. It has become clear that ongoing efforts to understand, share and apply complexity principles has been a recursive and messy process for each group member and remains a 'work in process'. For example, while the first focus group highlighted how members of the group were comfortable using the ecological frame as the starting point for much of their practice, everyone was more tentative about their understanding and use of complexity principles. Two years later, the group was more confident about some of these principles, more willing to share their views with each other and to draw upon the principles to inform their own practice. Later, in 2015, individual interviews revealed that more progress had been made in the group's emotional engagement with complexity and members use of the principles to inform their practice. In particular, the group now talked about how complexity influenced their views on learning and how a combination of principles, namely self-organisation, emergence, ambiguous boundaries, 'edge of chaos' and recursive elaboration, was directly informing their practice. More recently, an emerging theme has been the recognition that the group are now putting complexity 'into practice' and subsequently using these experiences to hone an understanding of the principles. Thus, the study is helping the group recognise how this recursive process has been in play throughout the group's evolution as complexity principles influence both collective thinking and the capacity to work in ways that are governed less by notions of control and certainty and more by self-organisation, emergence and messiness. Crucially, having worked with complexity thinking for several years, this ongoing engagement with key principles has impacted on the way each member approaches the learning process in their own practice. While the early focus group revealed inward struggles to gain some degree of understanding and mastery over key concepts, the more recent interviews demonstrate how the group members have developed an understanding of key principles and increasingly use them to inform their practice. The following two examples from the individual interviews highlight this emerging impact on group members' practice.

Example 1

Louisa, reflecting on her work in schools with children, noted how she confidently embraced key complexity principles when she said:

> the self-organisation and the emergence, it's been a real eye-opener for me to be able to watch my children almost from a different lens and just widen the lens . . . and widen the opportunities of the tasks that you give the children, and just to see what actually does emerge . . . what learning does emerge from just giving a variety of different tasks.

Example 2

Reflecting on her professional development work with teachers, Juliette was now delivering her courses differently based on complexity thinking because it now:

> gives me enough confidence to actually delegate a lot of the stuff to the people who come along so that they can find their way through the complexity of it, the maze that is all of these things.

With specific reference to her outdoors work with teachers, Juliette enthused that

> without doubt what emerges there is unpredictable, it's very open-ended and you've got to be quite brave in the early stages and that's what I usually say to teachers who come on training, that you really have to be brave and step back and let the learning emerge, let the children self-organise and do all of these things . . . the outcome is much richer for the bravery.

This iterative process seems to be helping the group push forward with a more adaptive and innovative agenda to develop complexity thinking as part of a re-envisioning of primary physical education and, as we now discuss, impact upon its professional learning work.

Concurrent with the group's personal efforts to understand and apply complexity thinking, professional learning activities with students and teachers have evolved and changed in a similarly messy manner. Conscious of the drawbacks inherent in the traditional larger scale, short and offsite courses, the group has made numerous attempts to reorient these professional learning efforts. As noted earlier, central to this change has been the work with over 500 primary teachers on the PgCert in 3–14 Physical Education. While the early delivery of the PgCert programme still tended towards a 'safer' top-down approach, as the group became more confident with complexity thinking, recent iterations of the programme have seen a much more participative, interactive and situated experience for the teachers. This change in approach has been facilitated by the long-term and recursive nature of the PgCert, which has enabled DPEG members to experiment with ideas as they support the teachers as self-organising professional learners whose development follows non-linear trajectories in their personal 'bounded' contexts. This self-organising and emergent view of professional learning has heralded a distinct move away from an approach 'imbued with order and fixed certainty' (Rayner, 2008, p. 42), in which participants are treated as 'empty' vessels (Morrison, 2008, p. 25).

By increasingly sharing complexity principles with PgCert teachers, and focussing on a balance of complexity-informed curriculum and pedagogy ideas alongside the teachers' personal professional learning journeys, the DPEG has grown to actively support the recursive, self-organising, collaborative, situated and emergent nature of the teachers' learning. This complexity-informed approach, however, has required the DPEG members to develop a broader and more adaptable 'pedagogical repertoire' that enables them to amend task boundaries and help teachers to consolidate learning, be challenged and display creativity as they engage with the learning process. In addition, while this complexity-informed pedagogical approach sets fluid boundaries across the different elements of the programme it also offers teachers the opportunity to situate their learning within their own contexts, share their experiences with fellow programme members and explore their future roles in physical education contexts. In particular, this approach encourages teachers to adopt leadership roles in their schools and communities: roles that support the development of primary physical education learning communities that produce new and rich behaviours, knowledges and practices (Morrison, 2008) and reflect contemporary innovation agendas (Carse, 2015). This move towards complexity thinking has therefore provided the DPEG with the confidence to more effectively engage with the self-organising, recursive, non-linear and unpredictable nature of professional learning as an essential feature of its innovation agenda.

However, while the group members may now be more confident taking this complexity approach in its university-based work with students and teachers, it has found it particularly difficult to sustain ongoing professional learning relationships with the teachers after they complete the PgCert programme. Attempts to introduce tutor programmes for the teachers, local professional learning communities and wider networks have all had some success, but have also proved to be very difficult to maintain due to time commitments by DPEG members and teachers, different teacher contexts and the ever-changing imperatives at the school and national levels. Subsequently, from these experiences, and in agreement with Kirk (2010), the group have been increasingly attracted to the potential of universities and local schools working together to develop the type of partnerships that offer in-depth collaborations that can sustain innovative projects in practice. In complexity terms, these partnerships offer the opportunity to develop the recursive relationships that recognise teachers, schools and universities are self-organising systems that have different starting points but also have the capacity to interact and support individuals and groups in their negotiation, sharing, consolidation and extension of the professional learning trajectories that ensue. Consequently, as the DPEG enters the next phase of its professional learning journey, it is once again adapting its agenda to concentrate on its relationship with teachers from local schools within its nearest local authority, the City of Edinburgh. With one member of the DPEG currently employed as a development officer in the city, the group's latest efforts are now focussed on working with local authority staff and teachers in an effort to support future primary physical education developments. In its early stages, this partnership is focused on the development of a co-constructed practitioner enquiry project involving members of the DPEG and a small number of teachers who have completed the PgCert. This new pilot project extends the DPEG's own self-study to include an additional ten teachers so that future professional learning activities can be self-initiated by the teachers and DPEG members but can also be supported, developed and shared in a collective learning community. Informed by the principles from complexity thinking discussed in this chapter, the project also connects with the recent professional update requirements put in place by the General Teaching Council of Scotland (GTCS, 2012). As such, while many of the previous professional learning projects have had limited ongoing success, the group are confident that this more focussed and more collaborative effort has the potential to further develop the group's understanding and capacity to share and disseminate its work.

In conclusion, as this chapter progressed it developed the view that teachers' professional learning should be a much more complex and transformative endeavour than is often assumed. Using examples from the DPEG's own professional learning experiences, it has portrayed how the traditional professional learning approach depicted by short, off-site and de-contextualised courses delivered/transmitted by 'experts' is unlikely to have much success in terms of its impact on teachers' professional learning. Consequently, the chapter discusses how principles from complexity and ecological thinking present an opportunity to develop a more theoretically informed approach to teachers' long professional learning. However, by exploring how the DPEG members have spent many years grappling to understand and apply complexity principles in their own practice, the chapter highlights how theory/practice synergy is far from being a simple and straightforward process. Building on this reflective self-study, the chapter concludes by proposing that all those involved in teachers' professional learning, particularly teacher educators and those leading professional learning, should be aware of the self-organising, interactive, recursive, situated and emergent nature of the professional learning process. As such, the chapter presents a strong case for a move towards a more transformative career-long professional learning approach that actively supports teachers' individual and collective capacity to cope with, negotiate and actively influence their own and others' learning.

Future directions

As governments continue to have a significant influence on the direction of education, and physical education in particular, this chapter has presented the view that traditional linear conceptions of teachers' professional learning focussed on policy implementation are both simplistic and unworkable if we are to create a teaching profession that can both cope with and influence the complex nature of learning in the twenty-first century. Although it may appear counter-intuitive to policymakers, the chapter has proposed that ideas from complexity thinking can offer important insights for the future direction of teacher's professional learning. By acknowledging the self-organising nature of the key education stakeholders as complex systems, it is important to recognise that teachers and schools have many differences and will all have different starting points as they engage in the development process (Jess et al., 2016). As such, there is a need for professional learning experiences that are participative, collaborative, situated, recursive and emergent.

For this to happen, however, we propose a need to create the national and local conditions that set out to enable the type of reflective practitioner enquiry and self-study that support a teaching profession who view professional learning as a career-long, complex and valuable process. From a primary physical education perspective we suggest it is critical that those involved in leadership roles acknowledge and understand the complex nature of teachers' professional learning. Accordingly, while traditional professional learning 'courses' undoubtedly have a part to play in this development process, there is a need for more strategic, long-term and situated approaches to primary physical education developments: approaches that help teachers and schools build the capacity to create the primary physical education learning experiences that are developmentally appropriate for all children across their primary school years. Seeking the collective 'buy-in' for a long-term project of this nature is a complex cognitive and emotional process and will require professional development leaders from schools, local authorities, national organisations and universities to rethink the way they approach the creation of professional learning cultures in primary schools. Although it may be a slow and time-consuming process, this reorientation in approach is critical if the time, effort and money spent on professional learning is to succeed in moving primary physical education forward in the future.

Summary of key findings

- Professional learning is now recognised as a key feature of career-long teacher education.
- Linear conceptions of professional learning consisting of short courses transmitted *to* teachers in one-off, off-site sessions by experts are increasingly

viewed as overly simplistic and having limited impact on teachers' thinking and practice.

- A professional learning approach informed by principles from complexity and ecological thinking is presented as a view that connects with much of the contemporary literature on professional learning.
- Those involved in teachers' professional learning, particularly teacher educators and professional learning leaders, should recognise the self-organising, interactive, recursive, situated and emergent nature of the professional learning process.
- A complexity-informed career-long professional learning approach actively seeks to support teachers' individual and collective capacity to cope with, negotiate and influence their own and others' learning.

Reflective tasks

- Reflect on the professional learning courses you have attended and discuss the impact they have had on your professional learning.
- How could the government create an appropriate national context to effectively support teachers' professional learning?
- Consider how important it is for professional learning to be informed by a theoretical perspective.
- From a personal perspective, what would be the most appropriate way you could be supported to develop your professional learning as a career-long endeavour?
- Discuss the importance of collaborative and co-constructed professional learning.

Further readings

Elliot, D., Atencio, M., Jess, M., & Campbell, T. (2013). From PE experiences to PE teaching practices? Insights from Scottish primary teachers' experiences of PE, teacher education and professional development, *Sport, Education and Society*, *18*(6), 749–766.

Keay, J. & Lloyd, C. (2011). *Linking Children's Learning with Professional Learning: Impact, Evidence and Inclusive Practice*. Rotterdam: Sense.

Ovens, A., Hopper, T., & Butler, J. (Eds.). (2013). *Complexity Thinking in Physical Education: Reframing Curriculum, Pedagogy and Research*. London: Routledge.

Note

1 The Scottish Executive was renamed the Scottish Government in 2007.

References

Armour, K. (2006). Physical education teachers as career-long learners: A compelling research agenda, *Physical Education & Sport Pedagogy*, *11*(3), 203–207.

Atencio, M., Jess, M., & Dewar, K. (2012). It is a case of changing your thought processes, the way you actually teach: Implementing a complex professional learning agenda in Scottish physical education, *Physical Education & Sport Pedagogy*, *17*(2), 127–144.

Ball, S., Maguire, M., & Braun, A. (2012). *How Schools Do Policy: Policy Enactments in Secondary Schools*. London: Routledge.

Bransford, J., Brown, A., & Cocking, R. (2000). *How People Learn: Brain, Mind, and Experience & School*. Washington, DC: National Academy Press.

Carse, N. (2015). Primary teachers as physical education curriculum change agents, *European Physical Education Review*, *21*(3), 309–324.

Cilliers, P. (1998). *Complexity and Postmodernism*. London: Routledge.

Davis, B. & Sumara, D. (2001). Learning communities: Understanding the workplace as a complex system, *New Directions for Adult and Continuing Education*, *92*, 85–95.

Deglau, D.A. & O'Sullivan, M. (2006). The effects of a long-term professional development program on the beliefs and practices of experienced teachers, *Journal of Teaching in Physical Education*, *25*(4), 379–396.

Drew, V., Priestley, M., & Michael, K. (2016). Curriculum development through critical collaborative professional enquiry, *Journal of Professional Capital and Community*, *1*(1), 92–106.

Fleet, A. & Patterson, C. (2001). Professional growth reconceptualized: Early childhood staff searching for meaning, *Early Childhood Research & Practice*, *3*(2), 1–11.

GTCS. (2012). The Standards for Registration: mandatory requirements for Registration with the General Teaching Council for Scotland, Edinburgh: General Teaching Council for Scotland.

Helterbran, V. & Fennimore, B. (2004). Collaborative early childhood professional development: Building from a base of teacher investigation, *Early Childhood Education Journal*, *31*(4), 267–271.

Jess, M., Atencio, M., & Carse, N. (2016). Integrating complexity thinking with teacher education practices: A collective yet unpredictable endeavour in physical education?, *Sport, Education & Society*. Retrieved from http://www.tandfonline.com/doi/full/10.1080/13573322.2016.1225195.

Jess, M., Atencio, M., & Thorburn, M. (2011). Complexity theory: Supporting curriculum and pedagogy developments in Scottish physical education, *Sport Education and Society*, *16*(1), 179–199.

Jess M., Dewar, K., and Fraser, G. (2004) Basic Moves: Developing a Foundation for Lifelong Physical Activity. *British Journal of Teaching in Physical Education*, *35*(2), 23–27.

Jess, M., Keay, J., & Carse, N. (2016). Primary physical education: A complex learning journey for children and teachers, *Sport, Education and Society*, *21*(7), 1018–1035.

Jess, M. & McEvilly, N. (2013). Traditional and contemporary approaches to career-long professional learning: A primary physical education journey in Scotland, *Education 3–13: International Journal of Primary, Elementary and Early Years Education*, *43*(3), 225–237.

Jess, M., McEvilly, N., & Carse, N. (2016). Moving primary physical education forward: Start at the beginning, *Education 3–13: International Journal of Primary, Elementary and Early Years Education*. Retrieved from http://www.tandfonline.com/doi/full/10.1080/03004279.2016.1169482.

Kirk, D. (2010). *Physical Education Futures*. London: Routledge.

LaBoskey, V. (2004). 'The methodology of self-study and its theoretical underpinnings.' In: J. Loughran, M. Hamilton, V. LaBoskey & T. Russell (Eds.) *International*

Handbook of Self-Study of Teaching and Teacher Education Practices (pp. 817–869). Dordrecht: Kluwer Academic Publishers.

Lingard, B., Hayes, D., & Mills, M. (2003). Teachers and productive pedagogies: Contextualising, conceptualising, utilising, *Pedagogy, Culture & Society, 11*(3), 399–424.

MacNaughton, G. (2005). *Doing Foucault in Early Childhood Studies: Applying Poststructural Ideas*. Abingdon, Oxon: Routledge.

Mason, M. (2008). What is complexity theory and what are its implications for educational change?, *Education Philosophy and Theory, 40*(1), 135–149.

Morrison, K. (2003). Complexity theory and curriculum reforms in Hong Kong, *Pedagogy, Culture and Society, 11*(2), 279–302.

Morrison, K. (2008). Educational philosophy and the challenge of complexity theory, *Education Philosophy and Theory, 40*(1), 19–34.

Ovens, A., Hopper, T., & Butler, J. (2013). *Complexity Thinking in Physical Education: Reframing Curriculum, Pedagogy and Research*. London: Routledge.

Prigogine, I. (1976). 'Order through fluctuations: Self organization and social system.' In: E. Jantsch & C. Waddington (Eds.) *Evolution and Consciousness: Human Systems in Transition* (pp. 93–130). Reading, MA: Addison-Wesley.

Rayner, S. (2008). Complexity, diversity and management: Some reflections on folklore and learning leadership in education, *Management in Education, 22*(2), 40–46.

Rovegno, I. (2006). 'Situated perspectives on learning.' In: D. Kirk, D. Macdonald & M. O'Sullivan (Eds.) *The Handbook of Physical Education* (pp. 262–274). London: Sage.

Scottish Executive. (2003). *Let's Make Scotland More Active: A Strategy for Physical Activity*. Edinburgh: HMSO.

Scottish Executive. (2004). *The Report of The Review Group on Physical Education*. Edinburgh: HMSO.

Scottish Government. (2011). *Teaching Scotland's Future: Report of a Review of Teacher Education in Scotland*. Edinburgh: Scottish Government.

Sheridan, S., Pope Edwards, C., Marvin, C., & Knoche, L. (2009). Professional development in early childhood programs: Process issues and research needs, *Early Education and Development, 20*(3), 377–401.

Wenger, E. (1998). *Communities of Practice: Learning, Meaning, and Identity*. Cambridge: Cambridge University Press.

Part III
The school perspective

5 Start young

The possibilities of primary physical education

Mike Jess

Introduction

While primary physical education has traditionally been positioned on the margins of education, there have been some encouraging signs recently as it has begun to receive more attention from across the political, professional and academic sectors. This change in fortune has primarily come from a growing belief that these formative experiences have the potential to help combat many of the concerns currently being voiced about children's health and wellbeing, physical activity levels and sport participation (Petrie & Hunter, 2011), and not necessarily from any shift in perception about the subject's educational value. Accordingly, while this increased interest is to be welcomed, the ongoing lack of clarity about the educational purpose of physical education (e.g. Kirk, 2010) and the long-term disquiet about the quality of primary physical education (e.g. Harris, Cale & Musson, 2011; Morgan & Bourke, 2008; Tsangaridou, 2014) would suggest that significant development may still be some way off, certainly in educational terms. In fact, this sudden rise in perceived importance may place primary physical education in a precarious position as an ever-increasing number of interested parties from the education, politics, sport, health, commerce and community sectors seek to claim a degree of 'legitimate' ownership of the primary physical education domain (e.g. Petrie, 2016). At the heart of this complex predicament is the realisation that these different stakeholder groups often hold different, even contradictory, views about the purpose and nature of primary physical education. For example, at the United Kingdom policy level an agenda focussed on sport and competition drives primary physical education developments in England (Department for Education, 2013), while the Scottish policy imperative is firmly directed towards a more holistic health and wellbeing agenda (Scottish Government, 2009). As a consequence of these quite different political perspectives, primary physical education in England has increasingly been 'outsourced' to agencies from the sport and private sectors (Griggs, 2016), while in Scotland physical education remains firmly entrenched as part of the primary school (Jess, Carse & Keay, 2016). It is, subsequently, becoming increasingly difficult to recognise what is, and who has, the 'real' primary physical education.

It is with this background in mind that this chapter seeks to build on much of what has been written in the previous two chapters by proposing the need for a transformative agenda to drive the future direction of primary physical education. This agenda is based on the belief that primary physical education is a much more complex phenomenon than it has traditionally been viewed. More specifically, primary physical education is presented as an educational endeavour that functions concurrently at three inter-related levels: as a subject area in its own right, integrating across the primary school curriculum and also acting as a catalyst for children's engagement in a physically active life beyond the school gates. Consequently, given the multiple interpretations of primary physical education currently 'doing the rounds', it will be argued that this layered educational aspiration is critical to the subject's future because it seeks to position primary physical education as a key part of the world of education while concurrently developing connections and partnerships with health, sport and other arenas.

Primary physical education: A complex educational agenda

Informed by the complexity and ecological ideas discussed in Chapter 3 and 4, the chapter discusses how three key ecological factors act to frame this educational agenda for primary physical education, i.e. the primary physical education curriculum and its related pedagogy, teachers' primary physical education professional learning and the stakeholders influencing primary physical education (see Jess, Keay & Carse, 2014 for a more detailed discussion about the rationale behind these three factors). From a complexity perspective it is important to stress that each of these three factors are not viewed as stable, fixed entities but as emergent and adaptable phenomena that have the capacity to self-organise and change over time as they interact with each other and with a range of other factors. While the degree of self-organisation and interaction activity between these three factors has traditionally been quite limited in the context of primary physical education, the recent increase in attention being offered the subject area has resulted in more interactive activity, albeit leading to developments that are messy, uncertain and not necessarily educational in nature. By strategically viewing curriculum and pedagogy, teachers' professional learning and the key stakeholders through this complexity lens, the chapter considers how this shift in perspective represents an opportunity to view primary physical education from a clear educational perspective.

The primary physical education curriculum and pedagogy

In a book chapter written a number of years ago (Jess, 2012) I presented a personal experience of a specific physical education lesson I had observed in a primary school: a lesson encapsulating many of the issues that plague primary physical education. In this example, I stopped my car to observe a physical education lesson in which a class of children (about 10 years of age) were playing rounders[1] in the school playground. The term 'playing', as I discuss, is being used loosely.

For the next 20 minutes I watched as almost all the children spent most of their time standing or sitting watching one of their classmates trying to use a small bat to hit a ball that was being bowled by the teacher. The teacher and children were in their normal school clothes. For periods of time, half of the class stood in the 'field', while the other half waited in a line before getting their chance to bat. Throughout the session, the teacher focussed on bowling and organising the batters, although she occasionally made some comment to individual children about the technical aspects of how to hold and swing the bat whilst also chastising the fielders for not behaving and trying hard enough. Almost all the children got a chance to bat, although quite a number failed to hit the ball on three consecutive attempts and simply returned to the end of the batting line. Most of the children who hit the ball managed a weak strike to send the ball dribbling along the ground to a fielder close by. Twice during my observation a batter delivered a big hit and everyone clapped. I watched for 20 minutes and, although I could say the children seemed to be enjoying themselves, I would also have to say that they were not doing much at all.

Since then I have presented this experience with many groups of teachers and students and could spend the rest of the chapter focussing on the myriad issues that have emerged from these discussions. However, three key issues are of particular importance to this chapter:

- compartmentalising primary physical education in the physical;
- the lack of apparent educational value;
- the importance of pedagogy.

Compartmentalising primary physical education in the physical

Throughout my observation of the lesson, while most of the children demonstrated some understanding of the rules of the game, the only learning the teacher seemed to spend any time highlighting, albeit minimally, was focussed on the physical technique of batting. While rounders, as a striking and fielding game, has many potential learning opportunities, the teacher only seemed to view the experience in terms of the physical aspects of the activity with virtually no attention being given to the more holistic and connective cognitive, social and emotional learning possibilities. From an educational perspective, this over-emphasis on the physical has long been a significant issue for primary physical education, and physical education in general, because it narrows the nature of the children's learning experience and results in primary physical education falling into a 'compartmentalisation trap'. As Gallahue and Donnelly (2003, p. 11) have previously highlighted, this 'compartmentalisation is a root cause for the difficulty that physical education has had historically in establishing itself as a legitimate aspect of the school curriculum'. With Cartesian views of a mind–body divide continuing to dominate much of Western education, this compartmentalisation traditionally positions physical education as being solely a physical learning experience and subsequently inferior to more cognitive subjects, particularly

English and mathematics (Pickup & Price, 2007). Accordingly, in the rounders example, physical education was not only being perceived to be a physical experience but also of limited educational importance to the teacher or children.

In a broader curriculum sense, this overemphasis on the physical has been evident in the multi-activity approach that has long dominated the overall physical education curriculum for many years and appears in a watered-down format in many primary schools (Griggs & Ward, 2012). With a 'sport-as-technique' focus (Kirk, 2010), this multi-activity approach offers a range of specific physical activities in short 5–8 week lesson 'blocks' during which time the main emphasis is on the technical performance of the movement skills related to the specific activity (Jewett & Bain, 1985). While this approach may still dominate practice in many parts of the world, its restricted 'one-size-fits-all' focus on the physical learning experience has been increasingly criticised as simply being a physical sampling exercise (Cothran, 2001) that offers fragmented and de-contextualised experiences (Siedentop, 1994) and fails to support transfer of learning across different contexts (Thorburn, Jess & Atencio, 2009). In essence, concerns about the educational value of this traditional curriculum approach are now commonplace (e.g. Casey, 2012; Jess & Gray, 2016; Kirk, 2013; Penney, 2008).

In addition to the multi-activity emphasis on movement skill, the recent (re-)emergence of health, obesity and physical activity imperatives has seen physical education's focus on the physical being further consolidated by way of the perceived biomedical connection between levels of physical activity and obesity (Johns, 2005). Subsequently, many health professionals now conflate the terms physical education and physical activity and propose moves towards 'learning' experiences focussed on heart rate elevation, calorific expenditure and the measurement of body mass index (Gard, 2008).

Consequently, while few are likely to contest the importance of the physical in primary physical education, this section has highlighted how an enduring overemphasis on the physical has traditionally resulted in physical education being positioned on the margins of the primary school curriculum. However, with primary physical education currently being more in the public domain, there is an opportunity to present the subject as one of educational value and begin a process that will move it beyond this compartmentalising that has limited its role in the primary school setting.

The lack of apparent educational value

Whilst moving the emphasis of primary physical education from a more reductionist physical focus will ultimately require a 'hearts and minds' shift for many key stakeholders, any change in direction will be predicated upon a clarification of the educational value of children's physical education. Specifically, there needs to be a much clearer articulation of how an educational future for primary physical education will logically and authentically connect to broader educational agendas. As was argued earlier in Chapter 3, by framing this educational agenda within a lifelong and lifewide learning perspective (Penney & Jess, 2004) it is suggested that primary physical education can be plausibly represented as the foundational learning experience that supports learners' engagement in an authentic active life. With physical learning undoubtedly a key feature of this more educationally-oriented approach, it is important to recognise that children also need to develop the cognitive, social and emotional knowledge and skills to help them effectively self-organise and interact in ways that support their long-term but non-linear engagement in physical activity. From a primary physical education perspective, the focus should consequently be on those learning experiences that consistently support connections within the subject area itself, across the primary curriculum in the school setting and also beyond the curriculum to children's lives (Penney & Jess, 2004). Children therefore need to be supported to not only develop the appropriate knowledge, understanding and skills to participate across a range of physical activity contexts but also need the self-organising, interactive and emergent capacities to help them become adaptable learners who can cope with, negotiate and influence the many different physical activity contexts they will meet across their lives.

In this vein, the notion of physical education as a 'connective specialism' acting as a 'hub' to link with educational and lifelong learning agendas is of particular interest (Penney, 2008). Working as part of the Developmental Physical Education Group (DPEG), and linking with complexity thinking ideas, we have been working to design and apply this more connective educational agenda in practice. More specifically, the group has been focussing on 'children's "core learning" as an evolving self-organising foundation that is a mix of similarities and diversities that can be applied and transferred to connect across a range of different physical activity contexts (applications) throughout life' (Jess & Carse, 2016, p. 7). As such, two interrelated elements have consistently been at the heart of this work: core learning and applications (Jess, 2004; Jess, Atencio & Thorburn, 2011; Jess et al., 2016; Jess, Haydn-Davies & Pickup, 2007; Penney & Chandler, 2000). Core learning experiences focus on the holistic learning that helps children develop, consolidate, apply and transfer their generic learning across a range of formal and informal physical activity contexts (or applications). This core learning is viewed as a key feature of the educational vision for primary physical education because it refers to the complex and recursive interaction between the physical, cognitive, social and emotional aspects of children's and young people's learning (Bailey et al., 2009). As such, this interactive process helps children develop the efficiency, adaptability and creativity to participate in a wide range of physical activity contexts (Jess, Dewar & Fraser, 2004). Further, core learning is not viewed as a set of 'building blocks' or 'fundamentals' learned in a traditional 'blocked' or de-contextualised manner, but as a long-term recursive process that scaffolds the non-linear messiness of children's learning pathway. Consequently, as the DPEG has grappled to develop core learning experiences informed by complexity thinking it has not sought to create the 'silver bullet' programme that has the 'quick fix' answers for primary teachers. Conversely, the group itself has been recursively shaping and reworking those learning activities that develop and connect children's emerging core learning with a range of increasingly more complex and authentic applications (Jess, 2012; Jess, Atencio & Carse, 2013; Jess, Carse, McMillan & Atencio, 2012).

The importance of pedagogy

Aligned to these complexity-informed curriculum ideas, it is important to acknowledge the key role that pedagogy plays in creating a positive and effective learning environment. Returning to the earlier rounders example, the pedagogy employed by the teacher in this instance could be described as transmissive or behaviourist, limited and even self-indulgent as she controlled the key bowling role. In this sense, the only person who seemed to be consistently absorbed in the learning experience was the bowler i.e. the teacher. Most of the children had a limited engagement as they received occasional instructions or comments about their lack of 'effort'. For many years, this top-down behaviourist teaching approach has been presented as the stereotypical physical education pedagogy in which children become the passive recipients of technical information transmitted by the teacher (e.g. Kirk, 2010). With this in mind, the DPEG has spent a number of years suggesting that primary (and secondary) teachers should seek to explore the possibilities of a 'pedagogy of emergence' based on the recognition that children's learning involves a self-organising, interactive, recursive and non-linear process (Jess et al., 2011). As such, the group suggests that teachers should look to develop a pedagogical repertoire that:

- recognises children's previous experiences and, subsequently, their different starting points;
- focuses on learning intentions that are less about certain outcomes but long term and not 'quick fixes';
- involves a process of recursive elaboration that supports children's adaptability so that they can apply and transfer their learning over many different applications;
- signposts connections within, across and beyond physical education.

In line with Chow and Atencio (2012) and others, it is important to recognise that teachers are therefore in a position to amend the different task and environmental factors in order to create a subtle mixture of tasks that support consolidation, challenge and creativity at different times in the children's learning process. These dynamic and ever-changing tasks encourage the children to learn through a combination of exploration, success and error (Jess et al., 2011). As such, this complex emergent approach to pedagogy engages children more actively in the learning process, helps them explore and create their own learning experiences and also supports their developing capacity to recognise and acknowledge the unpredictable nature of the many physical activity contexts they will meet over the years.

Combining this move towards a more educationally focussed curriculum and 'pedagogy of emergence' creates a vision for primary physical education that is very different from the rounders' example. Critically, this educational view seeks to position primary physical education as a key feature of children's overall learning experience in a way that offers them the opportunity to recognise different learning trajectories and connections across many parts of their collective lives. This more contemporary educational vision for primary physical education has received some support from people, like myself, who work as primary physical education specialist teachers or teacher educators. However, getting a similar 'buy-in' to this vision from primary teachers and the other key stakeholders remains a more difficult proposition. Consequently, the chapter now turns to these two groups because they have a key role in the delivery of primary physical education and in framing the direction of the subject area in the future. As such, the focus will first be on the professional learning of primary teachers who, in the main, are the main delivery agents of physical education in primary school settings, before turning to the other key stakeholders.

Teachers' professional learning

For many years, much has been written about the nature and the quality of primary teachers' professional development in physical education. Reports about initial teacher education have consistently highlighted experiences that are limited and often inappropriate, while the professional learning opportunities for in-service primary teachers have traditionally been depicted as infrequent, short, off-site courses that usually involve the transmission of different types of specific knowledge, e.g. lesson plans, activity-specific skill development etc. (e.g. Keay & Spence, 2012). These professional learning experiences usually ignore the previous experiences and needs of students and teachers, focus on the products as opposed to the process of learning and generally appear to have little impact on the confidence and/or competence of the teachers in their delivery of physical education (HMIE, 2001; Morgan & Bourke, 2008). Therefore, if primary teachers are to be expected to acknowledge and engage with an educational vision for primary physical education a significant challenge lies ahead because of the current conception of physical education held by many teachers, the low levels of confidence and competence when teaching physical education and, critically, the nature of the professional learning experiences that appear to dominate the primary sector. To witness a shift in the quality of primary physical education there is a need to not only acknowledge the importance of teachers' professional learning but also recognise it as a complex process that cannot have as its basis a simplistic linear 'quick fix' approach. As complex systems, teachers, like the children and classes they teach, self-organise their learning at different rates, in different contexts and pass along different non-linear professional learning pathways. It is therefore proposed that professional learning should be designed to help teachers develop the capacity to self-organise their professional learning journeys in ways that impact upon their practice in relation to the physical education learning of their children and colleagues. This shift should therefore be towards a professional learning approach that is more emergent, collaborative, situated and, crucially, recursive in nature.

However, given the way that primary physical education is often viewed in primary schools, this form of professional learning will position many teachers in an uncomfortable position as it necessitates a move beyond a 'PE is easy' scenario towards an understanding and acknowledgement of the educational value of physical education, a curriculum framework that supports this vision and also a pedagogical approach that enables the enactment of this vision. While short, knowledge-based courses will have a role to play in this complex view of professional learning, there is also a need to recognise other key considerations that will influence this professional learning process. Chapter 4 contains more detail about these professional learning considerations but four of the key interrelated considerations are now discussed.

- Primary teachers will need to be supported in viewing their physical education professional learning as a recursive process that begins in their initial teacher education and involves a process of regular revisiting focussed on improving their physical education practices. This recursive process is key because it encourages teachers to develop their thinking and practice over time as they explore possibilities, consolidate ideas and skills, challenge themselves and even make errors, much in the complex way their children will learn. By focussing on their professional learning in this way, teachers, individually and collectively, will not only develop the capacity to meet their children's needs, but will also be able to identify their professional learning needs and, subsequently, provide evidence of their own professional learning (GTCS, 2012; Keay & Lloyd, 2011).
- Because teachers are situated within larger nested systems tasked with the shared development of physical education across the primary years, it is important they come together regularly to develop some key similarities that will help bring a degree of order and connectedness to the children's physical education experiences across their primary years, e.g. shared educational vision, curriculum and pedagogy ideas.
- Primary physical education professional learning, as already alluded to, should not be an infrequent, isolated, add-on experience but one that is connected to the shared endeavour within the context the teachers are working. With physical education traditionally on the margins of the primary school, many primary teachers may not see the importance of integrating their primary physical education professional learning with the curriculum and pedagogical practices that take place within their classroom. As I discuss later, this change in mind-set towards physical education is not only important for primary teachers but also for the key stakeholders who influence the place of physical education within the education system.
- At a personal level, teachers will need to actively negotiate the ever-changing local and wider influences that impact on their thinking and practice around physical education. Making, or having, the time to reflect on how their previous experiences, personal interests and current capacities act as boundaries to their professional learning and practice would seem to be both a logical and necessary starting point for this process (Elliot, Atencio, Jess & Campbell,

2013; Lawson, 1983). By regularly reflecting on the impact of these changing boundaries, teachers will hopefully view their primary physical education professional learning as a long-term and recursive process and not simply as a 'quick fix' add-on to their 'real' work.

Given the complex but generic nature of the primary teacher role in most countries, it would not seem logical or appropriate to suggest that all primary teachers focus on physical education professional learning in this way. However, it would seem appropriate that all primary teachers should be supported to approach their overall professional learning in this way and that physical education should be a part of this complex, recursive process. However, for the future of primary physical education, there is a need, possibly an urgent need, for a capacity-building exercise that enables significant numbers of primary teachers to engage with a more detailed and recursive physical education professional learning experience, possibly in a similar fashion to the PgCert in 3–14 Physical Education that was discussed in Chapter 4. However, as the final section of the chapter now discusses, other key stakeholders have a significant role in helping create the enabling context across the layers of the education system that will support teachers' engagement in this type of educationally-informed professional learning.

The key stakeholders

While this chapter has sought to present a transformative complexity-informed agenda for the curriculum, pedagogy and professional learning in primary physical education, as just noted, the enactment of this educationally-oriented vision will ultimately be predicated upon a number of key enabling conditions being in place. While the higher profile of primary physical education at the policy level may be one key enabler, the escalated interest has created a more congested political arena in which the educational voice is often less in evidence (Petrie & Hunter, 2011). Consequently, while a shared educational vision for primary physical education across the stakeholder community may be some way off, efforts to pursue a 'shifting perspectives' agenda in this vein are likely to be critical for the short- and long-term development of the subject area. However, it is suggested that this 'shifting perspectives' agenda will need to be approached in a strategic manner by first identifying those who have the background, capacity and desire to initiate and enact an agenda of this nature.

In itself, this strategic approach creates a dilemma as a number of factors 'closer to home' are likely to mediate against this educational vision for primary physical education being voiced consistently. As discussed in Chapter 3, because the physical education profession concentrates most of its efforts on the more specialist-oriented secondary school years, primary physical education has generally been left on the margins of its own profession. As a result, the professional and academic voices speaking for primary physical education have consistently come from groups whose main focus and expertise lies in the more subject-centred arena of the secondary school. Consequently, while the physical education profession may be the most appropriate stakeholder to present a robust educational case for primary physical education, it is unclear how this case is best presented and by whom. There subsequently remains an internal need for the physical education profession to not only work to articulate the educational vision for primary physical education but also identify who should best represent primary physical education to the different stakeholders. While this internal negotiation may be daunting, uncomfortable and time consuming, it is unlikely that any significant progress can be made without it.

In addition to the complex nature of this internal dilemma, there is a simultaneous need for the physical education profession to work with the different stakeholders in efforts to create the capacity to shift the perspective on a larger scale (Fullan, 1999). Simply, if primary physical education is to move forward it must seek to engage with key educational, sport, health and other agendas by involving many cross-sector stakeholders in the development process. While children and teachers are directly involved at the micro level, a myriad of different stakeholders influence the current and future state of primary physical education. These stakeholders range from primary school management, local community groups, regional authorities, national agencies, professional learning providers, policymakers, parents, the wider general public and the media. Critically, as noted above, many of these stakeholders hold different visions for primary physical education so it is incumbent on the physical education profession to consider how best to work with these different groups in order to develop a more closely aligned or shared vision of what can move primary physical education forward more effectively. With such a variety of stakeholders now involved in primary physical education, progress towards this shared educational vision will require both a cognitive and emotional 'buy-in' by all parties. As such, it is important to recognise that this 'shifting perspective' agenda, while vital, will be a long-term, messy and potentially frustrating experience.

Conclusion

While primary physical education is currently witnessing something of a revival across the education section, this chapter has cautioned that many factors influencing the quality of children's physical education experiences will need to be addressed if this attention is to result in significant long-term benefits. By focussing on three complex interacting factors, i.e. curriculum and pedagogy, teachers' professional learning and a 'shifting perspectives' agenda, the chapter has argued that key ideas from complexity thinking have the potential to support an approach that will help primary physical education be developed as a more holistic and lifelong educational subject with significant cross-sector appeal. This educational vision sees primary physical education moving beyond the traditional compartmentalising within the physical domain to overtly incorporate key learning from the cognitive, social and emotional domains alongside a 'pedagogy of emergence' that acknowledges the self-organising, interactive and emergent nature of the learning process. It has been argued that this change in curriculum and pedagogy needs to be concurrently supported by a more informed approach to teachers' long-term professional learning: an approach that acknowledges teachers as complex learners who also self-organise and interact in a recursive process. In addition, it has also been argued that the more congested primary physical education landscape urgently requires a 'shifting perspective' agenda that not only moves primary physical education to the top of the physical education profession's development agenda but also seeks to find the most appropriate way to share the educational vision for primary physical education so that all key stakeholders may develop a shared vision for the future of the subject area. While this overall agenda may be ambitious, given more than a century on the margins, it is essential that those involved in primary physical education come together to help build the capacity for primary physical education to become a central feature of children's education in the future.

Key findings

- While primary physical education has long been on the margins of education it has recently received increased attention across the political, professional and academic sectors.
- Concerns remain about the quality of children's learning in primary physical education.
- The compartmentalising of primary physical education as only a physical subject has reduced its perceived educational value in schools.
- Complexity thinking principles are suggested as a way to help position primary physical education as a more holistic educational endeavour.
- Reorienting primary physical education is predicated upon key developments in curriculum, pedagogy, teacher's professional learning and a 'shifting perspectives' agenda.

Reflective tasks

- Discuss why primary physical education has recently become more visible in the policy, professional and academic sectors.
- Why do concerns about the quality of primary physical education remain?
- Why is it important for primary physical education to be viewed as a holistic educational endeavour?
- Discuss how teachers' professional learning can be developed to support the future of primary physical education.
- Discuss the importance of key stakeholders having a shared understanding of, and vision for, primary physical education.

Further readings

Bailey, R., Armour, K., Kirk, D., Jess, M., Pickup, I., & Sandford, R. (2009). The educational benefits claimed for physical education and school sport: An academic review, *Research Papers in Education, 24*(1), 1–27.

Fullan, M. (2004). *Learning to Lead Change, Building System Capacity: Core Concepts.* Toronto: Change Forces.

Note

1 Rounders is a striking and fielding game played in UK schools and has similarities to baseball and softball.

References

Bailey, R., Armour, K., Kirk, D., Jess, M., Pickup, I., & Sandford, R. (2009). The educational benefits claimed for physical education and school sport: An academic review, *Research Papers in Education, 24*(1), 1–27.

Casey, A. (2012). Models-based practice: Great white hope or white elephant?, *Physical Education and Sport Pedagogy, 19*(1), 18–34.

Chow, J. & Atencio, M. (2012). Complex and nonlinear pedagogy and the implications for physical education, *Sport, Education and Society, 19*(8), 1034–1054.

Cothran, D. (2001). Curricular change in physical education: Success stories from the front line, *Sport, Education and Society, 6*(1), 67–79.

Department for Education. (2013). *The National Curriculum: Framework Document.* London: Department for Education.

Elliot, D., Atencio, M., Jess, M., & Campbell, T. (2013). From PE experiences to PE teaching practices? Insights from Scottish primary teachers' experiences of PE, teacher education and professional development, *Sport, Education and Society, 18*(6), 749–766.

Fullan, M. (1999). *Change Forces the Sequel.* London: The Falmer Press.

Gallahue, D. & Cleland Donnelly, F. (2003). *Developmental Physical Education for All Children.* Leeds: Human Kinetics.

Gard, M. (2008). Producing little decision makers and goal setters in the age of the obesity crisis, *Quest, 60*(4), 488–502.

Griggs, G. (2016). Spending the primary physical education and sport premium: A west midlands case study, *Education 3–13: International Journal of Primary, Elementary and Early Years Education, 44*(5), 547–556.

Griggs, G. & Ward, G. (2012). Physical education in the UK: Disconnections and reconnections, *Curriculum Journal, 23*(2), 207–229.

GTCS. (2012). *The Standards for Registration: Mandatory Requirements for Registration with the General Teaching Council for Scotland.* Edinburgh: General Teaching Council for Scotland.

Harris, J., Cale, L., & Musson, H. (2011). The effects of a professional development programme on primary school teachers' perceptions of physical education, *Professional Development in Education, 37*(2), 291–305.

HMIE. (2001). *Improving Physical Education in Primary Schools.* Edinburgh: HMIE.

Jess, M. (2004). *The Basic Moves National Training Programme: Level 1 Manual.* Edinburgh: University of Edinburgh.

Jess, M. (2012a). 'Becoming and effective primary school physical education teacher.' In: K. Armour (Ed.) *Sports Pedagogy: An Introduction for Teaching and Coaching* (pp. 271–291). London: Prentice Hall.

Jess, M. (2012b). 'The future of primary PE: A 3–14 developmental and connected curriculum.' In: G. Griggs (Ed.) *An Introduction to Primary Physical Education* (pp. 37–54). Abingdon: Routledge.

Jess, M., Atencio, M., & Carse, N. (2013). 'Introducing conditions of complexity in the context of Scottish physical education.' In: A. Ovens, T. Hopper & J. Butler

(Eds.) *Complexity Thinking in Physical Education: Reframing Curriculum, Pedagogy and Research* (pp. 27–41). London: Routledge.

Jess, M., Atencio, M., & Thorburn, M. (2011). Complexity theory: Supporting curriculum and pedagogy developments in Scottish physical education, *Sport Education and Society, 16*(1), 179–199.

Jess, M., & Carse, N. (2016). Complexity Thinking and Early Childhood Physical Education, Paper presented at the 6th International TGfU Conference at the German Sports University, Cologne, Germany from 25–27 July.

Jess, M., Carse, N., & Keay, J. (2016). The primary physical education curriculum process: More complex that you might think!!, *Education 3–13: International Journal of Primary, Elementary and Early Years Education*. Retrieved from http://www.tandfonline.com/doi/full/10.1080/03004279.2016.1169482.

Jess, M., Carse, N., McMillan, P., & Atencio, M. (2012). Sport education in Scottish primary school: Emergence of an authentic application.' In: P. Hastie (Ed.) *Sport Education: International Perspectives* (pp. 41–57). London: Routledge.

Jess, M. & Gray, S. (2016). 'Curriculum reform and policy cohesion in physical education.' In: C. Ennis (Ed.) *Routledge Handbook of Physical Education Pedagogy* (pp. 143–156). London: Routledge.

Jess, M., Haydn-Davies, D., & Pickup, I. (2007). Physical education in the primary school: A developmental, inclusive and connected future, *Physical Education Matters, 2*(1), 16–20.

Jess, M., Keay, J., & Carse, N. (2016). Primary physical education: A complex learning journey for children and teachers, *Sport, Education and Society, 21*(7), 1018–1035.

Jewett, A. & Bain, L. (1985). *The Curriculum Process in Physical Education*. Madison, WI: Brown.

Johns, D. (2005). Recontextualizing and delivering the biomedical model as a physical education curriculum, *Sport, Education and Society, 10*(1), 69–84.

Keay, J. & Lloyd, C. (2011). *Linking Children's Learning with Professional Learning: Impact, Evidence and Inclusive Practice*. Rotterdam: Sense.

Keay, J. & Spence, J. (2012). 'Professional development in primary physical education.' In: G. Griggs (Ed.) *An Introduction to Primary Physical Education* (pp. 179–194). Abingdon: Routledge.

Kirk, D. (2010). *Physical Education Futures*. London: Routledge.

Kirk, D. (2013). Educational value and models-based practice in physical education, *Educational Philosophy and Theory, 45*(9), 973–986.

Lawson, H. (1983). Toward a model of teacher socialization in physical education: The subjective warrant, recruitment, and teacher education, *Journal of Teaching in Physical Education, 2*(3), 3–16.

Morgan, P. & Bourke, S. (2008). Non-specialist teachers' confidence to teach PE: The nature and influence of personal school experiences in PE, *Physical Education and Sport Pedagogy, 13*(2), 1–29.

Penney, D. (2008). Playing a political game and playing for position: Policy and curriculum development in health and physical education, *European Physical Education Review, 14*(1), 33–50.

Penney, D. & Chandler, T. (2000). Physical education: What futures?, *Sport, Education & Society, 5*(1), 71–87.

Penney, D. & Jess, M. (2004). Physical education and physically active lives: A life-long approach to curriculum development, *Sport, Education and Society, 9*(2), 269–287.

Petrie, K. (2016). Architectures of practice: Constraining or enabling PE in primary schools, *Education 3–13: International Journal of Primary, Elementary and Early Years Education.* Retrieved from http://www.tandfonline.com/doi/full/10.1080/03004279.2016.1169484.

Petrie, K. & Hunter, L. (2011). Primary teachers, policy, and physical education, *European Physical Education Review, 17*(3), 325–339.

Pickup, I. & Price, L. (2007). *Teaching Physical Education in the Primary School: A Developmental Approach.* London: Continuum.

Scottish Government. (2009). *Curriculum for Excellence: Experiences and Outcomes.* Retrieved from http://www.ltscotland.org.uk/curriculumforexcellence/experiencesandoutcomes/index.asp.

Siedentop, D. (1994). *Sport Education: Quality PE through Positive Sport Experiences.* Champaign, IL: Human Kinetics.

Thorburn, M., Jess, M., & Atencio, M. (2009). Connecting policy aspirations with principled progress? An analysis of current physical education challenges in Scotland, *Irish Educational Studies, 28*(2), 207–221.

Tsangaridou, N. (2014). Moving towards effective physical education teacher education for generalist primary teachers: A view from Cyprus, *Education 3–13: International Journal of Primary, Elementary and Early Years Education.* Retrieved from http://www.tandfonline.com/doi/full/10.1080/03004279.2014.952757.

6 Physical education teachers as agents of policy and curriculum change

Justine MacLean

Introduction

This chapter was written at a time when an understanding of the complexities of policy and design were evolving globally at a rapid rate. In recent years, schools have entered an era of educational reform with evidence of an epidemic of curriculum change worldwide (Levin, 1998). Scotland's new national policy initiative 'Curriculum for Excellence' (CfE) typifies the international trends in educational reform (Priestley, 2010) and was heralded as 'one of the most ambitious programmes of educational change ever undertaken in Scotland' (Scottish Government, 2008, p. 8). CfE was introduced in 2010 and aimed to ensure that, 'all children and young people in Scotland develop the knowledge, skills and attributes they need to flourish in life, learning and work, now and in the future,' (Scottish Executive, 2004). Physical education forms part of a collective alongside physical activity and sport, within the newly created curriculum area of 'Health and Wellbeing'. HWB is one of the core areas of the curriculum along with literacy and numeracy. The aims of CfE were ambitious and were 'designed to achieve a transformation in education in Scotland by providing a coherent, more flexible and enriched curriculum from 3 to 18' (Scottish Executive, 2004).

CfE is an example of modern-day curricular reform with top-down, government-led policy mediated by teachers initiating bottom-up curricular development as agents of change (Priestley, 2010). Two major principles are reflected in this kind of curricular reform: firstly, the acknowledgement that the school is a human social institution that requires to be responsive to its own environment and be allowed to develop in a way that suits that environment (Skilbeck, 1976). Secondly, the centrality of the teacher to modify, adapt, develop and create specific curricular to meet the needs of the individual pupil (Kelly, 2009). As such, teachers interpret a flexible curricular framework and exercise agency to recreate policy in their unique contextual setting. The policy text is 'less detailed and prescriptive than previous curriculum advice, it provides professional space for teachers and other staff to use in order to meet the varied needs of all children and young people' (Scottish Executive, 2004, p. 1)

Priestley (2011, p. 2) identifies a dichotomy developing in contemporary educational policy, one that either poses teachers as 'simple implementers of teacher proof curricula' or, alternatively, views teachers as 'active agents' in the change process. Policies generally do not tell the teacher exactly what to do: they seldom prescribe or define practice, but some more than others restrict the range of teacher response and involvement in the policy process. CfE sought to create a stronger component of ownership and creativity at school level and as such 'reflects the growing body of evidence that teachers are among the most powerful influences on learning and are best placed to determine how best to meet the needs of their pupils' (Donaldson, 2014, p. 181).

CfE – along with the New Zealand Curriculum, Australian Curriculum and more recently England's National Curriculum – displays typical features of this new type of policy trajectory. CfE required teachers to be actively involved at school level in the creation and design of the new curriculum and encouraged teachers to transform the curriculum to be fit for purpose and to promote best practice (Scottish Qualifications Authority, 2012). These aims reflected the needs of a rapidly changing society, and were not dissimilar from those introduced to Finnish education following the 1994 curricular reform (Vulliamy, Kimonen, Nevalainen & Webb, 1997). Likewise, the Australian curriculum is typical of this worldwide trend and is explicitly designed with inbuilt openness to enable authorities and schools to engage in reflective, individualised practice (ACARA, 2015). In this context, enabling curriculum innovation is probably less about the rigid adherence to policy (as inscribed in texts), but rather more akin to a process of teachers acting to bring policy intentions into being (MacLean, Mulholland, Gray & Horrell, 2015).

Given the complexities that surround the enactment of new policy in physical education this chapter invites readers to examine the tensions, issues and challenges that physical education teachers' face when *transforming* their practice to enact new curricular policy in their school setting. It begins by considering the complexities of policy, i.e. policy and transformational change and the importance of teacher voice in the policy process. Thereafter, the chapter considers the significance of teacher agency within the contextual dimensions of the school as important elements that enable teachers to enact and sustain change. Throughout the chapter references to specific research studies in Scotland, UK and internationally are analysed in order to highlight some of the complexities of transformational change in educational reform. The journey commences by examining the involvement of key stakeholders in the policy design process and concludes with some thoughts and projections into future directions of policy in physical education.

Main findings
Policy

It is useful from the outset to consider some of the meanings attached to terms that are common to policy discussions. What do we mean by 'policy', how can we understand it and how do we measure evidence of its effects? In an attempt to understand these issues, Ball (2015) provides a useful distinction between policy as *text* and policy as *discourse*. Policy as text explores the 'processes of interpretation and translation of policy through school actors enacting policy' (Ball, 2015, p. 307). This frequently engages teachers in a process of 'making sense of' the policy text and engaging in reviewing current practices to 'make space' for the new policy. However, all texts convey, endorse, subordinate or exclude particular interests and the concept of discourse is pivotal in understanding the characteristic of texts (Penney & Evans, 1999). Policy as discourse 'seeks to attend to the discursive possibilities for meaningful communication, perception and understanding and encompasses artefacts, organisational forms and practices' (Ball, 2015, p. 307). Policy as discourse approaches have been particularly important in recognising that various actors differ in their interpretation of the problem and different interpretations affect proposed solutions (Goodwin, 2011). The mere fact that we need to define these terms for the purpose of the analysis draws attention to the problem that definitions and meanings have, how they are context specific and (can be) highly contested. However, viewing policy as *discourse* provides an opportunity to examine 'the interplay between policy creation and response' (Adams, 2011, p. 59). In this sense, policy is considered to have a 'performative' function (Gergen, 1995) emphasising the interplay between policy constructors, policy text and the teacher where 'discourse presents a variety of representations from which action might be chosen' (Adams, 2011, p. 61). By contrast, the opposite stance is to take a managerialist view of policy, focussing on the generation and then implementation of policy when seeking to discover the effects of policy making. Conceptualising *policy as a process*, rather than solely the text, a moment or an event, helps to capture the interaction between policy constructors and teachers. This positions teachers as key stakeholders in the change process where they are regarded not merely as technicians delivering prescribed curricula but rather as co-producers and creators, designing and transforming curriculum. Considering policy in this way disregards the notion that policy text can simply be 'implemented', but rather places emphasises on policy *enactment* as a dynamic and non-linear process, which is not completed at any one point in time but is part of an evolving journey that brings policy intentions into being.

Transformational curriculum change

Educators and researchers have long acknowledged the problems associated with realising and sustaining curriculum change (Bekalo & Welford, 2000). Transformational curricular change requires time to enact: it is by its very nature ambitious (McLaren, 2015). Educational reform is not just simply a case of powerful people putting their ideas into practice. In fact, creating good ideas, having those ideas translated into text, having the text recontextualised by teachers in ways that produce the desired outcomes, is extremely difficult and almost never happens in the straightforward manner. As such, Levin (2001) suggests we should be surprised when efforts succeed rather than fail. These problems can, in part, be credited to teachers feeling 'at risk' when change is sought as the investment in certain discourses may promote some subjects and degrade others, for example, in the division of resources, primacy of subject arenas or in the allocation of time. Individuals or departments may be concerned that change could possibly undermine their present status and draw them into situations that may disadvantage them (Samuel, 1996). As such, attempts to introduce curricular change can often be met with resistance (MacPhail, 2007).

Frequently there can be a mismatch between what policymakers *say* will happen and what actually *does* happen as a consequence of policy (Elmore, 2007). For instance, a survey by Penney and Evans (1999) into the effectiveness of the implementation of the National Curriculum of Physical Education (NCPE) in England highlighted that teachers' practice and pupils' experience differed from the official aims. Swan and Brown (1997) reported similar findings during their evaluation of the 5–14 curriculum in Scotland. They revealed that teachers did not change their practice, but simply changed the curricular language and shaped the guidelines to 'fit' around their existing practice. These issues are not unique to the UK; Dyson, Wright, Amis, Ferry and Vardaman (2011, p. 376) investigating physical education policy in the United States (Mississippi and Tennessee), reported a lack of coordination between key actors, teachers, principals, and students which resulted in 'implementation failure'. Further, in Hong Kong, Johns (2003, p. 345) embarked on a post-structural case study of the physical education curriculum and noted that change could only be achieved by the 'transformation of the subjective realities experienced by teachers and the willingness of policymakers to understand those realities and include teachers in the process'. Therefore, considering *policy as discourse* allows us to disentangle the various components that contribute to the process and consider the extent of change that has been conceived at any given point in time. In this vein, Archer (1995) discusses concepts known as morphogenesis, morphostasis – terms that denote both change and continuity.

Morphogenesis and morphostasis

Margaret Archer's (1988) social theory is helpful in explaining the processes of change in schools as it makes an analytical distinction between the cultural system and the socio-cultural interaction. Archer uses the concepts morphogenesis and morphostasis to indicate change and stability in the social environment. These terms allude to processes that affect the extent of the transformation of dynamics within a context, or the restructuring of the previous system (Archer, 1995). Therefore, morphogenesis describes 'those processes which tend to elaborate or change a systems given form, structure or state' (Buckley, 1967, p. 58). In doing so, it 'captures both the possibility of radical and unpredictable re-shaping and the fact that the genus of this reshaping lies in the interplay between structure and agency' (Buckley, 1967, p. 75). For example, in a school (it is hoped) that policy generates new courses to be created and these would replace previous policy and practice (morphogenesis). However, this is frequently not the case and many schools continue with current practice with little or no change. This is described as 'morphostasis', and it considers 'those processes in a complex system-environment exchanges that tend to preserve or maintain a systems given form, organization or state' (Buckley, 1967, p. 58). As such, old ideas continue and the new policy is actively (or passively) rejected or resisted (Gillies, 2006). However, there is a mid-way model, a *form of morphogenesis*, where the new ideas merge with the old. Priestley (2011) suggests that this form is more common in schools, particularly where there are either instances of agreement and dissonance in the new policy, or when the difference between them is not important enough to cause conflict. Archer (1988), although not specifically concerned with educational innovation, captures the tension that teachers may experience in the face of a discourse that espouses 'transformational change' in curriculum and the complexities of continuing to work within the same temporal space and concludes that 'we can simultaneously feel bound to plod round the cultural treadmill yet also brim over with criticism and creativity – the tension between being conditioned to do things one way but being able to conceive of doing them differently' (Archer, 1996, p. xxiv).

Morphogenesis and morphostasis can only be apparent *after* there has been a disruption to the social structure and in this case it is the educational policy that forms the structural conditioning designed to bring about change. Archer's (1998) analysis of the morphogenetic relationship of agency and structure is concerned not only with the identification and elaboration of social structures, but in the cycles of structural conditioning, social interaction and structural elaboration. It is in the analysis of structural elaboration where judgements of morphogenesis and morphostasis or a form of morphogenesis are rendered possible. As highlighted previously, policy as discourse is not seen as a 'moment in time' but rather a process that at various points will be interpreted, constructed and reconstructed by those engaging with 'change'. By using this framework of analysis, it is possible to pinpoint morphostatic and morphogenetic forces at play (Rees & Gatenby, 2014), or in other words the key prevalent inhibitors and facilitators of the change process. Research indicates a plethora of factors that enable and constrain the transformation of practice as a result of policy reform and, while a list can never be exhaustive, some of the key factors will be discussed from national and international research studies. While the findings from research are not necessarily generalisable, there are international trends that resonate with the findings discussed in this section. This includes discussion around involving key stakeholders in the process of curriculum development, recognising and developing teacher agency and creating the right contextual conditions for teachers to act as agents of change. At the same time, there is a need to acknowledge those barriers and tensions that constrain teachers' accountability and the pressures of high-stake exams. Research in these areas is limited but there are some key findings that help identify the challenges that teachers face when enacting a flexible curriculum framework.

Involving key stakeholders

The extent of teacher involvement in the curriculum development process has been the concern of many authors (Kirk & MacDonald, 2001; MacPhail, 2007;

MacLean et al., 2015; Penney & Evans, 1999). Teachers worldwide have had to contend with national government reforms. However, in the political rush to bring about transformational change, teacher concerns have largely been dismissed and their opinions neglected or disregarded (Nutt & Clarke, 2002). In England, Penney and Evans (1999) reported that lack of teacher involvement in the creation of National Curriculum physical education resulted in decreased enthusiasm among teachers. In Scotland, MacPhail's (2007) research supports this view and suggested that if teachers are not involved in the curriculum process, it can only be expected that they subsequently require specific knowledge in order to understand and deliver it. Yet this reinforces a rather linear view of implementation where teachers are regarded as recipients and deliverers of a prescribed curriculum. However, if we envisage policy more as a process that requires to be coproduced, then it might be helpful to invite teachers and other stakeholders as partners in the creation of national policy. For example, in most Australian states, teachers are considered key stakeholders in the production of new curricula and adopt roles such as policy advisors and participants in school-based trials (Leahy, Burrows, McCuaig, Wright & Penney, 2016). Similarly, in Ireland, key stakeholders are considered central to the policy process and as a result teachers, researchers and academics in PE were invited by the government to create a consultative body. This example enables professionals to have a significant influence in the role of PE, to recognise and build on existing good practice and include innovative research in ways that shape future aspirations for their subject. Consultation in this sense could potentially be positive; however the selection of members may require a caveat. For instance, in Australia and the United States, the State is no longer the only player involved in the design of educational policy. Rather international and market actors are increasingly influencing the domain of education policy making (see Chapter 1). As a result, 'think tanks' were created to influence educational policy debates and reforms at international level (Savage, 2016). The think tanks contain policy elites who use their social, cultural, economic and political capital to add influence to policy debates. Inevitably, the voices of teachers are marginalised in this context. Priestley (2010, p. 34) outlines that 'the key point here is that there needs to be a clearly articulated process for engaging with innovation brought about by externally initiated policy'.

In order to understand the evolvement of policy, research was conducted by Gray, Mulholland and MacLean (2012) with ten policy constructors who contributed to the CfE policy text for PE in Scotland. The results indicated that the government had significant control over the process and this limited the extent to which the policy constructors could make a genuine contribution to shaping the vision for physical education. Thorburn (2010) also criticised the control of the government by explaining how national groups such as Education Scotland are formally invited to be involved in the policy-development process leaving key stakeholders such as teachers and academics on the periphery. Gillies (2001) describes such involvement as 'tokenism', where consultation is valued more as a public relations exercise than as a genuinely democratic process. All stakeholders affected by the curriculum should be involved in deciding its nature and purpose

(Ornstein & Hunkins, 1998). In addition, teachers should occupy a central position in curriculum decision-making so that they can construct new and relevant ideas about what physical education should be about now and in the future. Literature indicates that if physical education teachers are expected to act as agents of change in curricular reform then they need to be involved in the policy process. The earlier this happens in the policy cycle the more likely teachers are to engage in the policy process (Simmons & MacLean, 2016).

Teachers as agents of change

One way of understanding how teachers engage with and enact policy is to examine emerging research on *agency*, as this provides insight into how teachers relate to policy (Leander & Osborne, 2008). Teachers may use their agency to support new policy, develop a critical stance or even oppose educational change altogether (Sannino, 2010). Therefore, an understanding of what contributes to agency provides useful clues into the barriers and opportunities that can add or detract from a teacher's ability to support new policy. Teacher agency has often been associated with capacity, which teachers either do or do not possess. However, Priestley, Biesta and Robinson (2015, p. 34) argue that agency should be regarded 'as something that is achieved in and through concrete context-for-action'. Agency in this sense is considered as an ecological ongoing process that can be increased and nurtured in certain contexts, and exists as a configuration of past influences, present engagement and aspirations towards the future (Emirbayer & Mische, 1998). The temporal nature of agency is emphasised and focuses on the factors that inhibit or promote a heightened sense of agency. Agency, unlike capacity, is not something that teachers have but rather something to be achieved in certain situations – it denotes a 'quality' of the engagement of actors with temporal–relational contexts for action, not quality of the actors themselves' (Priestley, Biesta & Robinson, 2013, p. 189). Therefore, it defers emphasis away from what teachers *have* (capacity) onto what teachers *do* (by means of their environment that they act in and through). This demonstrates why 'capacity' is a misleading measure of teacher ability to enact policy, as it places value solely on teacher skills and knowledge rather than the interaction of what the teacher brings to the situation and the situation brings to the teacher. Priestley et al. (2013, p. 189) cautions 'that while teachers may come to a situation equipped with substantial capacity (skills and knowledge) and strong educational aspirations, innovation may simply prove to be too difficult or risky to enact'. Therefore, Priestley (2010) suggests that we consider those factors that increase teacher agency within the contextual dimensions of the school as a more productive way of understanding why some teachers enact policy and others feel powerless to do so.

Contextual dimensions

Research recognises certain forces that interact at the 'ground level' of policy enactment; these can include cultural, social and material structures that can act as enablers and constrainers. Cultural influences refer to the constraints and opportunities that are already in existence that shape the culture of the school. This may include shared values, knowledge, beliefs and ideas that contribute to the school culture. Laker (2002, p. 2) describes it as 'a system of shared values, meaning and symbols that enables societies and individuals to operate effectively without continually redefining these values, meanings, symbols and points of reference'. Social influences could include the relationships between different key stakeholders, the ethos of the school or the willingness of teachers to be collegiate and collaborate with others. For example, the leadership team in the school may actively encourage curriculum innovation and seek to empower teachers by pursuing specific strategies that enable them to be creative. However, the social environment can also constrain development as not everyone has an equal stake in curriculum design and, as a result, notions of control and direction will influence degrees of freedom in curriculum construction. Teachers are one of many key stakeholders working in and around schools who share responsibility for enacting new policies. Therefore, the social arena becomes an important space to share ideas, reflect and develop understanding – in fact, Adams (2011, p. 66) states, 'that it is the very opportunities for conversation and professional activity that form policy'. Material structures that contribute to the form policy takes include access to time, resources, finances and the layout of the school. This is particularly important in PE where differences in the range, condition, location and availability of facilities can influence curriculum opportunities (Penney & Evans, 1999). Time becomes paramount, not just in creating space for teacher preparation but also in the amount of time physical education is afforded in the timetable. In an already congested curriculum supremacy over time and opportunities for physical education shape the form that policy takes. So, tensions within the social and material structures in the school setting (can) offer both opportunities and constraints for teachers.

MacLean et al. (2015) investigated the factors that enabled physical education teachers to enact CfE in a climate that provided schools' and teachers with greater autonomy, flexibility and responsibility. Secondary school physical education teachers responded (n = 88) to a questionnaire that explored their perceptions of curriculum change. In addition, 17 physical education teachers within one local authority took part in semi-structured individual interviews. The results from the questionnaire indicated that two-thirds of teachers believed there was a need for change within the Scottish curriculum; however, just over half anticipated that they would make changes to their physical education curriculum. Times of change generally created feelings of uncertainty for teachers and, as such, their typical reaction was to resist change and hold onto existing practices. However, some schools were actively engaging with the new policy and showed evidence of heightened teacher agency. The results indicated that the schools that possessed a collaborative culture, before the introduction of CfE, were able to engage in practices that helped create policy in their schools (MacLean et al., 2015). Teachers welcomed discussions on constructing policy ideas with other colleagues and valued opportunities for cooperative learning supporting the findings of Bowins and Beaudoin (2011), who emphasise the importance of teacher collaboration to adapt and embrace change. However, MacLean et al's (2015) research took this notion one step further and reinforced Adams' (2011) research, which emphasised the importance of *teacher conversation and professional activity* as crucial in assisting teachers to create policy. Teachers valued conversations with senior management but also placed importance on informal conversations that took place between colleagues during lunch breaks and between classes. MacLean et al.'s (2015) research found that teachers who were actively making changes to curriculum organisation referred to an improvement and increase in collaborative practices throughout the whole school. As a result, individual *agency* enhanced the social structure for innovation in schools. Schools that embraced change also contained a social structure that sought to improve external links to *professional learning communities* (see Chapter 7) and internal links between subject areas in *interdisciplinary work*. In MacLean et al.'s (2015) research, teachers viewed themselves as professionals mediating flexible policy frameworks, and not as technicians carrying out prescribed policy. As a result, the findings indicated that the combining factors of teacher agency, culture and social and material structures along with the schools' capacity to manage new policy development were crucial in enabling teachers to enact and sustain change.

Accountability

Accountability discourses have reshaped the landscape of teacher professionalism and altered the way that the government, policymakers, administrators (and possibly teachers) view of what it means to be successful (Buchanan, 2015). Success in high-stake exams, and consequently teacher accountability, have become defining features of twenty-first century schools. Research conducted by Simmons and MacLean (2016) investigated the impact that high-stake exams place on PE teachers to act as agents of change when utilising a flexible curriculum framework. In order to address the research questions semi-structured individual interviews were conducted with five full-time PE teachers working in one secondary school in Scotland. The results indicated that teachers' first response to the policy process was to compare the structure of the course and the extent of the change from previous policy in order to evaluate how 'much space' was needed for the new course. Teachers recognised that it was necessary to engage with the exams and practices associated with the new course, but difficulties arose when attempting to merge this engagement with previous experience and approaches. Teachers chose to create a *form* of morphogenesis (Archer, 1995) rather than complete morphogenesis in the change process, in order to make links with the previous policy. The main reason given for this lack of compatibility with previous course experiences was the vast quantity of written assessment in the new course. Teachers found elements of the flexible nature of the new policy positive in principle; however, they became confused, insecure and exacerbated by the lack of coinciding, explicit documentation. Teachers understood that new course documents were being treated as blueprints to adapt to their individual school, but were concerned about the vagueness of crucial exemplars and assessment criteria:

> Reading the documents, they were so open and vague, which I know is probably the way they should be, but it meant it was open to interpretation from every single teacher who's reads it.
>
> (Teacher Male)

It became clear that there was a fine line between opportunities for teacher agency and engendering insecurity:

> I've no doubt there will have been creativity produced because of it, but I've also no doubt that there'll be teachers insecure – feeling they're a couple of lessons ahead of the pupils – and we know for a fact that's transmitted across to the children in the last couple of years. That's not healthy.
>
> (Teacher Male)

These findings echo those of previous research (MacLean et al., 2015; Priestley, 2010), and indicated that numerous interpretations of 'vague' policy text meant that teachers struggled to be sure of their course. Within the high stakes nature of the flexible policy framework, PE teachers unfortunately felt they lacked the necessary tools to be curriculum decision-makers. Ironically, teachers stressed that it would (perhaps) be easier for them to exercise agency within a more explicitly structured course. These results indicate that revolutionary change was somewhat stagnated by potent inhibitors such as a lack of collaboration with policymakers and vague course documentation. These were compounded by an inherent desire for pupils to succeed, which induced feelings of wariness and indecision among teachers. The flexible curriculum and guidance offered by policymakers was insufficient for teachers to confidently act as curriculum decision-makers, resulting in a call from the PE teachers for a more explicitly structured course. It became clear that when teachers are given responsibility to devise and develop policy they require support, collaboration and direction to empower their decision making (MacLean et al., 2015), particularly when faced with the high-stakes nature of the exam climate. Interestingly, Brown and Penney (2016) in a recent case study into the enactment of new curriculum policy in Victoria, Australia noted that past exams were fundamentally important in shaping teachers' enactment of the new policy. The examination texts were seen as an authoritative source for further understanding course expectations and helped to overcome the vagueness that was in the official course text.

Career-long professional learning

One such 'innovation' often considered pivotal in assisting teachers acting under new flexible policy frameworks is collaborative engagement in Career-Long

Professional Learning (CLPL). Research by Armour and Yelling (2007) indicated that, most often, schools do not readily adopt collaborative approaches to CLPL. However, following a large-scale study of physical education curriculum change in Hong Kong, it was identified that collaborative CLPL among university scholars, school teachers, and educational curriculum officers engendered greater security and confidence in the face of significant change (Ha, Lee, Chan & Sum, 2004). Research evidence suggests that appropriate CLPL can support the development of 'robust reflective, discursive, collaborative and inclusive teacher identities in practitioners' (Kelly, 2006, p. 515) and as such support teachers in the role of agents of change. This approach to teacher learning was a key concern of the new National Qualifications in Scotland and was strongly encouraged in the 'Building the Curriculum' CfE documents (Scottish Government, 2010). In Scotland teachers are encouraged to take responsibility for their own learning and development 'enabling (teachers) to embrace change and better meet the needs of children and young people' Education Scotland (2014). This was reinforced by Donaldson (2011, p. 15) in Teaching Scotland's Future:

> The most successful education systems invest in developing their teachers as reflective, accomplished and enquiring professionals who are able, not simply to teach successfully in relation to current external expectations, but who have the capacity to engage fully with the complexities of education and to be key actors in shaping and leading educational change.

However, research by Simmons and MacLean (2016) indicated that teachers placed value on the unstructured collaboration at local (department) level in preference to the rigid agendas associated with teacher CLPL. Teachers highlighted the importance of collaborative approaches when working under a flexible policy framework, proposing internal discussion and collegiality as key factors in refining the course to suit the individual context. Such collaboration was also said to provide a structural resource for those less experienced teachers in the department who have been said to rely more on colleague support and the structures of the department than their own reflexive deliberation (Kahn, 2009). The research concluded that for CLPL to be significant a collective policy-as-discourse approach from an early stage would allow both teachers and policymakers to form new policy collaboratively, in a discursive manner.

Future directions

In this chapter, we hope to have heightened awareness of the complexity of the policies and practices that we encounter in a way that demands continual careful reflection. Our research into the policy process in physical education has provided a modest insight into the complexities that surround the enactment of new policy in physical education and has identified not an exhaustive list but the social, cultural and material structures that need to be strengthened in order for the teacher to act as a creative, imaginative agent of change. We can both empathise and celebrate the value and potential for individual teachers. On the one hand, teachers are being treated as professionals, mediating flexible curriculum frameworks and not as technicians following prescribed curricular; however, on the other hand, there is an expectation that teachers will act as 'agents of change' transforming educational practice. While this is a recognition that is long overdue, equal recognition needs given to the contextual dimension of the PE teachers working environment in order that they are *enabled* to achieve educational transformation. In teachers' daily struggle to keep up with educational initiatives and increased demands of accountability compounded by associated paperwork, the fundamental aspects of teacher agency can be overlooked. As educational policy moves from mandates to capacity building, there is an argument that more attention needs to be given to teachers, as in the end it is teachers' commitment to the transformation of policy that shapes the success of initiatives. Teachers are among the most powerful influences on learning and are best placed to determine how to meet the needs of their pupils (Donaldson, 2014) yet in most educational reforms their involvement has been tokenistic. Teachers and other key stakeholders would welcome a real and acknowledged share in policy discussions. PE teachers, as agents of change, can make an invaluable contribution to the curriculum reform process and are strategic in preserving, protecting and safeguarding certain conceptions about what it means to be physically educated. Looking to the future, CfE is still 'in flux' as flexible frameworks are continually being reproduced and reassembled in ways that meet the needs of individual pupils. In time, it is possible that key stakeholders will recognise the conditions that are needed to achieve transformative change. Certainly, research into the Australian curriculum (Cowley & Williamson, 1998), where flexible curriculum frameworks have been in place for longer, indicated that teachers embraced the curriculum flexibility as it enabled them to fit policy guidelines to their local needs. It is hoped that in time, and with support, a similar response will be signalled by teachers in Scotland as they continue to grapple with new policy reform agendas, as agents of change.

Summary of key findings

- Archer uses the concepts morphogenesis and morphostasis to indicate change and stability in the social environment. Morphogenesis describes those processes that change a system's given form and morphostasis considers those processes that tend to preserve or maintain a system's given form.
- Curriculum reform with top-down, government-led policy mediated by teachers initiating bottom-up curricular development involves teachers to act as agents of change.
- By considering policy as discourse the focus is centred on the ongoing evolvement of policy as a process and emphasises the interplay between the policy constructor, the policy text and the teacher.
- Educators and researchers frequently experience difficulties in realising and sustaining curriculum change. This is particularly so when the aim of reform is to transform practice.

- Enabler studies have indicated that teachers need to be more involved in the policy construction process.
- Enabler studies indicated that teachers are able to act as agents of change when there is an interaction between teacher agency and the cultural, social and material structures of the school.

Reflective tasks

- What are the major challenges of large-scale reform?
- What kind of changes are teachers expected to contribute to?
- What conditions enable teachers to act as agents of change?
- What further support is required for teachers to engage in curriculum change?
- How can competing and conflicting interests be reconciled in the educational outcomes schools are seeking to achieve?

Further readings

Ball, S., Maguire, M., & Braun A. (2012). *How Schools Do Policy: Policy Enactments in Secondary School*. Oxon: Routledge.
Priestley, M., Biesta, G., & Robinson, S. (2015). *Teacher Agency: An Ecological Approach*. London: Bloomsbury.

References

Adams, P. (2011). From 'ritual' to 'mindfulness': Policy and pedagogic positioning, *Discourse: Studies in the Cultural Politics of Education, 32*(1), 57–69.
Archer, M. (1988). *Culture and Agency: The Place of Culture in Social Theory*. Cambridge: Cambridge University Press.
Archer, M. (1995). *Realist Social Theory: The Morphogenetic Approach*. Cambridge: Cambridge University Press.
Archer, M. (1996). *Culture and Agency: The Place of Culture in Social Theory*. Cambridge: Cambridge University Press.
Archer, M. (1998). 'Realism and morphogenesis.' In: M. Archer, R. Bhaskar, A. Collier, T. Lawson & A. Norrie (Eds.) *Critical Realism: Essential Readings* (pp. 356–381). London: Routledge.
Armour, K.M. & Yelling, M. (2007). Effective professional development for physical education teachers: The role of informal, collaborative learning, *Journal of Teaching in Physical Education, 26*(2), 177–200.
Australian Curriculum, Assessment and Reporting Authority (ACARA). (2015). Retrieved from http://www.acara.edu.au/default.asp.
Ball, S.J. (2015). What is policy? 21 years later: Reflections on the possibilities of policy research, *Discourse: Studies in the Cultural Politics of Education, 36*(3), 306–313.
Bekalo, S. & Welford, G. (2000). Practical activity in Ethiopian secondary physical sciences: Implications for policy and practice and match between the intended and the implemented curriculum, *Research Papers in Education, 15*(2), 185–212.
Bowins, W. & Beaudoin, C. (2011). Experienced physical education teachers adapting to a new curriculum: Perceived facilitators and inhibitors, *PHENex Journal, 3*(1), 1–15.

Brown, T.D. & Penney, D. (2016). Interpretation and enactment of senior secondary physical education: Pedagogic realities and the expression of Arnoldian dimensions of movement, *Physical Education and Sport Pedagogy*. Retrieved from http://www.tandfonline.com.ezproxy.is.ed.ac.uk/doi/abs/10.1080/17408989.2015.1123239.

Buchanan, R. (2015). Teacher identity and agency in an era of accountability, *Teachers and Teaching Theory and Practice, 21*(6), 700–719.

Buckley, W. (1967). *Sociology and Modern Systems Theory*. Englewood Cliffs, NJ: Prentice Hall.

Cowley, T. & Williamson, J. (1998). A recipe for success? Localized implementation of a (flexible) national curriculum, *The Curriculum Journal, 9*(1), 79–94.

Donaldson, G. (2011) Teaching Scotland's Future : Report of a review of teacher education in Scotland. Edinburgh: The Scottish Government.

Donaldson, G. (2014). Teacher education and curriculum change in Scotland, *European Journal of Education, 49*(2), 178–191.

Dyson, B., Wright, P.M., Amis, J., Ferry, H., & Vardaman, J.M. (2011). The production, communication, and contestation of physical education policy: The cases of Mississippi and Tennessee, *Policy Futures in Education, 9*(3), 367–380.

Education Scotland. (2014). Career-long professional learning: Guidance for teachers on approaches to professional learning: Education Scotland. Retrieved from http://www.educationscotland.gov.uk/professionallearning/clpl/index.asp.

Elmore, R. (2007). *School Reform from the Inside Out*. London: Harvard Education Press.

Emirbayer, M. & Mische, A. (1998). What is agency?, *American Journal of Sociology, 103*(4), 962–1023.

Gergen, K.J. (1995). 'Social construction and the educational process.' In: L.P. Steffe & J. Gale (Eds.) *Constructivism in Education* (pp. 17–40). New Jersey: Lawrence Erlbaum.

Gillies, D. (2001) The Scottish parliament and educational policy making. Unpublished MSc dissertation, University of Strathclyde, UK.

Gillies, D. (2006). A curriculum for excellence: A question of values, *Scottish Educational Review, 38*(1), 25–36.

Goodwin, S. (2011). 'Analysing policy as discourse: Methodological advances in policy.' In: L. Markauskaite, P. Freebody & J. Irwin (Eds.) *Analysis in Methodological Choice and Design Scholarship, Policy and Practice in Social and Educational Research* (Vol. 9, pp. 167–180). Netherlands: Springer.

Gray, S., Mulholland, R., & MacLean, J. (2012). The ebb and flow of curriculum construction in physical education: A Scottish narrative, *The Curriculum Journal, 23*(1), 59–78.

Ha, A.S., Lee, J.C., Chan, D.W., & Sum, R.K. (2004). Teachers' perceptions of in-service teacher training to support curriculum change in physical education: The Hong Kong experience, *Sport, Education and Society, 9*(3), 421–438.

Johns, D. (2003). Changing the Hong Kong physical education curriculum: A poststructural case study, *Journal of Educational Change, 4*(4), 345–368.

Kahn, P. (2009). Contexts for teaching and the exercise of agency in early-career academics: Perspectives from realist social theory. *International Journal for Academic Development 14*(30) 197–207

Kelly, A.V. (2009). *The Curriculum Theory and Practice* (6th ed.). London: Sage.

Kelly, P. (2006). What is teacher learning? A socio-cultural perspective, *Oxford Review of Education, 32*(4), 505–519.

Kirk, D. & MacDonald, D. (2001). Teacher voice and ownership of curriculum change, *Journal of Curriculum Studies, 33*(5), 551–567.

Laker, A. (Ed.). (2002). *The Sociology of Sport and Physical Education.* New York: Routledge Falmer.

Leahy, D., Burrows, L., McCuaig, L., Wright, J., & Penney, D. (2016). *School Health Education in Changing Times: Curriculum, Pedagogies and Partnerships.* New York: Routledge.

Leander, K.M. & Osborne, M.D. (2008). Complex positioning: Teachers as agents of curricular and pedagogical reform, *Journal of Curriculum Studies, 40*(1), 23–46.

Levin, B. (1998). An epidemic of educational policy: (What) can we learn from each other? *Comparative Education, 34*(2), 131–141.

Levin, B. (2001). *Reforming Education: From Origins to Outcomes.* London: Routledge Falmer.

MacLean, J., Mulholland, R., Gray, S., & Horrell, A. (2015). Enabling curriculum change in physical education: The interplay between policy constructors and practitioners, *Physical Education & Sport Pedagogy, 20*(1), 79–96.

MacPhail, A. (2007). Teachers' views on the construction, management and delivery of externally prescribed physical education curriculum: Higher grade physical education, *Sport, Education and Society, 12*(1), 43–60.

McLaren, S. (2015). 'Policy formulation and enactment: Linked up thinking.' In: K. Stables & S. Keirl (Eds.) *Environment, Ethics and Cultures: Design and Technology Education's Contribution to Sustainable Global Futures.* International Technology Education Series (pp. 133–152). Rotterdam: Sense.

Nutt, G. & Clarke, G. (2002). 'The hidden curriculum and the changing nature of teachers' work.' In: A. Laker (Ed.) *The Sociology of Sport and Physical Education* (pp. 148–166). New York: Routledge Falmer.

Ornstein, A.C. & Hunkins, F.P. (1998). *Curriculum: Foundations, Principles, and Issues.* Boston, MA: Allyn & Bacon.

Penney, D. & Evans, J. (1999). *Politics, Policy and Practice in Physical Education.* London: Routledge.

Priestley, M. (2010). Curriculum for excellence: Transformational change or business as usual? *Scottish Educational Review, 42*(1), 23–36.

Priestley, M. (2011). Whatever happened to curriculum theory? Critical realism and curriculum change, *Pedagogy, Culture and Society, 19*(2), 221–238.

Priestley, M., Biesta, G., & Robinson, S. (2013). 'Teachers as agents of change: Teacher agency and emerging models of curriculum.' In: M. Priestley & G. Biesta (Eds.) *Reinventing the Curriculum: New Trends in Curriculum Policy and Practice* (pp. 187–203). London: Bloomsbury.

Priestley, M., Biesta, G., & Robinson, S. (2015). *Teacher Agency: An Ecological Approach.* London: Bloomsbury.

Rees, C. & Gatenby, M. (2014). 'Criticial realism and ethnography.' In: P.K. Edwards, J. O'Mahoney & S. Vincent (Eds.) *Studying Organizations Using Critical Realism: A Practical Guide* (pp. 132–147). Oxford: Oxford University Press.

Samuel, I. (1996). *Organizations: Characteristics, Structures and Processes.* Israel: University of Haifa and Zemora Bitan.

Sannino, A. (2010). Teachers' talk of experiencing: Conflict, resistance and agency, *Teaching and Teacher Education, 26*(4), 838–844.

Savage, G.C. (2016). Think tanks, education and elite policy actors, *Australian Educational Research, 43*(1), 35–53.

Scottish Executive. (2004). *A Curriculum for Excellence.* Edinburgh: Scottish Executive.

Scottish Government (2008). Building the Curriculum 3: A Framework for Learning and Teaching. Edinburgh, Scottish Government.

Scottish Government. (2010). *Building the Curriculum 5: A Framework for Assessment.* Edinburgh: The Scottish Government.

Scottish Government. (2011). *Teaching Scotland's Future: Report of a Review of Teacher Education in Scotland.* Edinburgh: Scottish Government.

Scottish Qualifications Authority. (2012). *National 5 Physical Education Course Specification.* Glasgow: Scottish Government.

Simmons, J. & MacLean, J. (2016). PE teachers' perceptions of factors that inhibit and facilitate the enactment of curriculum change in a high stakes exam climate, *Sport, Education and Society.* Retrieved from http://www.tandfonline.com/doi/full/10.1080/13573322.2016.1155444.

Skilbeck, M. (1976). *School-Based Curriculum Development in Open University Course 203, Unit 26.* Milton Keynes: Open University Press.

Swan, J. & Brown, S. (1997). The implementation of a national curriculum and teachers classroom thinking, *Research Papers in Education, 12*(1), 91–114.

Thorburn, M. (2010). Opportunities and challenges for physical education. In Thorburn, M. & Gray, S. (eds) *Physical Education: Picking up the Baton* (pp. 1–7), Edinburgh: Dunedin Academic Press.

Vulliamy, G., Kimonen, E., Nevalainen, R., & Webb, R. (1997). Teacher identity and curriculum change: A comparative case-study analysis of small schools in England and Finland, *Comparative Education, 33*(1), 97–116.

7 The role professional learning communities play in school-based curriculum development

Andrew Horrell and Rosemary Mulholland

Introduction

A primary objective of curriculum reform is the transformation of what takes place in schools. Ultimately, the curriculum in each school comes into being as a result of the interplay between contextual factors and the professional action of teachers (Day, 2014; Priestley, Biesta & Robinson, 2015). This chapter explores in detail how professional learning communities play an important role in building teachers' capacity for school-based curriculum development (SBCD). The chapter presents selected findings from an interpretive study of nine schools, which revealed the role professional learning communities played in supporting teachers to reimagine and recast physical education (Horrell, 2016). Focusing on the lead teachers tasked with designing a new curriculum for physical education within a newly formed curriculum area of health and wellbeing, the study sought to explore how they engaged in SBCD. Analysis of data and the discussion of findings for that study are presented in detail elsewhere (see Horrell, 2016). However, in this chapter we present important insights about the role of professional learning communities.

It is important to note that although we draw on the findings from Horrell's (2016) study, we have also been involved as teacher educators and researchers in a number of projects examining change processes teachers have engaged in following the introduction of Curriculum for Excellence (CfE) (Gray, MacLean & Mulholland, 2012; MacLean, Mulholland, Gray & Horrell, 2015). Our experiences, research and scholarship have led us to develop an appreciation of how schools and teachers have responded to the introduction of a flexible curriculum framework. Chapter 6 presented concepts about teacher agency and this chapter presents important insights about the interplay between culture, educational structures and individual teachers that led to the development of professional learning communities across schools and within departments. We present research findings that indicated that during a period of curriculum change teachers engaged in professional learning activities which led to transformations in their approach to SBCD.

Clarke and Hollingsworth's (2002) perspective on teacher change is particularly relevant as they argue that there has been an overemphasis on decontextualised 'one-off' formal professional development events as a mechanism to address deficits in teacher knowledge. Professional development has been considered as something that teachers require to enable changes in curriculum, pedagogy and assessment to take place in practice. The starting point for professional development approaches has been all too often that teachers start in some form of deficit and require training so that they can 'implement' change. Therefore, the starting point for professional development approaches has been to view teachers' knowledge and/or skills as insufficient and requiring development through the input of those external to schools. The approach has often been to provide training for teachers so that a curriculum can be straightforwardly implemented to bring about the aspirations of policymakers. However, as Chapter 6 highlighted, there have been changes to the ways in which policymakers view the curriculum development process: there has been an explicit shift towards conceptualisation of teachers as active learners with the capacity to undertake self-directed professional learning and engage with others in a participatory process of professional growth.

In support of this shift and in contrast to much of the preceding literature which assumes that professional development led by 'experts' is required to enable teachers to engage in change processes, we offer an alternative perspective – one that values and acknowledges that teachers can and do engage in professional learning activities to develop their ability to undertake their roles in school, without the need to engage in formal professional development events led by 'experts'. The findings show that issues addressed in previous chapters which have stressed the importance of developing an appreciation of societal and theoretical perspectives, can aid in developing an appreciation of the transformations that take place in schools when considering curriculum change.

The curriculum framework for schools in Scotland did not change overnight; there was a long period of consultation and development, guidance documents were published and drafts of the curriculum circulated. Even after the 'final' publication of the curriculum, guidance papers continue to be issued. Curriculum change is, therefore, less of a moment and more of a process; the underpinning rationale for change requires careful scrutiny. In the case of the introduction of the CfE, the Scottish Executive (2004, p. 10) stated that "Scottish schools and education authorities will continue to be accountable for the decisions they take about the curriculum they offer, with the expectation that they will use arrangements creatively and flexibly and in ways which raise levels of achievement and attainment for all young people". This reveals raising achievement and attainment as the key drivers for change. The other clear message is that schools, education authorities and, by implication, teachers continue to be accountable for their actions during a period of curriculum change.

Main findings

The role of education authorities

In Scotland, although there are schools in the independent sector, the majority of teachers and students attend schools under local authority control.[1] There are

32 local authorities of varying sizes who oversee educational provision. At the time of the introduction of CfE, the Scottish Government and its agencies published curriculum guidance and expected local authorities to support the introduction of the new curriculum. It was the responsibility of individual local authorities to determine the best course of action to support curriculum development. Some local authorities produced their own guidance documents for HWB which were circulated widely through informal professional networks within the physical education community.

The Horrell study (2016) took place in one particular local authority, which was given the title the Terrane1 Local Authority. This authority decided not to focus first on the health and wellbeing (HWB) curriculum area but on the areas of literacy and numeracy. This had the effect of making curriculum leaders' roles more challenging and provided a barrier to SBCD. One of the teachers articulated their concerns as follows:

> John – Topaz School: And at the moment the health and wellbeing is lagging behind because [Terrane has] never once come out and said this is the [Terrane] Council Improvement Plan for every school in [Terrane] to drive forward. They have for literacy and they have for numeracy. So we're still waiting.
> (Horrell, 2016, p. 137)

John's frustration stemmed from the absence of specific guidance about HWB; it marginalised HWB as a 'responsibility for all' teachers. None the less, even Terrane Local Authority had chosen to focus on literacy and numeracy, a participant in the study, Susan, in her role as a Quality Improvement Officer for the Authority, noted that many headteachers were keen to address all the areas outlined in CfE as 'a responsibility for all'.

In the local authority where the research took place, HWB had a whole-school focus and this enabled Susan, as a quality improvement officer for HWB, to marshal support for two authority-wide professional development events. These events were not the focus of Horrell's (2016) research questions, but in the interviews with the teachers they had a degree of prominence that merited presenting in more detail in this chapter. The opportunities to meet with other teachers and share ideas appeared to have a powerful influence on the way they conceptualised and approached SBCD. It was a responsibility of individual local authorities to determine the best course of action to support curriculum development. Some local authorities produced their own guidance documents for HWB, which were circulated more widely through informal professional networks within the physical education community. The two professional development days represented an alternative approach to supporting teachers in Terrane Local Authority where the study took place. In her interview, Susan indicated that she viewed her role as one of support and sought to help teachers feel less anxious about the task they faced. Uncertainty about what HWB would mean for the subject area of physical education featured in their interviews. One thematic representation of their concerns was 'loss'. Their decision-making process involved considering if changes in curriculum would require them to change their practice in such a way that rather than making experiences 'better' for learners it would lead to a loss of experiences. As teachers, they had a well-established repertoire of practices that in their assessment were valued by pupils. Changes to curriculum and practice as a result of physical education's place within HWB could lead to a loss of what they valued.

The professional learning community that formed in Terrane had a significant impact on how teachers viewed the proposed curriculum.

> James – Ruby School: I think the way Terrane went about it last year was exceptional. We got together, every department was represented, mostly by two or three individuals to be honest and we set into different groups, working parties, sub-groups within that, and we trialled [units of work we created]. We didn't just write a course and say this is what we're going to do. We went away and trialled the experiences and outcomes in different ways, with different activities.
>
> (Horrell, 2016, p. 145)

The events organised by the local authority to support teachers led to the development of a professional learning community that facilitated teachers' active engagement in SBCD. This active engagement required careful tailoring of new developments to the constraints and affordances of their individual schools. The initial processes associated with learning about the curriculum was complex; rather than reading the documents and seeing these as a blueprint for action, the teachers actively considered what would be required if physical education was now within HWB.

Forming a professional learning community

Central to the formation of a professional learning community is the perceived need to engage collectively (Stoll et al., 2006). In preparation for meeting with peers at the development meetings, teachers reported reading policy texts associated with CfE, so that they could discuss ideas about how existing practice in physical education may or may not be appropriate within the context of CfE. There was a depth to their engagement with these texts which reflected their desire to engage collectively in a process to understand what the introduction of CfE would mean for their context. This active engagement required careful tailoring of new developments to the constraints and affordances of their individual schools. The initial processes associated with learning about the curriculum was complex, rather than reading the documents and seeing these as a blueprint for action, the teachers actively considered what would be required if physical education was now within HWB.

These levels of engagement challenged previous accounts of teachers' responses to curriculum change, which have reported superficial or strategic engagement with policy texts and curriculum guidance. Teachers from within Terrane Local Authority ran the sessions, and to do so they had committed a considerable amount of their own time to learning about CfE and considering their intended responses. Therefore, rather than 'experts' presenting their interpretation or solutions for curriculum, it was the teachers' actions that led to the formation of the professional learning community.

They were able to lead these sessions and shared their ideas with their colleagues because they had detailed knowledge of the guidance documents. Their approach modelled to other teachers that developing an understanding about CfE was not about passively listening to 'experts' or being told what to do; it was possible to learn about the curriculum and consider their own response. During the day, teachers formed working groups within their department or across different schools with the intention of planning units of work and then trialling these with classes. In the interviews, teachers explained that the curriculum was organised into 'blocks', 'courses' or 'units'. These terms were used interchangeably to describe each school's formal documented plan for the learning outcomes, learning activities and approaches to assessment for a sequence of lessons. However, in this chapter we have chosen to use the term 'unit' to refer to the pilot work they undertook. These units were often developed collectively by the teachers with the intention to create learning experiences that would address the broad aims of CfE and subject-specific content in physical education. The teachers reported that as they trialled the units of work they would discuss with colleagues in department meetings or through other informal professional networks their experiences.

Learning from and with other teachers

The second development day took the form of practical workshops with teachers sharing their approaches and discussing their thoughts about the appropriateness of what they had planned and their evaluation of pupils' learning during their pilot work. The event was for all teachers in the authority, but time constraints dictated that not all those who had information to share could provide an input into the day. Those teachers who had a central role within the professional learning community, and were active in the process of developing units, trialling them and then leading the workshops provided the input. This meant that at this event, some teachers were more on the periphery listening to and learning from peers.

One of the curriculum leaders, John, using his IT skills, created a 'wiki'[2] for the purpose of sharing the units of work created by the working groups. This innovation helped teachers to review the materials created by teachers at a later date with the possibility of downloading and editing the documents to suit their own purposes. The wiki was mentioned as a source of support for professional learning, but as Sarah noted, her aspirations that the wiki would save her time were not realised.

> Sarah – Coral School: I mean, I looked at quite a lot of it and thought, oh, I can't use that and yet the whole point was to try and not to make us have to

reinvent the wheel and be duplicating work, but I still feel that we will end up doing [our own units].

(Horrell, 2016, p. 162)

In Horrell's (2016) study one of the phases of data collection involved curriculum leaders discussing with the researcher their plans for the physical education curriculum in response to CfE. Although the teachers had access to the units that the working groups created, it was evident from the planning shown during the interview sessions that, as a result of the professional development experiences, they reimagined and recast their own units to suit their context. This was certainly the case for the department Sarah worked in and, as the following comments from Emma about the wiki make clear, the dialogic processes that took place as a result of the professional development opportunities were highly valued:

> Emma – Jade School: [John] fostered some of the approaches that he was showing that day. But yeah, they help; they definitely help [being able to access the wiki]. I prefer the conversations that you can have with each other; that sort of, 'Oh, what are you doing?'; 'Oh, go and show me that; what does that look like on paper?'; 'What does it look like in a lesson?' And listen to what some people are doing. I mean, it's quite amazingly different to what . . . but yeah, that for me has been really useful.

(Horrell, 2016, p. 146)

There was strong evidence that the professional learning opportunities supported curriculum leaders' engagement with the process of SBCD. Professional learning was not an isolated activity restricted to reading curriculum documentation. The two professional development events arranged by Susan enabled curriculum leaders to engage in face-to-face conversations, observe practical examples and, at a later date, revisit units of work via a wiki.

Professional learning and accountability

Regimes of accountability exert a powerful influence on teachers' thinking about their role and their work in schools. When curriculum leaders were engaging in the process of curriculum development, they sought reassurance that their planning would be acceptable to 'others'. The professional development events helped curriculum leaders develop their understanding of the process and they reported becoming more confident in their abilities to create a physical education curriculum aligned with the principles of CfE:

> Katie – Sapphire School: Like I say, that's why the sharing of practice and experiences with other schools was beneficial, because you're sort of giving yourself a bit more confidence, say, well what we're doing is maybe along the right lines now because other schools are doing something very similar. But,

then you're thinking, well why are we all doing this, why were we not given a clearer structure at the start?

(Horrell, 2016, p. 163)

The doubts Katie expressed highlighted how professionally challenging engaging in curriculum development had been for her. CfE was designed to allow teachers to exercise professional judgement and Katie's comments point up how the flexibility of the curriculum framework contrasted with curriculum leaders' desire for clear guidance. At the same time, Katie indicated the support provided by Terrane's professional development events were formative experiences, which made her more confident that her approach to planning for CfE would be on 'the right lines'.

It is important to explore what 'on the right lines' meant in Katie's statement. The 'other' featured strongly in curriculum leaders' descriptions of their decision making, and reflected their perception of how their actions would be evaluated within and outwith the school. In Scotland, as in many education systems around the world school inspections take place. The inspection framework for schools was revised and published during the development phase for CfE, and it was clear that curriculum leaders were giving prominence to how their actions would be judged. Thus curriculum leaders' responses reflected how significant they felt external measures of accountability and attainment were.

Our analysis of the interview transcripts detected that teachers were acutely aware of the powerful influence Her Majesties Inspectorate of Education (HMIE)[3] had on the decision making of local authorities and senior leadership teams in schools. The teachers own professional learning efforts were often focused on concerns related to inspection and in part the professional learning community that formed to support the introduction of CfE reflected a view that getting the curriculum 'right' was important as they would be accountable for what they had planned during any inspection process.

Despite this, the concerns reported by teachers did not reflect an obsessive anxiety that excluded concerns about pupils or the learning process. There was care and concern for what took place in physical education with the desire to ensure that the experiences were meaningful and worthwhile for pupils. It was quite simply that, at this early phase of planning the curriculum when the interviews took place, there was more of a focus on getting it right in the eyes of school senior management teams, Terrane Local Authority and HMIE. Regimes of accountability played an important part in the need for the teachers to learn about the curriculum.

Curriculum leaders' engagement with national and local curriculum guidance texts and the professional development events did not lead to a single interpretation of what CfE would mean for their context. In the quotation below, taken from Barry's first interview, three important and related points emerge. Firstly, as already indicated, the events organised by Terrane provided reassurance and helped to reduce the concerns curriculum leaders had. Secondly, his comments about existing practice being consistent with the text of the experiences and outcomes for HWB is telling and this is evidence of CfE being reinterpreted by curriculum leaders. Finally, the events provided opportunities to share approaches to curriculum design in physical education, but he did not seek directly to replicate in practice what was shared at the events and on the wiki. The formation of the professional learning community to create and make the development days possible were, in his words, 'the turning point', providing an important context for his professional learning:

> Barry – Opal School: that took some of the fear and anxiety out of it, I think. Because they felt encouraged and thought, well actually that's stuff that I do. Okay, so rather than just have a football blog, we'll put the kids into teams and we'll create a table and we'll call it the African Cup of Nations and they'll all wear the colours of Egypt and that team will be the Cameroon and blady blady bla, which was stuff that we'd been doing for years and years. And I think that's where we came to a point where actually, we can go away and now write a course because we feel confident. That CPD was kind of the turning point, I felt.
>
> (Horrell, 2016, p. 148)

In summary, this chapter has identified that the operation and actions of Terrane Local Authority had a significant role in the formation of a professional learning community. In addition, it shows that regimes of accountability played an important role in the process of curriculum development. Horrell's (2016) study has revealed that curriculum change in physical education is not simply a matter for individual curriculum leaders or groups of teachers working together within a department. The task curriculum leaders were presented with – of developing the physical education curriculum within the framework of CfE – was patterned by the policy context. Drawing on policy documents relevant to CfE at national and local authority level, the findings presented in this chapter reveal the complex interplay between the policy context, regimes of accountability and the support available to curriculum leaders. Peer-led professional development events were significant in that they appear to have provided a very important source of support for curriculum leaders as they engaged in SBCD. Both days provided an opportunity to share practice and the pilot work that had been undertaken within the authority. Curriculum leaders then sought to develop the curriculum within the context of their school.

Future directions

Our finding lend support for research methodologies which seek to uncover the professional learning teachers engage in during a process of curriculum change. MacLean et al.'s (2015, p. 93) recent study of physical education teachers across Scotland stated 'many teachers reported "lip service" changes to current practice with little or no change'. In contrast, the research approach adopted by Horrell (2016) which engaged teachers in detailed discussions, uncovered considerable engagement with the links between curriculum change and teaching practice. It also brings into focus the role professional learning communities can play in developing teachers' capacities to understand the possible responses when new policy emerges at national, local authority or school level.

In the absence of the kind of systematic programme of teacher development advocated by Elliott (1993), McKernan (2008) and Stenhouse (1975), teachers had to engage in their own sense-making practices to support curriculum development. Teachers did not report engaging with research related to physical education. They reported learning from each other and reading curriculum guidance to learn about CfE. Future research could productively explore from the perspective of teachers what professional learning they value and engage in. Our research and analysis indicates that teachers can and do engage in professional learning activities as part of wider communities of teachers and as individuals. The learning that takes place may not always bring about transformations in practice, which align practice with external conceptions of the transformations required, but do reflect processes of professional learning about what are possible enactments of curriculum and pedagogy for their specific context of practice.

There has been a tendency for research on teachers' practice to take as the starting point an implementation view of policy. This approach creates an illusion that the ideal form of the curriculum is already known, requiring 'appropriate' actions from teachers and schools (Kelly, 2009; Kimpston, 1985; Sabatier, 1986; van den Berg, 2002). The findings presented here provide further evidence that there is value in research approaches that seek to value teachers' interpretations of policy rather than seeking to predict and account for the outcomes or take-up of policy (Spillane, Reiser & Reimer, 2002). Transformations to curriculum and practice are by their very nature not predictable or always aligned with the intentions of policymakers. Further research with teachers may productively employ the approaches adopted by Enright, Hill, Sandford and Gard (2014), which sought to provide a nuanced, appreciate enquiry of how teachers learn, so that scholars in the field of physical education can develop a deeper appreciation of the interplay between professional learning communities, the professional learning activities of teachers and the processes of curriculum enactment.

Summary of key findings

- Professional learning communities played an important role in supporting teachers to reimagine and recast physical education.
- Regimes of accountability played an important role in shaping the way that teachers approached and engaged in the process of school-based curriculum development.
- Research methodologies that uncover the professional learning teachers engage in during curriculum change can help to develop new perspectives on the role of professional learning communities to support curriculum developments.
- Different conceptions of teacher change and teachers' professional development have implications for teachers as active learners during professional development.

Reflective tasks

- Over time there have been different conceptions of teacher change and teacher professional development. What, in your view, are the implications when schools are viewed as learning communities and when teachers are considered to be active learners able to undertake their own professional development?
- Identify what you consider to be important factors that lead to the development of professional learning communities.
- Recent developments in information technology enable teachers to interact with teachers beyond their local context. What possibilities might this afford for curriculum development and change in physical education?
- After professional learning communities are formed, what might be important factors that help them to provide sites where teacher learning and growth is supported?
- Why might professional learning communities reinforce existing practice rather than lead to a transformation of curriculum and pedagogy?
- If there is a shift from a view that teachers need professional development to change, to one where teachers are capable of learning and leading change, what are the implications for policymakers?

Further reading

McKernan, J. (2008). *Curriculum and Imagination: Process Theory, Pedagogy and Action Research.* London: Routledge.

Opfer, V. & Pedder, D. (2011). Conceptualizing teacher professional learning, *Review of Educational Research, 81*(3), 376–407.

Notes

1   Terrane is the pseudonym given to the local authority in Horrell's (2016) study. Terrane is a geological term used to describe a fragment of the earth's crust that has broken off from one tectonic plate and is 'sutured' to an adjoining plate; the fragment preserves its own distinctive geological history. In this study Terrane Local Authority has its own distinctive 'geological'/'educational' history and can also be considered to be 'sutured' to the Scottish Government.

2   The wiki as a shared editable web application allowed teachers within the authority to view all of the materials created.

3   Her Majesty's Inspectorate of Education (HMIE) was an executive agency of the Scottish Government, responsible for the inspection of public and independent, primary and secondary schools, as well as further education colleges, community learning, local authority education departments and teacher education. HMIE and Learning and Teaching Scotland were merged in 2011 to create Education Scotland.

References

Clarke, D. & Hollingsworth, H. (2002). Elaborating a model of teacher professional growth, *Teaching and Teacher Education, 18*(8), 947–967.

Day, C. (2014). Teacher Quality in the Twenty First Century: New Lives, Old Truths. In: X, Zhu and K. Zeichner, K (Eds.), New Frontiers in Educational Research, (pp. 21–38). Dordrecht: Springer.

Elliott, J. (1993). What have we learned from action research in school-based evaluation?, *Educational Action Research, 1*(1), 175–186.

Enright, E., Hill, J., Sandford, R., & Gard, M. (2014). Looking beyond what's broken: Towards an appreciative research agenda for physical education and sport pedagogy, *Sport, Education and Society, 19*(7), 912–926.

Gray, S., MacLean, J., & Mulholland, R. (2012). Physical education within the Scottish context: A matter of policy, *European Physical Education Review, 18*(2), 258–272.

Horrell, A. (2016). Pragmatic innovation in curriculum development: A study of physical education teachers' interpretation and enactment of a new curriculum framework. (Unpublished doctoral thesis). University of Edinburgh, Edinburgh.

Kelly, A.V. (2009). *The Curriculum Theory and Practice*. London: Sage.

Kimpston, R.D. (1985). Curriculum fidelity and the implementation tasks employed by teachers: A research study, *Journal of Curriculum Studies, 17*(2), 185–195.

MacLean, J., Mulholland, R., Gray, S., & Horrell, A. (2015). Enabling curriculum change in physical education: The interplay between policy constructors and practitioners, *Physical Education & Sport Pedagogy, 20*(1), 79–96.

McKernan, J. (2008). *Curriculum and Imagination: Process Theory, Pedagogy and Action Research*. London: Research.

Opfer, V. & Pedder, D. (2011). Conceptualizing teacher professional learning, *Review of Educational Research, 81*(3), 376–407.

Priestley, M., Biesta, G., & Robinson, S. (2015). *Teacher Agency: An Ecological Approach*. London: Bloomsbury.

Sabatier, P.A. (1986). Top-down and bottom-up approaches to implementation research: A critical analysis and suggested synthesis, *Journal of Public Policy, 6*(1), 21–48.

Scottish Executive. (2004). *A Curriculum for Excellence: The Curriculum Review Group*. Edinburgh: Scottish Executive.

Soll, L., Bolan, R., McMahon, A., Wallace, M., & Thomas, S. (2006). Professional learning communities: A review of the literature, *Journal of Educational Change, 7*(4), 221–258.

Spillane, J.P., Reiser, B.J., & Reimer, T. (2002). Policy implementation and cognition: Reframing and refocusing implementation research, *Review of Educational Research, 72*(3), 387–431.

Stenhouse, L. (1975). *An Introduction to Curriculum Research and Development*. London: Heinemann.

van den Berg, R. (2002). Teachers' meanings regarding educational practice, *Review of Educational Research, 72*(4), 577–625.

Part IV
The practice perspective

Part IV

The practice perspective

8 Creating autonomy-supportive learning environments to improve health and wellbeing in physical education

Shirley Gray, Fiona Mitchell and C.K. John Wang

Introduction

In many developed countries around the world, schools and, in particular, physical education departments, are seen to be environments where children and young people can be provided with opportunities to engage in physical activity, and develop their understanding of ways to lead a healthy and active lifestyle. Importantly, official policy text for physical education, health and wellbeing describe a broad conception of health, one that takes account of young peoples' social, emotional and mental health. For example, in Scotland the key aims of the Health and Wellbeing curriculum (where physical education is positioned) are to develop learners' 'knowledge and understanding, skills, capabilities and attributes which they need for mental, emotional, social and physical wellbeing now and in the future' (Scottish Government, 2009, p. 1). In countries such as Australia, New Zealand and Canada, the subjects of physical education and health education have similarly been brought together to form what is now known as health and physical education, with policy text describing health in an holistic way, referring to the development of mental, social, emotional as well as physical wellbeing (Australian Curriculum, Assessment and Reporting Authority, 2012; Gouvernement du Quebec, 2007; Ministry of Education, 1999).

Given that traditionally teachers of physical education have seen their role primarily in terms of developing physical health and performance, this offers an exciting opportunity for professional learning, to support a holistic view of health *in* and *through* physical education. This will provide teachers with the capacity to create positive learning experiences in physical education that enhance learning and extend the development of learner wellbeing beyond the concept of physical wellbeing. However, alongside this optimism for the future of physical education is a concern about the challenge that this poses for teachers. This concern is related to the view that the term health and wellbeing may not be well understood by physical education teachers (MacLean, Mulholland, Gray & Horrell, 2015) and that this may impact on the way in which the physical education curriculum is interpreted and delivered. This chapter seeks to examine the nature of these concerns and, in doing so, suggests that by engaging more with psychological theories of learning, physical education teachers can enhance their understanding of the relationship between their own practice and learner experience. More specifically, this chapter presents Self-Determination Theory (SDT; Deci & Ryan, 1985) as a useful mechanism to support teachers as they attempt to better understand the needs of their learners and the positive impact their practice can have on learning, health and wellbeing. As Quinn (cited in Anding, 2005) explains, if we want to change our learners, then we need to change ourselves. Developing a theoretical understanding of teaching and learning creates more possibilities for change that can ultimately lead to becoming a transformational teacher. However, change is not easy and is often hindered by the many challenges that teachers face in their day-to-day lives. Following this introduction, we identify some of the challenges faced by teachers in light of recent curricular reforms. We then highlight the importance of placing the learner at the centre of the teaching and learning process to enhance learning and wellbeing. Thereafter, we introduce SDT and explore how this theory might help teachers to better understand their learners and their learning contexts. In doing so, we suggest that creating autonomy-supportive learning environments may be effective in enhancing learning *and* intrinsic motivation. Critically, when learners are intrinsically motivated, they are more likely to experience positive affective outcomes (Kirby, Byra, Readdy & Wallhead, 2015).

Main findings
Challenges for teachers

Teachers face a number of challenges when developing and implementing a new curriculum. For example, understanding and interpreting curriculum documentation, understanding and constructing curriculum models and implementing relevant and effective pedagogies (Gray, MacLean & Mulholland, 2012; MacLean et al., 2015). Part of the difficulty with interpreting curriculum policy and making decisions about how to 'teach' health and wellbeing in the physical education context, stem from the perception that the primary role of physical education is to promote physical activity for physical health (Gray et al., 2012; Horrell, Sproule & Gray, 2012). This perspective is somewhat problematic, with claims by Horrell et al. (2012) that it could result in a form of physical education that is more like 'managed recreation', where the teacher's role is reduced to one of setting up and managing physical activity. Echoing this concern, Thorburn and Gray (2010) warn that an emphasis on activities that are aligned with health and wellbeing may result in 'activity sampling' rather than learning. Some may call for physical education to be focused more on increasing physical activity participation and providing health-related physical activities. However, this narrower perspective of physical education limits what can be learned, how it is learn, and who can be successful in physical education. For example, those who are physically active, physically fit and physically able may thrive in this context, while those who 'are not' are more likely to be isolated and labelled as demotivated and problematic (Astrom, 2012).

The subject of physical education aligned with health and wellbeing can offer much more than physical activity for the sake of physical health. Rather it can be rich, diverse and develop a wide variety of motor, cognitive and affective skills linked to learning and performance in a range of sports and physical activities (Bailey, 2006; Gray, Sproule & Wang, 2008; Scottish Executive, 2004). Importantly, the key to successful and positive learning in physical education is teacher pedagogy (Bailey, 2006; Gray et al., 2008), as well as positive and collaborative learner–teacher relations, where the teachers listen to their learners and value their opinions (Mitchell, Gray & Inchley, 2015).

Under the right conditions, the learning environment created in physical education by the teacher can provide enjoyable and educationally valuable sport and physical activity learning experiences while, simultaneously, promoting positive mental, social and emotional wellbeing (Bailey, 2006). Notably, it is suggested that providing learners with positive mental, social and emotional experiences in physical education may be even more important than simply increasing physical activity levels in the pursuit of living a healthy lifestyle (Gard, 2011). For example, positive learning experiences in physical education are said to promote high self-esteem, which in turn is associated with positive affective responses and high levels of intrinsic motivation (Reinboth & Duda, 2006; Standage & Gillison, 2007). The individual's learning experience within the physical education context is strongly influenced by factors such as teacher expectations, peer evaluations, position or status as well as more personal factors, such as perception of ability. Significantly, physical education teachers can have some control over these factors, for example through the pedagogies they adopt, the relationships they have with their learners, and the way in which they understand their learners' emotional experiences and feelings in and about physical education. Despite this, there is some evidence to suggest that physical education teachers do not attribute learners' negative perceptions or experiences in physical education to their own practice. Instead, they assume that learners do not feel good about themselves in physical education due to factors such as lack of parental support or lack of interest and ability (Astrom, 2012). Many physical education teachers, therefore, see little point in modifying their practice to change the views and experiences of disengaged or demotivated learners. However, we argue that even demotivated learners can have positive experiences in physical education and this can be achieved, in part, with a greater understanding of how teacher behaviour and pedagogy influence learning and wellbeing. This understanding may provide physical education teachers with the knowledge and skills that will enable them to contribute to the goals of a health and wellbeing curriculum while simultaneously attend to the performance outcomes that continue to play a major role in most physical education curricula.

Understanding physical education pedagogy

There are pedagogical strategies available to the teacher that can help them to create learning environments that support wellbeing and simultaneously promote 'physical' learning in physical education (Morgan, Sproule & Kingston,

2005; Reinboth & Duda, 2006). For example, it is suggested that when the physical education teacher sets tasks that are differentiated to meet the needs of all learners, when learners are encouraged to make decisions, when groups are heterogeneous and cooperative, and recognition and rewards are on effort and improvement, then positive self-esteem and affect are supported (Reinboth & Duda, 2006). Such pedagogical strategies encourage a mastery motivational climate for learning, a learning environment that is positively associated with gains in cognition, affect and behaviour (Morgan et al., 2005). Thus, understanding motivational climate and the pedagogical issues associated with a mastery motivational climate may go some way to assist physical education teachers in promoting health and wellbeing (see Chapter 9 for extended details on this matter). However, to apply any teaching strategy appropriately, effectively and flexibly, it is essential that teachers understand how they impact on the learner and the ways in which individual differences and needs can affect how the learning environment is perceived.

The learner plays a critical role in the teaching and learning process, a principle that is key to transformational teaching (Slavich & Zimbardo, 2012). Yet there remains a limited understanding of the precise nature of this role, and its influence over teacher planning and pedagogy. Bailey, Armour, Kirk and Jess (2009) have called for more research to be carried out on the processes of learning in physical education in order to further enhance our understanding of how contextual factors impact on learner experience and learning. Astrom (2012) also calls for a greater understanding of the interaction between the learner and the teacher within the physical education context to develop a clearer understanding of student motivation and to challenge current approaches to teaching physical education. It is suggested a deeper understanding of such processes can be enhanced, in part, by considering how theory underpins participation and learning in physical education. Understanding theory that considers the role and the experience of the learner in the learning process has the potential to provide teachers with the knowledge and tools to create a much more meaningful and effective learning environment, one that offers flexibility according to the needs of each individual. Self-Determination Theory (SDT; Deci & Ryan, 1985) is a social cognitive theory of motivation that has dominated the literature in motivation over the past five years (Wang, 2016). Other social cognitive theories of motivation, for example Achievement Goal Theory (Ames, 1992) (see chapter 9), highlight the way in which individual goal perspectives can influence learning and behaviour. However, SDT offers a much more comprehensive perspective, one that takes account of the differentiated content of goals, regulatory processes and the ways in which these are influenced by the individual's interaction with the learning environment (Wang, 2016).

Self-Determination Theory

Self Determination Theory (SDT) is a theory of motivation based on the assumption that all humans have innate tendencies to succeed, to thrive and to engage in activities that develop and support a sense of self. It is a useful framework for understanding learning and wellbeing in physical education because it recognises the role of both the learner and the environment in the individual's learning endeavours (Deci & Vansteenkiste, 2004). SDT proposes that the type and quality of a learner's engagement in a learning task is related to the way in which the environment satisfies three main psychological needs: feelings of relatedness, competence and autonomy. The concept of *relatedness* is the degree to which an individual feels a sense of belonging to, or connection with, the learning environment – for example, when a learner feels accepted among peers and teachers and experiences a high degree of social support (Perlman & Goc Karp, 2010). *Competence* is the learner's desire to interact effectively with the environment and experience success and control (Koka & Hagger, 2010) and *autonomy* is their feeling of agency, free will and choice within the environment (Ryan & Deci, 2006). Given this focus on the basic needs of the individual, SDT is a useful framework for exploring the teaching and learning contexts in physical education as it has the capacity to 'illuminate individual differences and how well each need is satisfied within a given practice context' (Sanli, Patterson, Bray & Lee, 2013, p. 2). Additionally, 'SDT posits that the fulfilment of the basic psychological needs for autonomy, competence, and relatedness is necessary for wellbeing to be attained and maintained' (Gagné, Ryan & Bargmann, 2003, p. 375). When basic needs are satisfied, learners feel good about learning; they make clear progress in their learning and, generally, experience positive wellbeing and performance outcomes (Burton, Lydon, D'Alessandro & Koestner, 2006). Furthermore, learning environments that satisfy the individual's basic needs contribute to the development of the learner's concept of 'self' that is closely aligned with intrinsic aspects of the core self (Hodgins & Knee, 2002), and that is very similar to the concept of self-esteem. Indeed, it has been reported that when basic needs are met in the learning context, over time self-esteem is enhanced (Deci, Schwartz, Sheinman & Ryan, 1981; Niemiec & Ryan, 2009).

SDT also emphasises the role of motivation in learning. Specifically, SDT suggests that intrinsic motivation and more self-determined forms of extrinsic motivation are enhanced in learning environments that satisfy the three basic needs. Additionally, autonomous motivation is positively associated with enjoyment in learning, positive mood, vitality and positive coping strategies (Burton et al., 2006). Burton et al. (2006) note that 'overall, research has indicated that having an autonomous self-regulatory style is associated with psychological well-being and positive behavioural outcomes'. When individuals feel more self-determined they are more likely to make decisions and carry out actions because of the inherent value of doing so. They are not overly concerned about outcomes or consequences and are not negatively affected by negative outcomes (Hodgins, Brown & Carver, 2007). Niemiec et al. (2006), for example, found that high school students high in autonomous motivation for attending college reported high levels of wellbeing in the form of vitality and life satisfaction. By contrast, when basic needs are not met, individuals become externally motivated and this can result in negative affect responses, for example anxiety or distress (Ryan &

Deci, 2006). This is because when individuals perceive the environment to be more controlling, their sense of self-worth is called into question. A more controlling environment inhibits the extent to which individuals feel like they can be themselves. They behave in a particular way because they believe that they should, rather than out of a sense of freedom, intrinsic interest or enjoyment. In educational contexts, this is often caused by the relationship learners have with their teacher (Reeve, 2002). For example, Ryan, Stiller and Lynch (1994) found that adolescents who did not feel a sense of belonging in terms of their relationship with their teachers attempted to cope with emotional concerns on their own. This resulted in negative consequences for both autonomous self-regulation and wellbeing, including low self-esteem.

The role of the teacher, therefore, is critical in terms of creating a learning environment that satisfies their learner's basic needs, allowing intrinsic motivation to flourish and supporting their wellbeing. This can also be achieved while attending to more formal learning outcomes, since autonomous regulation is also associated with greater conceptual learning and academic performance (Burton et al., 2006). Accordingly, when teachers focus less on the outcome of the learning activity and more the learning experiences, within a climate of trust and respect, intrinsic motivation is enhanced and both learning and wellbeing are positively affected (Mitchell et al., 2015). Consequently, to realise the aspirations of physical education curricula that aim to contribute to the positive and holistic health and wellbeing of young people in schools, a shift in pedagogy may be required and, for some, this will necessitate the development of theoretical insight, positive teacher–learner relations and practice (Ten Cate, Kusurkar & Williams, 2011).

Basic psychological needs and physical education pedagogy

In the following sections, we analyse each basic need separately, beginning with competence, followed by relatedness and, finally, autonomy. We do so to develop a more in-depth understanding of each in the physical education context. In addition to this, we present research examples that offer some insight into how teachers might create learning environments in physical education that satisfy the basic needs of their learners. These examples provide a useful insight into the ways in which basic needs can be met in physical education and also complement the aims being taken forward in Chapter 9.

Developing learner competence

SDT posits that the ways that learners understand their own competence levels impacts on their motivation, participation and wellbeing in physical education, and can influence subsequent motivated behaviours, such as selecting challenging tasks, applying effort and persistence (Weiss & Ferrer-Caja, 2000). Resultantly, learning environments that facilitate improvements in competence and in perceived competence increase the likelihood that students will continue to participate in physical education and physical activity (Klint & Weiss, 1987). This is important because research has repeatedly shown that children with the poorest motor skills are most at risk from leading sedentary lifestyles (Okely, Booth & Patterson, 2001; Wrotniak et al., 2006). In contrast, increased proficiency in physical education is linked to the development of positive attitudes towards physical education, enjoyment in physical education and continued participation in youth physical activity (Biddle, Whitehead, O'Donovan & Nevill, 2005; Wrotniak et al., 2006). Importantly, high perception of competence alone is not enough to impact on autonomous forms of motivation, learning and wellbeing. The learners' perception of competence has to be accurate and therefore closely aligned with improvements in actual performance. When actual competence is high, perceived competence is high, even for adolescent girls who are known to be more likely to drop out of physical activity than adolescent boys (Sport Scotland, 2007; Whitehead & Biddle, 2008). Thus, effective pedagogies for improvements in actual performance, while simultaneously raising the learners' awareness of their improvements in performance, are key to increasing intrinsic motivation and wellbeing in physical education. No one pedagogical practice will be effective for all learners. However, the principles that underpin learner-centred pedagogies, for example problem-solving and goal-setting, by their very nature are more likely to offer individualised learning experiences more closely aligned to the needs of learners. In developing further an understanding of such pedagogies, Gray and Sproule (2011) found that a learner-centred, game-focused teaching approach (see Chapter 9) that aimed to develop game understanding and whole team involvement/performance resulted in improvements in both perceived and actual performance in a 4 v 4 basketball game. In particular, the secondary school students that took part in the study reported a more sophisticated awareness of their role as a player off the ball, which contributed to their increased competence within the team context. The teachers provided the students with different roles during each lesson (for example a defender, attacker, observer and teacher), thus accommodating different aspirations and interests. They also provided different types of task (cognitive, social, physical) as well as tasks that varied in level of difficulty. The authors suggested that this afforded opportunity for all the students to be meaningfully engaged in the lesson, experience success and, importantly, improve their perceived and actual competence in basketball (Gray & Sproule, 2011).

Relatedness

Although enhancing actual and perceived competence are important in terms of promoting intrinsic motivation, learning and wellbeing, feeling a sense of relatedness has also been shown to be important for positive wellbeing in the physical education context. For example, Weiss and Stuntz (2004) suggest that physical education can be an effective medium for enhancing learners' feelings of relatedness to others in the class by providing experiences that focus on communication, cooperation and problem solving. These activities emphasise group support and trust, and are similar to those explored in Chapter 9 in relation to cooperative grouping. For the present, the quality of the relationship between the learner and the teacher is also very important (Reeve, 2002) and, in physical education, this is especially important for girls (Gibbons, 2014; Shen et al., 2012). Research findings (Bailey et al., 2009; Brooks & Magnusson, 2006; Flintoff & Scraton, 2001; Inchley, Kirby & Currie, 2008) have also demonstrated that the physical education teacher has an important influence on engagement, learning and affective experiences in the physical education environment. Relatedness is deeply associated with the learner feeling that a teacher genuinely likes, respects and values them (Niemiec et al., 2006). Research suggests that having a supportive physical education teacher, one who helps the student in their learning, shows them how to do new activities and promotes a sense of fun, is a significant factor in shaping learners' attitudes towards physical education (Inchley et al., 2008). By contrast, negative perceptions of physical education are expressed when teachers are perceived to be unapproachable or too critical (Inchley et al., 2008). Furthermore, in their study that examined the experiences of disengaged girls in a 'fit for girls' programme (Scottish Government funded), Mitchell et al. (2015) demonstrated that when teachers provided their learners with opportunities for consultation and support in the physical education environment, they generally had more positive physical education experiences. The students in their study felt like they had a voice and that their voices were listened to and acted upon to inform future curriculum decisions. For this to be achieved, it required a teacher–learner relationship based on trust, understanding and respect (Mitchell et al., 2015). Creating space and time during physical education lessons for the development of positive learner–teacher relationships is something that all physical education teachers should strive to achieve, both informally and implicitly, as well as explicitly as part of the planning, teaching and learning processes. Gibbons (2014) offers further insight as to how this might be achieved, for example by using encouraging and inclusive language, explicitly addressing issues such as bullying or harassment and asking learners what they need to feel safe in the learning environment. She also calls for further research to be carried out in this area so that teachers might have clearer ideas about ways in which they can create more socially-supportive learning environments in physical education.

Autonomy and autonomy support

Although the satisfaction of all three needs is related to the development of intrinsic motivation, learning and positive affect, perception of autonomy is a necessary condition for the development of intrinsic motivation and it is expected to play a key role in the development of learning and wellbeing (Ryan & Deci, 2006). Furthermore, the degree to which teachers support autonomy, as opposed to controlling behaviour, is a strong predictor of engagement and learning (Ryan & Deci, 2006). Autonomy refers to the individual's feeling that they have some control and responsibility for their own learning, very similar to the concept of self-regulated learning, which will be explored in the next chapter. One means by which the teacher can nurture the learner's inner motivational resources is to provide the learner with choice about what is learned and how it is learned. In a literature review that investigated learner choice in the context of motor learning, Sanli et al. (2013) found that when choice was offered (choice about when and what type of feedback to receive, the level of task difficulty and choice about the rate of progression through each practice), motor skill acquisition improved. Sanli et al. (2013) theorised that these learning conditions supported the basic psychological needs of the learner and thus increased intrinsic motivation. Additionally, they claim that choice and control over the learning environment increases learner accountability and this, they suggest, encourages the learner to apply more effort to their learning, improving performance and satisfying their sense of challenge. There is evidence, therefore, to demonstrate that offering learners choice in physical education (about what they learn and how they learn) can be effective in term of developing their motivation to persist in learning tasks and, ultimately, improving their performance in those tasks.

Enhancing learners' feelings of autonomy also offers a developmental perspective on the teaching and learning process. As Reeve (2009) notes:

> The developmental perspective is so important to an autonomy-supportive style because autonomy support itself is defined as the instructional effort to involve, nurture, and develop students' inner motivational resources and capacity and responsibility for self-motivation. Thus, a student's engagement in a learning activity centres not only around learning that particular lesson but further around developing the capacity and sense of personal responsibility to generate and regulate autonomous motivation of one's own.
>
> (p. 168)

Creating an autonomy-supportive learning environment, is not only created by providing learners with choice. Reeve (2009) describes three conditions that have the potential to create an autonomy-supportive learning environment. They are: adopting the learners' perspective, accepting their thoughts and feelings, and supporting their motivational development and capacity for self-regulation. This, Reeve suggests, is achieved when teachers attend to the learners' interests and preferences, provide clear rationales for their learning, avoid using controlling language (encouraging problem solving), are patient with their students and acknowledge that they can have valid reasons for feeling negative about their learning experiences. Consequently, creating autonomy-supportive learning environments that nurture learners' inner motivational resources and provides opportunities for self-regulated learning is critical to the development of positive classroom functioning, improved educational outcomes and positive psychological wellbeing (Burton et al., 2006; Cheon & Reeve, 2015; Reeve, 2009). For example, in an investigation that implemented an intervention to help teachers develop an autonomy-motivating style, Cheon and Reeve (2015) found that the students in the 'autonomy-support' group reported greater psychological need satisfaction, greater engagement, and less amotivation than did students of teachers in the control group. In the physical education setting, Kirby et al. (2015) found that autonomy-supportive environment was created when the practice and inclusion styles (Mosston & Ashworth, 2002) were used (further detail around Mosston and Ashworth's work is presented in Chapter 9). This was primarily because the learners had numerous opportunities to make their own decisions about their practice, which in turn, positively influenced their basic psychological need satisfaction and level of self-determined motivation. In a review of the SDT literature in physical education, Van den Berghe, Vansteenkiste, Cardon, Kirk and Haerens (2012) found that teachers who were more flexible with their students, offered more choice and opportunities for self-initiative, created learning environments that led to greater enjoyment, better task orientation and more autonomous functioning. Indeed, several studies have demonstrated that feelings of autonomy in physical education enhance student motivation, learning and wellbeing outcomes (Kirby et al., 2015; Mandigo et al., 2008; Moutatidis, Barkoukis & Tsorbatzoudis, 2015).

Supported by SDT, the research described above suggests that, when presented appropriately, physical education teachers can create learning experiences that will contribute to learners' overall positive wellbeing. Presenting physical education appropriately is a challenging task, one that is not overcome by simply following one particular pedagogical model. In order to present physical education appropriately, physical education teachers must take time to get to know their learners: who they are, their interests, their aspirations, their perceptions and their abilities. Understanding SDT, and the relationship between teacher behaviour, pedagogy and the satisfaction of basic needs therefore, is critical for the development of flexible, informed, meaningful and effective pedagogy within the physical education context. Physical education teachers have at their disposal information and ideas about how to implement various teaching approaches, for example, Teaching Games for Understanding (Bunker & Thorpe, 1982), Mosston's Spectrum of Teaching Styles (Mosston & Ashworth, 2002) and Cooperative Learning (Dyson & Casey) (see Chapter 9 for more detail on each approach). However, a greater understanding of their learners, their basic psychological needs and how they can be met through various physical education pedagogies will enable them to structure their lessons in a more motivationally adaptive way (Ntoumanis & Standage, 2009).

Conclusion

Many countries around the world have established physical education as a logical site for the development of young peoples' health and wellbeing. This is a relatively new position for physical education and provides the profession with an exciting opportunity to analyse and review its aims and purposes. It offers teachers the opportunity to move the subject forward in line with curricular and societal expectations by more explicitly and meaningfully supporting student learning and the development of their physical, mental, social and emotional wellbeing. This is not an easy task and one that is made more difficult by the fact that many physical education teachers view their role as primarily associated with the promotion of physical activity for physical health. However, we argue that the concept of health and wellbeing far exceeds the limits of physical health and represents a much more holistic perspective, encompassing social, emotional and mental health. This chapter has demonstrated that if teachers are to impact positively on young peoples' health and wellbeing in the physical education context, then a greater focus on the individual learner is required. Guided by SDT, the chapter has highlighted that satisfying learners' need to feel competent, related and autonomous are critical in the promotion of intrinsic motivation, learning and wellbeing. Furthermore, these outcomes are more likely to be achieved with a greater understanding of the relationship between teacher behaviour, pedagogy and basic needs so that more meaningful and autonomy-supportive pedagogies can be applied in a flexible and effective way. Becoming a transformational teacher is not achieved by following a blueprint for 'effective' or 'innovative' practice. Transformation comes from understanding learners and the ways in which they contribute and shape the learning process. From this perspective, teaching is a developmental process that nurtures the inner resources of the learner so that they become independent, motivated, and self-directed learners – issues that will be further explored in Chapter 9.

Summary of key findings

- Physical education teachers around the world have been given more responsibility for the development of student health and wellbeing in the school context.
- There are pedagogical approaches in physical education that claim to promote student health and wellbeing. However, it is important to understand the needs of the learner and the impact that teaching approaches have on the learner.
- SDT is a theory of motivation based on the assumption that all humans have innate tendencies to succeed, to thrive and to engage in activities that develop and support a sense of self. SDT recognises the role of both the learner and the environment in the individual's learning endeavours.
- SDT proposes that the type and quality of a learner's engagement in physical education is related to the way in which the environment satisfies three main psychological needs: feelings of relatedness, competence and autonomy.
- The satisfaction of all three basic psychological needs is related to the development of intrinsic motivation, learning and positive affect.
- Enhancing feelings of autonomy in physical education is particularly important because it offers a developmental perspective on the teaching and learning process.
- An autonomy-supportive learning environment is created when teachers attend to the learners' interests and preferences, provide clear rationales for their learning, avoid using controlling language (encouraging problem solving), are patient with their learners and acknowledge that learners can have valid reasons for feeling negative about their learning experiences.

- A greater understanding of basic needs and how they can be met through various physical education pedagogies will enable teachers to structure their lessons in a more motivationally adaptive way.

Reflective tasks

- Do you agree that teachers of physical education are primarily concerned with improving their learners' performance and physical health?
- Should teachers of physical education be responsible for students' health in the school context?
- What were your positive and negative experiences of physical education as a student? Can you identify something that the teacher did that contributed to these experiences?
- To what extent do your teaching practices control your students' learning as opposed to promoting their autonomous learning?
- What do you perceive to be the relative strengths and weaknesses of adopting an autonomy-supportive teaching approach in your own teaching context? How might any weaknesses be overcome?
- How could you facilitate the psychological needs of your learners? What specific examples can you draw from the text to support your ideas?
- Does SDT provide a framework to better understand teaching approaches?

Further readings

Wang, C.K.J. (2016). 'Maximizing student motivation in physical education: A self-determination theory perspective.' In: C.D. Ennis, K. Armour, A. Chen, A. Garn, E. Mauerberg-deCastro, D. Penney, S. Silverman, M. Solmon & R. Tinning (Eds.) *Routledge Handbook of Physical Education Pedagogy* (pp. 594–606). London: Routledge.
Van den Berghe, L., Vansteenkiste, M., Cardon, G., Kirk, D., & Haerens, L. (2012). Research on self- determination in physical education: Key findings and proposals for future research, *Physical Education & Sport Pedagogy, 19*(1), 97–121.

References

Ames, C. (1992). Classrooms: Goals, structures, and student motivation, *Journal of Educational Psychology, 84*, 261–271.
Anding, J.M. (2005). An interview with Robert E. Quinn: Entering the fundamental state of leadership: Reflections on the path to transformational teaching, *Academy of Management Learning & Education, 4*, 487–495.
Astrom, P. (2012). Teachers' discursive representations of pupils 'low motivated' for physical education and health, *European Journal for Sport and Society, 9*, 119–138.
Australian Curriculum, Assessment and Reporting Authority. (2012). *The Shape of the Australian Curriculum: Health and Physical Education*. Sydney: ACARA Copyright Administration.
Bailey, R. (2006). Physical education and sport in school: A review of benefits and outcomes, *Journal of School Health, 76*(8), 397–401.

Bailey, R., Armour, K., Kirk, D., Jess, M., Pickup, I., Sandford, R., & Pearce, P. (2009). The educational benefits claimed for physical education and school sport: An academic review, *Research Papers in Education, 24*(1), 1–27.

Biddle, S., Whitehead, S., O'Donovan, T.M., & Nevill, M.E. (2005). Correlates of participation in physical activity for adolescent girls: A systematic review of recent literature, *Journal of Physical Activity and Health, 2*(4), 423–434.

Brooks, F. & Magnusson, J. (2006). Taking part counts: Adolescents' experiences of the transition from inactivity to active participation in school-based physical education, *Health Education Research, 21*(6), 872–883.

Bunker, D. & Thorpe, R. (1982). A model for the teaching of games in the secondary school, *Bulletin of Physical Education, 10*, 9–16.

Burton, K.D., Lydon, J.E., D'Alessandro, D.U., & Koestner, R. (2006). The differential effects of intrinsic and identified motivation on well-being and performance: Prospective, experimental, and implicit approaches to self-determination theory, *Journal of Personality and Social Psychology, 91*(4), 750–762.

Cheon, S.H. & Reeve, J. (2015). A classroom-based intervention to help teachers decrease students' amotivation, *Contemporary Educational Psychology, 40*, 99–111.

Deci, E.L. & Ryan, R.M. (1985). *Intrinsic Motivation and Self-Determination in Human Behavior*. New York: Plenum Press.

Deci, E.L., Schwartz, A.J., Sheinman, L., & Ryan, R.M. (1981). An instrument to assess adults' orientations toward control versus autonomy with children: Reflections on intrinsic motivation and perceived competence, *Journal of Educational Psychology, 73*, 642–650.

Deci, E.L. & Vansteenkiste, M. (2004). Self-determination theory and basic need satisfaction: Understanding human development in positive psychology, *Ricerche di Psicologia, 27*, 17–34.

Flintoff, A. & Scraton, S. (2001). Stepping into active leisure? Young women's perceptions of active lifestyles and their experiences of school physical education, *Sport, Education and Society, 6*(1), 5–21.

Gagné, M., Ryan, M., & Bargmann, K. (2003). Autonomy support and need satisfaction in the motivation and well-being of gymnasts, *Journal of Applied Sport Psychology, 15*, 372–390.

Gard, M. (2011). A meditation in which consideration is given to the past and future engagement of social science generally and critical physical education and sports scholarship in particular with various scientific debates, including the so-called 'obesity epidemic' and contemporary manifestations of biological determinism, *Sport, Education and Society, 16*(3), 399–412.

Gibbons, S.L. (2014). Relatedness-supportive learning environment for girls in physical education, *Learning Landscapes, 7*(2), 139–150.

Gouvernement du Quebec. (2007). *Quebec Education Program: Secondary Cycle 2: Personal Development*. Ministère de l'Education. ISBN 2–550–49680–0. Bibliothèque Nationale du Québec.

Gray, S., MacLean, J., & Mulholland, R. (2012). Physical education within the Scottish context: A matter of policy, *European Physical Education Review, 18*(2), 258–272.

Gray, S. & Sproule, J. (2011). Developing pupils' performance in team invasion games: A comparative study within a Scottish context, *Physical Education and Sport Pedagogy, 16*(1), 15–32.

Gray, S., Sproule, J., & Wang, C.K.J. (2008). Pupils' perceptions of and experiences, in team invasion games: A case study of a Scottish secondary school and its three feeder primary schools, *European Physical Education Review, 14*(2), 179–201.

Hodgins, H.S., Brown, A.B., & Carver, B. (2007). Autonomy and control motivation and self-esteem, *Self and Identity, 6,* 189–208.

Hodgins, H.S. & Knee, R.C. (2002). 'The integrating self and conscious experience.' In: E.L. Deci & R.M. Ryan (Eds.) *Handbook of Self-Determination Research* (pp. 87–100). New York: University of Rochester Press.

Horrell, A., Sproule, J., & Gray, S. (2012). Health and wellbeing: A policy context for physical education in Scotland, *Sport Education and Society, 17*(2), 163–180.

Inchley, J., Kirby, J., & Currie, C. (2008). *Physical Activity in Scottish Schoolchildren (PASS) Project: Physical Activity among Adolescents in Scotland: Final Report of the PASS Study.* Child and Adolescent Health Research Unit. Edinburgh: University of Edinburgh.

Kirby, S., Byra, M., Readdy, T., & Wallhead, T. (2015). Effects of spectrum teaching styles on college students' psychological needs satisfaction and self-determined motivation, *European Physical Education Review, 21*(4), 521–540.

Klint, K.A. & Weiss, M.R. (1987). Perceived competence and motives for participating in youth sports: A test of Harter's competence motivation theory, *Journal of Sport Psychology, 9,* 55–65.

Koka, A. & Hagger, M. (2010). Perceived teaching behaviours and self-determined motivation in physical education: A test of self-determination theory, *Research Quarterly for Exercise and Sport, 81,* 74–86.

MacLean, J., Mulholland, R., Gray, S., & Horrell, A. (2015). Enabling curriculum change in Scotland: Physical education teacher and policy constructors' perceptions compared, *Physical Education and Sport Pedagogy, 20*(1), 79–96.

Mandigo, J., Holt, N., Anderson, A., & Sheppard, J. (2008). Children's motivational experiences following autonomy-supportive games lessons *European Physical Education Review,* 14(3), 407–425.

Ministry of Education. (1999). *Health and Physical Education in the New Zealand Curriculum.* Wellington: Learning Media.

Mitchell, F., Gray, S., & Inchley, J. (2015). 'This choice thing really works . . .': Changes in experiences and engagement of adolescent girls in physical education classes, during a school-based physical activity programme, *Physical Education and Sport Pedagogy, 20*(6), 593–611.

Morgan, K., Sproule, J., & Kingston, K. (2005). Teaching styles, motivational climate and pupils' cognitive and affective responses in physical education, *European Physical Education Review, 11*(3), 1–27.

Mosston, M. & Ashworth, S. (2002). *Teaching Physical Education* (5th ed.). San Francisco: Benjamin Cummings.

Moutatidis, A., Barkoukis, V., & Tsorbatzoudis, C. (2015). The relation between balanced need satisfaction and adolescents' motivation in physical education, *European Physical Education Review, 21*(4), 421–431.

Niemiec, C.P., Lynch, M.F., Vansteenkistec, M., Bernstein, J., Deci, E.L., & Ryan, R.M. (2006). The antecedents and consequences of autonomous self-regulation for college: A self-determination theory perspective on socialization, *Journal of Adolescence, 29,* 761–775.

Niemiec, C.P. & Ryan, R.M. (2009). Autonomy, competence, and relatedness in the classroom: Applying self-determination theory to educational practice, *Theory and Research in Education, 7*(2), 133–144.

Ntoumanis, N. & Standage, M. (2009). Motivation in physical education classes: A self-determination theory perspective, *Theory and Research in Education, 7*(2), 194–202.

Okely, A., Booth, M., & Patterson, J. (2001). Relationship of physical activity to fundamental movement skill among adolescents, *Medicine and Science in Sports and Exercise, 33,* 1899–1904.

Perlman, D.J. & Goc Karp, G. (2010). A self-determined perspective of the sport education model, *Physical Education and Sport Pedagogy, 15*(4), 401–418.

Reeve, J. (2002). 'Self-determination theory applied to educational settings.' In: E.L. Deci & R.M. Ryan (Eds.) *Handbook of Self-Determination Research* (pp. 183–203). Rochester, NY: University Of Rochester Press.

Reeve, J. (2009). Why teachers adopt a controlling motivating style toward students and how they can become more autonomy supportive, *Educational Psychologist, 44*(3), 159–175.

Reinboth, M. & Duda, J.L. (2006). Perceived motivational climate, need satisfaction and indices of well-being in team sports: A longitudinal perspective, *Psychology of Sport and Exercise, 7,* 269–286.

Ryan, R.M. & Deci, E.L. (2006). Self-regulation and the problem of human autonomy: Does psychology need choice, self-determination, and will?, *Journal of Personality, 74*(6), 1557–1585.

Ryan, R.M., Stiller, J., & Lynch, J.H. (1994). Representations of relationships to teachers, parents, and friends as predictors of academic motivation and self-esteem, *Journal of Early Adolescence, 14,* 226–249.

Sanli, E.A., Patterson, J.T., Bray, S.R., & Lee, T.D. (2013). Understanding self-controlled motor learning protocols through the self-determination theory, *Frontiers in Movement Science and Sport Psychology, 3,* 1–17.

Scottish Executive. (2004). *A Curriculum for Excellence.* Edinburgh: Scottish Executive.

Scottish Government. (2009). *Curriculum for Excellence: Health and Wellbeing: Experiences and Outcomes.* Edinburgh: Scottish Government.

Shen, B., Rinehart-Lee, T., MaCaughtry, N. & Li, x. (2012). Urban African-American Girls' Participation and Future Intentions Toward Physical Education, *Sex Roles, 67*(3), 323–333.

Slavich, G.M. & Zimbardo, P.G. (2012). Transformational teaching: Theoretical underpinnings, *Educational Psychology Review, 24,* 569–608.

Sport Scotland. (2007). Population and participation profiles: Key equity figures for 2006, Sportscotland Research Update (2007). Retrieved from: https://sportscotland.org.uk/documents/participation/populationandparticipationprofiles.pdf

Standage, M. & Gillison, F. (2007). Students' motivational responses toward school physical education and their relationship to general self-esteem and health-related quality of life, *Psychology of Sport and Exercise, 8,* 704–721.

Ten Cate, T.J., Kusurkar, R.A., & Williams, G.C. (2011). How self-determination theory can assist our understanding of the teaching and learning processes in medical education. AMEE Guide No. 59, *Medical Teacher, 33,* 961–973.

Thorburn, M. & Gray, S. (2010). 'Professionalism and professional development.' In: M. Thorburn & S. Gray (Eds.) *Physical Education: Picking Up the Baton: Policy and Practice in Education* (pp. 48–67). Edinburgh: Dunedin Academic Press.

Van den Berghe, L., Vansteenkiste, M., Cardon, G., Kirk, D., & Haerens, L. (2012). Research on self- determination in physical education: Key findings and proposals for future research, *Physical Education & Sport Pedagogy, 19*(1), 97–121.

Wang, C.K.J. (2016). Maximizing Student Motivation in Physical Education: A Self-Determination Theory Perspective, In C.D. Ennis, K. Armour, A. Chen, A. Garn, E. Mauerberg-deCastro, D. Penney, S. Silverman, M. Solmon, & R. Tinning (Eds.) *Routledge Handbook of Physical Education Pedagogy*, (p. 594–606), London: Routledge.

Weiss, M.R. & Ferrer-Caja, E. (2000). Predictors of intrinsic motivation amongst adolescent students in physical education, *Research Quarterly for Exercise and Sport, 71*(3), 267–279.

Weiss, M.R. & Stuntz, C.P. (2004). 'A little friendly competition: Peer relationships and psychological development in youth sport and physical activity contexts.' In: M.R. Weiss (Ed.) *Developmental Sport and Exercise Psychology: A Lifespan Perspective* (pp. 165–196). Morgantown, WV: Fitness Information Technology.

Whitehead, S. & Biddle, S. (2008). Adolescent girls' perceptions of physical activity: A focus group study, *European Physical Education Review, 14*(2), 243–262.

Wrotniak, B.H., Epstein, L.H., Dorn, J.M., Jones K.E. & Kondilisc, V.A. (2006). The relationship between motor proficiency and physical activity in children, *Pediatrics, 118*(6), 1758–1765.

9 Pedagogy for motivation, learning and development in physical education

Shirley Gray, Kevin Morgan and John Sproule

Introduction

Traditionally, the focus for learning in physical education has been either the development of sport specific motor skills (Moy, Renshaw & Davids, 2015) or to increase physical activity levels in order to improve physical health (Gray, MacIsaac & Jess, 2015). To do so, teachers have typically adopted direct teaching approaches where they:

- set the specific learning goals that emphasise the physical learning domain;
- organise the tasks that aim to support the attainment of those learning goals;
- provide learners with feedback about how to achieve those learning goals;
- decide when learners are ready to progress to the next learning task.

This is a very teacher-intensive and educationally narrow approach to teaching physical education. It reduces the learning opportunities to those decided upon by the teacher. It is 'performance' focused, privileging those learners that are skilful, fit and strong, while marginalising those who are not. For example, only emphasising the physical domain in physical education lessons means that those learners who have low self-perceptions of their physical ability are likely to see little relevance in participating. Furthermore, with such a public focus on the body, fitness and physical performance, those less able and less fit can be made to feel inadequate, embarrassed and morally judged by others. Unless the teacher differentiates between learners of different physical abilities and fosters an inclusive learning environment, this can lead to the development of low self-esteem and poor perception of body image (Gray, MacIsaac & Jess, 2015). A key focus for physical education teachers, therefore, should be to create an inclusive learning environment, one that emphasises a broad range of learning outcomes, where the aims and personal benefits to the learner are explicit and where there is a clear emphasis on developing personalised learning and self-confidence.

In addressing these issues, this chapter presents three alternative approaches to teaching and learning, each focusing less on the content for learning and more on the learner, their learning and their development. In presenting these perspectives, we do not intend to undermine the role of motor skill learning, or the development of physical health in the physical education context. Learning how to move in various sport and physical activity contexts is clearly an important goal for all physical educationalists. However, learning in physical education can, and we argue should, also be developmental in nature. That is, learning should also facilitate the development of the learner's personal, social and cognitive skills, thus providing them with a platform for effective and self-regulated learning now and in the future. Teaching approaches that have the capacity to do this are not founded on the idea of the teacher 'transmitting' knowledge to the learner who 'receives' this knowledge. Rather, these teaching approaches are founded on the notion that the teacher has a trusting relationship with the learner, understands their basic needs and the various contexts in which they learn. They are also based on the notion that, for effective learning to take place, the learner must be actively involved in these learning contexts, contexts that are meaningful, relevant and inherently social. In an attempt to provide more detail about how this is achieved, we present three pedagogical approaches that offer a broader perspective on teaching and learning in the physical education context: learner-centred games teaching, a mastery motivational climate and self-regulated learning. We also argue that for learners to become self-regulating they require a teacher who is an effective leader, one who inspires, challenges and empowers. Indeed, we hope that it becomes clear towards the end of the chapter that all three approaches have the capacity to transform the learning and the lives of young people.

Main findings
Learner-centred, game-focused teaching and learning

Traditionally, team invasion games such as hockey, rugby and soccer have played an important and prominent role within many physical education curricula around the world (Gray & Sproule, 2011). However, it has been suggested that many learners in schools no longer see the relevance of games in more contemporary times, and this is partly why they become disengaged from physical education (Whitehead & Biddle, 2008). Reflecting many of the views presented in the previous chapter, we support the idea that games (not only invasion games, but other game forms such as badminton, volleyball and softball) should be part of a balanced physical education curriculum that can provide rich and diverse learning experiences and develop a wide variety of motor, cognitive and affective skills (Bailey, 2006). Importantly, key to successful and positive learning is teacher pedagogy and the creation of a trusting and safe learning environment (Mitchell, Gray & Inchley, 2015). Under the right conditions, the learning environment can provide experiences that not only enhance their learners' motor performance in games, but also the learning process and their overall growth and development (Bailey, 2006). It is imperative, therefore, that the teacher both understands and explicitly conveys the holistic learning benefits of participation in games to the learners, so that they can be more fully engaged despite the fact that they may not go on to pursue these activities in later life.

Traditional approaches to games teaching

Games in physical education have traditionally been taught using a teacher-centred, skill-focused approach with the aim of developing and refining specific game skills out with the context of the game (Moy et al., 2015). Only once the skills have been practised are the learners provided with opportunities to apply the skills in the game. The skills are usually practised through repetition in progressive tasks that move from closed to open situations. In this way, learners can focus on key technical components of the skill in order to replicate a model performance prescribed to them by the teacher. The teacher directs this process by providing feedback to the learners, often in the form of corrective feedback based on previous errors in performance. In adopting this skills-first approach, learners frequently find it difficult to transfer their previously 'learned' skills into the game. This is because when the skills are removed from the game context, learners do not develop an understanding of the situations during the game that necessitate the application of such skills. In other words, they do not develop decision-making skills. Lack of game knowledge and inability to make decisions about when and why to execute skills can make the transfer from practice to game-play very difficult. This can result in increased errors in game performance and subsequent lack of motivation, effort and enjoyment (Ridgers, Fazey & Fairclough, 2007). This is especially the case for less able and less confident learners and, for some, can result in humiliation, marginalisation and disengagement from physical education (Harvey & Jarrett, 2014; Moy et al., 2015)

Alternative approaches

A number of alternative approaches have been developed to address issues associated with the skills-first approach, for example: Game Sense (den Duyn, 1997), Deliberate Play (Cote & Hay, 2002), the Tactical Approach (Griffin, Mitchell & Oslin, 1997) and Play Practice (Launder, 2001). These approaches focus on understanding the game context, rather than on learning game-specific skills, and aim to develop players' technical *and* tactical performance by teaching through simplified and modified games. The origins of most, if not all, game-focused approaches derive from a teaching approach that was developed in the 1980s called Teaching Games for Understanding (TGfU) (Bunker & Thorpe, 1982). This is a tactical approach where *understanding the game through games play* is the main goal. It did not claim to be a new, innovative model for games teaching (Hopper, Butler & Storey, 2009), rather it was seen as a way of organising and implementing pre-existing pedagogies for games in a way that had not previously been done. This perhaps explains (partly) why so many nuanced variations were subsequently developed (Stolz & Pill, 2014). Significantly, although TGfU was largely developed to enhance learning and performance experiences in games, it also seemed to address other shortcomings of the traditional approach, including low motivation in games and the perceived lack of relevant educational outcomes in physical education (Stolz & Pill, 2014).

With many of these game-focused approaches, games are categorised to highlight the similarities between games in terms of their structure and objectives (invasion, net and striking/fielding). Teachers, therefore, become facilitators of game knowledge, rather than facilitators of game-specific motor skills. While there are some differences between each of the models presented above, what they have in common is the idea that game understanding and decision making can and should be developed in authentic and meaningful game contexts. Consequently, teacher have a less direct role, employing pedagogical techniques such as modified games, problem-solving tasks and questioning. The intention with these techniques is to encourage players to explore the game environment, to recognise tactical situations and work out for themselves (individually or in teams) the most appropriate tactical *and* technical options. In doing so, learners have to solve problems, think critically, observe and discuss, thus taking more responsibility for their own learning. Not only is this more authentic, social and meaningful learning environment more likely to facilitate the improvement of learners' game playing performance (Gray & Sproule, 2011), it has also been shown to enhance key affective constructs such as enjoyment, value and intrinsic motivation, primarily because learners have control over their own learning (Moy et al., 2015)

Learning theories

Two theories of learning that have commonly been used to explain learning within game-centred approaches such as TGfU, are constructivism (Wright, 2004) and situated learning (Kirk & MacPhail, 2002). Constructivism focuses on the active role of learners in constructing their own understanding and performance. Consequently, because the learner is at the centre of the learning process, content becomes more meaningful and is learned more easily which can result in an increase in motivation (Mawer, 1999). Situated learning theory (Lave & Wenger, 1991) is a form of constructivism that focuses on the social settings that construct and constitute learning. From this perspective, social and cultural contexts are fundamental components of what is learned and how it is learned. Resultantly, knowledge is constructed through social interactions within communities of practice, communities that are framed in culture. Within these communities, knowledge is shared and developed, and ideas are negotiated and agreed within authentic tasks to which all of the members of that community can relate. Light (2008) describes 'complexity theory' (See Jess et al., Chapter 4) to demonstrate the commonalities between different forms of constructivism. He explains that teachers should understand learning as a more complex process, one that is shaped by the learners' individual and social experiences. Here, an 'embodied' approach is presented, one that highlights the complexity and interdependence of the cognitive, physical, social and biological factors that shape learning

(Davids, Button & Bennett, 2008). Consequently, the separation of knowledge and movement, and the individual from the specific learning contexts is unrealistic in explaining how learning occurs.

An alternative theory that has been used to explain game-focused teaching and learning is Newell's Constraints Theory (Newell, 1986). This theory of learning focuses less on the acquisition of game knowledge and more on the ways in which functional (decision-making) movements emerge in games contexts. Like the 'complex' theories presented above, Constraints Theory also supports the notion that human intentions are 'embodied', constrained by a number of social, physical and environmental factors (Davids, Araujo, Button & Renshaw, 2007). More specifically, this theory suggests that movements emerge from the interaction of constraints that lie within the task (for example the equipment, rules and boundaries of the game), the environment (for example the surface, weather, light) and the performer (for example height, strength, attention and motivation). In terms of games teaching, the interaction of the task, performer and the environment provides the 'boundaries' for goal-directed and dynamic behaviours to emerge. The emergence of dynamic behaviours also suggests that the existence of a common optimal motor pattern for performing a skill is misleading. Learners have an abundance of movement possibilities available to them. This empowers them to seek their own optimal movements to reach the task goal, developing functional movements that are aligned with their own characteristics, experiences and abilities rather than to those of a 'model' performer. Exploratory activity in contexts that mirror the performance environment (albeit a simplified performance environment) therefore is both inherent and essential in learning, and perceptual information is used to guide the learner to goal-directed behaviour. Proponents of this theory describe 'non-linear' pedagogy to explain how teachers might facilitate learning in games (Chow et al., 2007). Similar to other game-focused approaches, modified and simplified games are advocated as they maintain key informational sources that guide the learner's movements. The teachers adopt a facilitative role, creating contexts for learning that encourage exploratory movements, individualised goal attainment and 'interactive practice and cooperative learning for problem resolution' (Moy et al., 2015, p. 5).

Research evidence

There is a body of research evidence to suggest game-focused approaches can have a positive impact on game performance outcomes in physical education (Gray & Sproule, 2011; Harvey & Jarrett, 2014; Miller et al., 2015; Nathan & Haynes, 2013). However, there is also evidence to suggest that game-focused approaches can facilitate the attainment of other important goals in physical education, for example, the development of social and emotional skills. Much of the research in this area has looked at the ways in which game-focused approaches have impacted on self-determined motivation, given that intrinsic motivation in physical education is associated with high levels of engagement, improved learning outcomes and positive wellbeing (see Chapter 8). In aligning game-focused teaching (or non-linear pedagogy) to the satisfaction of basic needs in physical education, Moy et al. (2015) highlight how the principle of self-organisation under constraints can enhance learners' perception of physical competence and autonomy. This is because learners are given the freedom to explore the practice environment and find their own solutions to the task problem thus 'enabling them to match performance problems with their unique individual characteristics and action capabilities to experience success' (p. 5).

Similarly, Mandigo, Holt, Anderson and Sheppard (2008) found that their version of TGfU, a version that promoted autonomy-supportive teacher behaviours, increased the number of positive affective experiences reported by participants. They also found relatively high levels of motivation in participants, as measured by enjoyment, optimal challenge, autonomy support, perceived competence. They reported differences between boys and girls in relation to their experiences in each lesson, with the girls reporting higher levels of enjoyment, optimal challenge and autonomy support, while the boys reported higher levels of perceived competence. These findings are interesting because they suggest that individuals can react differently to the same motivational experiences. Mandigo et al. (2008) suggest that, even though boys and girls have the same basic needs, social and cultural factors may mediate how individuals react to the same environment.

Consequently, while adopting game-based approaches may impact positively on the learning and affective outcomes for many, as alluded to in the previous chapter, the learner must lie at the heart of the teaching and learning process. Indeed, some have criticised approaches such as TGfU (and the Tactical Approach) because their focus is more on the application of the model rather than individual learning and development. Stolz and Pill (2014), for example, propose that although TGfU and the Tactical Approach are presented as cyclical models, they remain linear in nature given that teachers must adhere to a progressive series of steps toward game performance. By contrast, they suggest that Game Sense (den Duyn, 1997) and non-linear pedagogy are approaches that are more iterative, where the learners' needs (or constraints of the learner) are critical to the design of the learning task. Moy et al. (2015) liken this to SDT and the need to recognise learners' basic psychological needs to facilitate intrinsically motivated behaviour.

Approaches to teaching games, including and emanating from TGfU, that provide opportunities to learn through the game (often simplified or modified), facilitate individualised goal attainment and provide opportunities to work with others to solve problems, have the potential to create effective environments for learning in physical education. More importantly, when such approaches are organised according to the learning and developmental needs of the individual, we suggest that they have the potential to contribute to the learner's motivation for learning as well as their personal growth and development. Closely aligned to the focus on individual progress and learning are the concepts of motivational climate and, in particular, teaching approaches/behaviours that facilitate the creation of a mastery motivational climate.

Motivational climate

A key factor in determining motivation and learning is the motivational climate that has been created by the teacher and the way in which this is perceived by the learner. Motivational climate has been predominantly considered from a psychological perspective, with a particular focus on Achievement Goal Theory (AGT) (Nicholls, 1984). AGT (Nicholls, 1984) identifies the two different definitions of success as: normatively focused (ego), where the goal is to outperform others by comparing one's own ability to theirs; and self-referenced (task/mastery), where success is seen as improving one's personal best performances (Ames, 1992a). Importantly, AGT argues that these two different states of goal involvement are a consequence of the teacher's behaviours (teacher-created motivational climate) in combination with a learner's goal orientations, or predispositions to be self-referenced (task oriented) or comparative with others (ego oriented) (Ames, 1992a; Duda & Balaguer, 2007).

When a teacher emphasises self-referenced improvement, individual progress, effort and persistence then it is more likely that the motivational climate will be perceived as mastery/task involving. If, the climate encourages normative comparisons between learners, then there is a stronger likelihood that an ego involving climate will prevail (Duda & Balaguer, 2007; Roberts, 2001). Perceptions of a mastery climate have been consistently associated with positive motivational responses such as beliefs that success is dependent on effort, high levels of satisfaction and enjoyment, choice of challenging tasks, intrinsic motivation and low levels of boredom (Goudas & Biddle, 1994). Perceptions of an ego climate, however, have been related to a belief that success is dependent on ability, a choice of less challenging tasks, higher levels of boredom, lower levels of enjoyment and satisfaction, and a greater likelihood of cheating and unethical behaviours (due to a win-at-all-costs attitude) (Kavussanu & Roberts, 2001). Recently, while acknowledging the role of AGT and psychological processes in motivational climate, Morgan (2016) has argued that the pedagogical and sociological aspects of the motivational environment should be equally considered.

From a pedagogical perspective, few areas of the school curriculum generate such contrasting motivational responses as physical education (Biddle, 2001). For some learners, physical education is the highlight of their day, whereas for others it is perceived as a major source of stress and anxiety. Teachers' behaviours and the motivational strategies they adopt play a significant role in shaping learning, attainment and the quality of the learners' experiences (Reeve, 2009). Presenting challenging and enjoyable learning opportunities that motivate students to participate, exert effort and learn should, therefore, be an overriding principle of a teacher's philosophy (Morgan, Milton & Longville, 2015). Manipulating the TARGET (task, authority, recognition, grouping, evaluation and time) structures (Ames, 1992a; Epstein, 1988) to be mastery focused has been found to foster positive motivational responses such as: higher levels of perceived competence, satisfaction and enjoyment, less boredom, a stronger preference for engaging in more challenging tasks, higher mastery goal orientations and a stronger belief that success was the result of effort (Hassan & Morgan, 2015).

TARGET

According to Ames (1992a, 1992b) a mastery motivational climate can be fostered by manipulating the TARGET structures to set self-referenced, differentiated and varied tasks, provide learners with a sense of individual autonomy, recognise effort and progress, organise heterogeneous and cooperative groups, individualise formative evaluation/assessments and allow flexible time to learn. Connecting the previous section of this chapter on game-focused approaches with motivational climate, Gray, Sproule and Morgan (2009) found that a game-focused approach to teaching basketball with secondary age learners changed the TARGET behaviours of the teacher from more ego-orientated to more mastery-focused. Specifically, while adopting a more game-focused approach, the teacher focused more on self-referenced learning goals, provided more autonomy and decision-making opportunities, reduced comparative feedback, facilitated more mixed ability cooperative grouping and increased activity time. Although it is acknowledged that the TARGET structures all inter-relate (Ames, 1992a), for the remaining part of this section on motivational climate, each of these TARGET structures will be considered individually with a particular emphasis on learners' personal, social and cognitive development.

Task – The primary focus of the task structure is threefold: to promote personalised learning goals; to differentiate the tasks for inclusion and optimal challenge; and to include a variety of tasks to maintain interest and engagement (Ames, 1992a). Developing the ability to set realistic and achievable goals is an essential life skill for personal development. Initially, in a physical education context, this process is likely to be shared between teacher and learner. Over time, however, the aim should be to develop learners' ability to set their own personalised goals so that they can maintain an active and healthy lifestyle. Inclusion values the achievement of everyone equally and promotes the notion that all learners can achieve success irrespective of ability and personal circumstances (Stidder & Hayes, 2013). Designing tasks in such a way that the different levels of physical and cognitive ability are not overtly evident is, therefore, a key consideration for teachers in facilitating an inclusive environment. Learners need to feel comfortable to opt into tasks that best suit their level of achievement and a mastery task structure encourages this choice. In such a learning environment, learners' confidence and perceived ability levels are protected and enhanced (Ames, 1992a). The teacher is instrumental in fostering this mastery climate, which links well to a 'nurturing' pedagogical agenda where the emotions and personal development of the individual participants are considered paramount (Almond & Whitehead, 2012).

Authority – The authority structure relates to the balance of decision making between teacher and learners during the lessons. Consistent with game-focused approaches to physical education, a mastery climate encourages learners to take on leadership roles and participate in decision making. Involvement in decision making has been associated with positive motivational responses such as feelings of self-competence, responsibility, independence and greater levels of self-determination and engagement in learning (Ames, 1992b). Several teaching styles from Mosston and Ashworth's (2002) physical education Spectrum promote shared decision making. Indeed, the Spectrum is a continuum of teaching strategies categorised according to who (teacher or learner) makes the decisions before, during and after the lesson tasks. At one end of the spectrum is the Command style in which the teacher makes all the decisions across all three stages. At the other end of the spectrum is the Learner-Initiated style in which the learner makes almost all the decisions and the teacher acts as a facilitator. Between these two styles, Mosston and Ashworth (2002) identified a series of other styles, each categorised according to the decisions made by the teacher and learner. Styles such as Reciprocal, Inclusion, Guided Discovery and Problem Solving are particularly focused on learner autonomy. Research by Morgan, Sproule and Kingston (2005) demonstrated that such styles foster a more mastery involving motivational climate than the more traditionally used teacher-led styles.

Recognition – What teachers recognise and reward within their lessons plays a crucial role in motivating learners and engaging them in the lesson activities. The distribution of recognition and rewards has important consequences for learning, interest, satisfaction and feelings of self-worth (Morgan et al., 2015). It is paramount, therefore, that teachers also recognise other achievements such as sustained effort, individual progress, cognitive development, understanding, creativity, cooperation and team work (particularly evident in games-focused approaches) if all learners are to receive equal opportunity for recognition within physical education lessons. This is consistent with a mastery climate (Ames, 1992a) and inclusive practice in physical education (Stidder & Hayes, 2013).

Although often given by the teacher with good intention, recognition and rewards given publicly and on a differential basis invite social comparison between learners and emphasise an ego involving motivational climate. To foster a mastery motivational climate, teachers should aim to give individual recognition to learners, so that their feelings of satisfaction derive from improving personal standards rather than doing better than their peers. In physical education settings, providing individual feedback and distributing this equally is a significant logistical challenge for teachers but one that they should persevere with. By providing one-to-one feedback the teacher recognises every learner's individual needs, which is more likely to enhance their self-esteem and levels of confidence.

Grouping – According to Ames (1992a), when the teacher promotes mixed ability and varied grouping arrangements, it is more difficult for the learners to interpret performance comparatively and, consequently, a mastery climate is more likely to be perceived. Furthermore, cooperation within groups is an essential requirement of a mastery climate. This is consistent with the Cooperative Learning model in physical education (Dyson & Casey, 2012), where learners work together in small, structured, heterogeneous groups to master the subject matter. To ensure that a group is cooperative, educators must understand the basic elements that need to be carefully structured within every cooperative group. According to Dyson and Casey (2012), for groups to be truly cooperative the following elements need to be in place: clearly perceived positive interdependence; considerable 'face-face' interaction; clearly perceived 'individual accountability';

personal responsibility to achieve the group's goals; frequent use of relevant interpersonal and small-group skills; and frequent and regular 'group processing' of current functioning to improve the group's future effectiveness. Fostering such team dynamics is essential to the success of game-focused approaches to physical education, and to enhancing learners' feelings of relatedness as discussed in the previous chapter.

Another important aspect of the TARGET grouping structure is the use of varied grouping arrangements that involves regrouping learners on a regular basis, both within and between lessons. The interpersonal and small-group skills this grouping arrangement developed allowed free and easy communication between group members (Dyson & Casey, 2012). According to Dyson (2001), these skills include listening to others, taking responsibility, giving and receiving feedback, sharing decision making and encouraging each other. Such interactions are only possible when effective cooperation exists within groups. Regrouping learners on a regular basis can make it more challenging to build 'positive interdependence' and 'individual accountability' due to potentially difficult interpersonal relationships between different group members. However, such varied grouping arrangements have the potential for significant gains in learners' personal and social development as they need to practise their interpersonal skills with a wider group of peers.

Evaluation – Evaluation or assessment is one of the most important features of the physical education environment and consequently learners' motivation can be easily undermined by it (Morgan et al., 2015). Evaluation that emphasises normative assessment and peer comparisons promotes an ego climate that can impair learners' perceived ability, intrinsic interest and self-esteem (Nicholls, 1989). In contrast, when evaluation is mastery based on improvement, progress towards individual or team goals, participation and effort all learners have equal opportunity to achieve. Effective evaluation strategies for the promotion of a mastery motivational climate are consistent with Assessment for Learning (AfL) (Assessment Reform Group, 1999). Such strategies include informing learners of the criteria against which they are being evaluated and including them in the evaluation of themselves (self-evaluation) and others (peer-evaluation). By becoming more aware of their own and others' strengths and weaknesses, learners are more likely to understand their learning and to be able to set themselves goals for improvement. Recognising where the learners are, communicating their strengths and areas for development and identifying steps required to further improve are all essential elements of effective evaluation (Newton & Bowler, 2015). The use of teacher questioning, combined with self and peer-evaluations are all important strategies for evaluating learning and in fostering a positive motivational environment (Newton & Bowler, 2015).

Time – Consistent with the pedagogical concepts of 'time on task' and 'active learning time' in physical education (Metzler, 1989), the final TARGET structure is time. Active learning time has been defined as the time learners are engaged in motor and other learning activities in order to achieve the learning outcomes (Metzler, 1989). The 'other' learning time referred to in this chapter considers cognitive and social learning. From a mastery and inclusion perspective, the key concept is to allow for flexible learning time to accommodate learners with different prerequisite skills (Ames, 1992a). If this is neglected, teachers will deny differences in learning rates and reduce the number of effective learners (Epstein, 1988). Considering the practical implications for physical education teachers, the pace of instruction and the time allotted for completing tasks significantly influences motivation. In promoting a mastery motivational climate, the use of extension tasks is an effective strategy for those learners that finish the task early. Similarly, allowing additional time for those who require it will allow learners to progress at their own optimal rate of learning. However, some caution is advised here as, depending on the maturity and experience of the learners, allowing too much flexibility in time has the potential to result in a loss of focus and for the pace of learning to drop to unsatisfactory levels.

In summary, a mastery motivational climate is created when the teacher organises tasks that are multi-dimensional, designed for variety and enjoyment and are differentiated to meet the needs of all learners. In addition, a mastery climate is achieved when the teacher encourages the learners to make decisions, when groups are heterogeneous, varied and cooperative, and recognition and rewards are focused on effort and improvement. Finally, time on task should be maximised and evaluation should be self-referenced. When this is achieved, intrinsic motivation is enhanced and this in turn promotes higher levels of enjoyment, perceptions of competence and a positive attitude towards physical education (Morgan et al., 2005; Ommundsen & Kvalo, 2007).

In the previous chapter, it was argued that intrinsic motivation is facilitated by contextual conditions that reflect an autonomy-supportive learning environment, thus satisfying the basic needs of competency, relatedness and autonomy. For example, the inclusion of learners in decision-making processes facilitates the satisfaction of the need for autonomy (Roberts, 2001; Sproule et al., 2013), and is more likely to make learners' perceptions of competence more resilient (Standage, Duda & Ntoumanis, 2005). This demonstrates the similarities between game-focused teaching approaches and the conditions required for a mastery motivational climate and, in doing so, highlights the potential that they both have in promoting self-determined motivation (Moreno, González-Cutre, Sicilia & Spray, 2010). Congruent with intrinsic motivation and self-determination is the ability to effectively self-regulate one's behaviour. Indeed, it has been argued that to remain on task and fully engaged in learning requires good self-regulation skills (Blair & Razza, 2007).

Self-regulated learning

Grounded in social cognitive theory, self-regulated learning (SRL) is a theoretical approach attending to processes that enable learners to control cognition, behaviour and motivation (Kaplan, 2008). Self-regulated learners are highly reflective and come to understand what and why they are learning. They achieve this through the implementation of learning strategies, including planning, goal setting, self-monitoring and self-evaluation, all key aspects of TARGET, as identified in the previous sub-section. As a result, they apply effort in their learning, become more successful learners and, importantly, value this learning. This relationship between learning, motivation and self-regulation is important because self-regulation theorists endorse the view that attaining high self-efficacy determines the capacity for self-regulation (Gordon, 2001; Zimmerman, 1989). The importance of providing learners with appropriate and meaningful opportunities for successful and autonomous learning has already been highlighted in this chapter. However, this also suggests that these conditions are not only important in terms of enhancing motivation for learning, but also important for the development of self-regulated learning since self-efficacy beliefs and self-regulation are intrinsically inter-related (Bandura, 1997). Indeed, some consider it essential that the curriculum is structured in a manner that scaffolds motivational aspects of SRL (e.g. Egan, 2011). Unfortunately, given the traditional focus on the transmission of 'content' in physical education, many teachers neglect to teach their learners *how* to self-regulate (Dignath-van Ewijk & van der Werf, 2012; Perry, Hutchinson & Thauberger, 2008). We argue that teachers have a critical role in the development of self-regulating learners, highlighting Reeve, Ryan, Deci and Jang's (2008) idea that 'although autonomous self-regulation is the destination, the road goes through social regulation, reflecting the ancient Chinese proverb, *Start with your master, end with yourself* (p. 239).

Consistent with the self-referenced focus of TARGET, Zimmerman (2000) suggests that self-regulated learning occurs by engaging in a process that begins with a cognitive phase involving goal setting and strategic planning, and moves through to a performance phase where feedback and monitoring strategies are used to guide learning. Finally, self-regulated learners take time to reflect on their learning, where they make an evaluative judgment about their learning that informs future goals setting and planning for the next learning cycle. Based on these principles, Zimmerman (2000) proposed a four-level model of self-regulation development: observation, emulation, self-control, and self-regulation. From this, Goudas, Kolovelonis and Dermitzaki (2013) have developed an instructional approach to teaching physical education that helps students become self-regulated learners. According to this approach, in the early stages of learning, learners should be supported by the modeling, instruction, monitoring, and guidance activities of teachers or peers. Learning new skills, therefore, begins with observational learning, followed by practice and social feedback from their teacher or from their peers. As the learner progresses, practice becomes more self-directed so that the learner becomes more able to adapt their performance to changes in internal and external conditions. Consequently, social feedback is gradually withdrawn and replaced by self-generating feedback and learners practise skills in changing or more challenging conditions. The result of which is a process 'whereby learners personally activate and sustain cognitions, affects and behaviours that are systematically oriented toward the attainment of personal goals' (Zimmerman & Schunk, 2011, p. 1).

Transformational teaching

The successful development of self-regulated learning, a mastery motivational climate and game-focused approaches are all highly dependent upon the skills of the teacher to foster an effective learning environment. Creating learning environments that enhance learning/performances *and* that nurtures the learners' development and capacity for learning is made more difficult by external pressures caused by, for example, high-stakes examinations and league tables. However, if teachers are to make a positive impact on learning *and* development, then they need to move beyond the view that teaching is the 'transmission of knowledge', towards the view that teaching can be transformational. A primary goal of transformational teaching is to create independent, self-regulated, and self-motivated physically educated citizens. Transformational teaching and learning involves empowering learners not only to fly their own plane; it also enhances the self-efficacy of learners to land and take off the plane safely and at places of *their* choice. In part, this can be achieved by the application of learner-centred teaching strategies. However, effective leadership is also critical to successful transformation, organisational and system performance, and sustainability. Transformational teaching involves the demonstration of behaviours that empower and inspire learners, transcend teachers' own self-interests, and give learners the confidence to achieve higher levels of functioning (Beauchamp et al., 2014). It is important, therefore, that teachers can lead, engage others, achieve results aligned with vision and values, build internal and external relationships to successfully navigate socio-political environments, and demonstrate critical thinking, innovation and strategic orientation to transform the lives of learners.

Transformational Leadership Theory (Bass & Riggio, 2006; Burns, 1978) proposes that transactional (task-focused) leaders achieve minimum standards and transformational (team-oriented) leadership inspires performance beyond expectations and improves team behaviour (Hu et al., 2016). Furthermore, Hu et al. (2016) suggest that transformational leadership is additive, rather than inversely correlated, to transactional leadership. Therefore, Hu et al.'s findings support transformational leaders who demonstrate a high moral standard, gain the respect and trust of learners. Therefore, one path for engaging learners is to consider the use of transformational leadership as a pedagogical theory, because a transformational teacher can connect with learners' needs and motives to help them reach their fullest potential. Thus, undertaking leadership is for everyone, including teachers of physical education. The skills required for leadership (e.g. motivating and influencing, time management, planning and coping with pressure) are those that will enable teachers to not only adapt to a changing world, but also create an experience that is relevant and aligned to what is valued both by learners and society. For example, teachers should not just teach learners to do physically activity, when they could teach them to take responsibility for their own physical activity. This involves taking a lead role and setting a new direction, or by taking an actively supportive followership role (e.g. autonomy supportive) to see initiatives through and make them sustainable. This could be achieved within a spiral curriculum model of physical education, built on the intention to teach key concepts, not all at once, but in different contexts over time, and based on the belief in learning as a constructivist and active process. For example, Bruner (1996) argued that concepts are neither independent nor discrete, but dynamic changing ideas, and learning should be participatory, proactive, communal, collaborative and given over to the construction, rather than the reception, of meanings. Thus, spiral curricula have emerged, with conceptual insights being revisited at different levels interspersed with periods of stasis (Kinchin, 2010).

The significant role that leadership plays is evident in Beauchamp et al.'s (2014) conceptualisation of transformational teaching where teaching involves four dimensions: idealised influence; inspirational motivation; intellectual stimulation; and individualised consideration. Idealised influence takes place when teachers interact with learners through the demonstration of values-based principles, foster trust and respect among learners, and act as role models. Inspirational motivation takes place when teachers communicate high expectations to their learners, display optimism, articulate a compelling vision of what is possible, and inspire learners to achieve their goals. Intellectual stimulation involves engaging the rationality of learners, encouraging them to see issues from multiple perspectives and question commonly held assumptions. Finally, individualised consideration occurs when teachers display empathy and understanding of learners' unique personal and psychological needs.

In addition, it should be noted that aspects of transformational leadership offer unique conceptual extensions that only recently have been the sustained focus of inquiry within school physical education settings. Recently, for example, Bourne et al. (2015) found that when physical education teachers made use of transformational teaching behaviours with adolescents that this was positively related to both in class physical activity and leisure-time physical activity. Thus, while recognising that the pursuit of physical activity during class time is an important goal, we contend that physical education also should involve stimulating learners intellectually to consider how they can benefit from sustained engagement in physical activity as a lifestyle choice. This perspective is supported by Bennie, Peralta, Gibbons, Lubans and Rosenkrantz (2016) who have shown that motivational teaching strategies such as explaining relevance and offering choice are perceived to be effective when part of physical education lessons.

Future directions

This chapter set out to offer a broader view of teaching and learning in the physical education context; one that moves beyond a focus on motor skill development towards a perspective where the learner and their learning *and* development are central to the teaching process. In doing so, we have highlighted the potential that a learner-centred, game-focused approach to games teaching might have in terms of promoting individualised, yet social opportunities for autonomous learning and development. We have also highlighted teaching behaviours that have the potential to create a mastery climate that fosters high levels of effort, enjoyment, satisfaction and intrinsic motivation. We have evidenced, for example, that when a teacher emphasises self-referenced improvement, individual progress, effort and persistence, that positive motivational responses and increased opportunities for successful learning will follow. However, in focusing on the role of the learner, and in our endeavours to promote learning that has the potential to change the way that learners approach their learning, we have also highlighted the need for teachers to develop learners' capacity for self-regulated learning. Here, learners are supported in the early stages of the learning process to understand their learning, so that, over time, learning becomes self-directed towards the attainment of their own personal goals (Zimmerman & Schunk, 2011).

Finally, in bringing together these three different pedagogic approaches we have described many of the characteristics of the transformational teacher; the teacher who facilitates learning while also promoting personal development and disposition toward learning (Slavich & Zimbardo, 2012). Rosebrough and Leverett (2011) state that this form of education inspires rather than informs and that transformational teachers facilitate the development of both skills *and* attitudes for overcoming challenges. Transformational teachers are also transformational leaders who can inspire their learners to reach their potential individually and collectively, while simultaneously realising their shared vision (Slavich & Zimbardo, 2012). From this perspective education and teaching can change lives, where 'great teachers call upon ordinary students to embrace their own greatness' (Anding, 2005, p. 488).

Summary of key findings

- Traditionally, teaching approaches in physical education have been very performance focused and teacher-centred.
- Game-focussed teaching approaches are more learner-centred and aim to facilitate the attainment of a broad range of educational goals, including those that are cognitive and social.
- Research on game-centred teaching approaches on learning has shown improved decision-making, increased enjoyment and feelings of autonomy support.
- A mastery motivational climate is perceived when a teacher emphasises self-referenced improvement, individual progress, effort and persistence.
- The behaviour of the teacher plays a significant role in shaping the learning, attainment and quality of the learners' experiences.
- Manipulating the TARGET structures to be mastery focused fosters positive motivational responses such as: higher levels of perceived competence, satisfaction and enjoyment, less boredom, a stronger preference for engaging in more challenging tasks, higher mastery goal orientations and a stronger belief that success was the result of effort.
- To remain on task and fully engaged in learning, learners require good self-regulation skills. Self-regulated learners are highly reflective and come to understand what and why they are learning.
- Self-regulated learning is developed initially through supported practice.

- A primary goal of transformational teaching is to create independent, self-regulated, and self-motivated physically educated citizens.
- Transformational teachers are effective leaders. The skills required for leadership are those that will enable physical education teachers to create experiences that are relevant and aligned to what is valued both by learners and society.

Reflective tasks

- How do the three approaches described relate to the ideas presented in the previous chapter?
- What do you think might be the challenges of adopting each approach when working with your learners? How might these challenges be overcome?
- Reflect on the similarities between a mastery motivational climate and self-regulated learning and how one approach can help to enhance the other.
- Outline why transformational teaching is important for learner relevance and lifestyle choice.
- Why is it important for (student) teachers of physical education to develop their leadership skills?

Further readings

Alderman, K.M. (2008). *Motivation for Achievement*. New York: Routledge.
Wright, J., Macdonald, D., & Burrows, L. (2004). *Critical Inquiry and Problem-Solving in Physical Education*. London: Routledge.

References

Almond, L. & Whitehead, M. (2012). Translating physical literacy into practice for all teachers, *Physical Education Matters, 7*, 67–70.
Ames, C. (1992a). 'Achievement goals, motivational climate, and motivational processes.' In: G.C. Roberts (Ed.) *Motivation in Sport and Exercise* (pp. 161–176). Champaign, IL: Human Kinetics.
Ames, C. (1992b). Classrooms: Goals, structures, and student motivation, *Journal of Educational Psychology, 84*, 261–271.
Anding, J.M. (2005). An interview with Robert E. Quinn: Entering the fundamental state of leadership: Reflections on the path to transformational teaching, *Academy of Management Learning and Education, 4*, 487–495.
Assessment Reform Group. (1999). *Assessment for Learning: Beyond the Black Box*. Cambridge: University of Cambridge School of Education.
Bailey, R. (2006). Physical education and sport in school: A review of benefits and outcomes, *Journal of School Health, 76*(8), 397–401.
Bandura, A. (1997). *Self-Efficacy: The Exercise of Control*. New York: W.H. Freeman & Co.
Bass, B.M. & Riggio, R.E. (2006). *Transformational Leadership* (2nd ed.). Mahwah, NJ: Lawrence Erlbaum.

Beauchamp, M.R., Barling, J., Li, Z., Morton, K.L., Keith, S.E., & Zumbo, B.D. (2014). Development and Psychometric Properties of the Transformational Teaching Questionnaire, *Journal of Health Psychology, 15*(8), 1123–1134.

Bennie, A., Peralta, L., Gibbons, S., Lubans, D., & Rosenkrantz, R. (2016). Physical education teachers' perceptions about the effectiveness and acceptability of strategies used to increase relevance and choice for students in physical education classes, *Asia-Pacific Journal of Teacher Education*, 1–18. DOI: 10.1080/1359866X.2016. 1207059

Biddle, S.J.H. (2001). 'Enhancing motivation in physical education.' In: G.C. Roberts (Ed.) *Advances in Motivation in Sport and Exercise* (pp. 101–128). Champaign, IL: Human Kinetics.

Blair, C. & Razza, R.P. (2007). Relating effortful control, executive function, and false belief understanding to emerging math and literacy ability in kindergarten, *Child Development, 78*, 647–663.

Bourne, J., Liu, Y., Shields, C.A., Jackson, B., Zumbo, B.D., & Beauchamp, M. (2015). The relationship between transformational teaching and adolescent physical activity: The mediating roles of personal and relational efficacy beliefs, *Journal of Health Psychology, 20*(2), 132–143.

Bruner, J. (1996). *The Culture of Education.* Cambridge, MA: Harvard University Press.

Bunker, D. & Thorpe, R. (1982). A model for the teaching of games in secondary schools, *Bulletin of Physical Education, 18*, 7–10.

Burns, J.M. (1978). *Leadership.* New York: Harper & Row.

Chow, J.Y., Davids, K., Button, C., Shuttleworth, R., Renshaw, I., & Araújo, D. (2007). The role of nonlinear pedagogy in Physical Education, *Review of Educational Research, 77*(3), 251–278.

Cote, J. & Hay, J. (2002). 'Children's involvement in sport: A developmental perspective.' In: J.M. Silva & D. Stevens (Eds.) *Psychological Foundations of Sport* (pp. 484–502). Boston, MA: Merrill.

Davids, K., Araujo, D., Button, C., & Renshaw, I. (2007). 'Degenerate brains, intermediate behaviour and representative tasks: Implications for experimental design in sport psychology research.' In: T. Reilly, J. Cabri & D. Araujo (Eds.) *Science and Football V* (pp. 537–550). London: Routledge.

Davids, K., Button, C., & Bennett, S. (2008). *Dynamics of Skill Acquisition: A Constraints-Led Approach.* Champaign, IL: Human Kinetics.

den Duyn, N. (1997). Game Sense: It's Time to Play!, *Sports Coach, 19*(4), 9–11.

Dignath-van Ewijk, C. & van der Werf, G. (2012). What teachers think about self-regulated learning: Investigating teacher beliefs and teacher behavior of enhancing students' self-regulation, *Education Research International.* Retrieved from http://dx.doi.org/10.1155/2012/741713.

Duda, J.L. & Balaguer, I. (2007). 'Coach created motivational climate.' In: S. Jowett & D. Lavellee (Eds.) *Social Psychology in Sport* (pp. 117–130). Champaign, IL: Human Kinetics.

Dyson, B. (2001). Cooperative learning in an elementary physical education programme, *Journal of Teaching in Physical Education, 20*, 264–281.

Dyson, B. & Casey, A. (2012). *Cooperative Learning in Physical Education: A Research Based Approach.* London, England: Routledge.

Egan, R. (2011). Adjusting curricular design to 'create' a culture of self-regulation, *The Canadian Journal for the Scholarship of Teaching and Learning, 2*(6), 1–15.

Epstein, J. (1988). 'Effective schools or effective students? Dealing with diversity.' In: R. Haskins & B. MacRae (Eds.) *Policies for America's Public Schools* (pp. 89–126). Norwood, NJ: Ablex.

Gordon, L.M. (2001). High teacher efficacy as a marker of teacher effectiveness in the domain of classroom management. Paper presented at the Annual Meeting of the California Council on Teacher Education, San Diego, CA.

Goudas, M. & Biddle, S.J.H. (1994). Perceived motivational climate and intrinsic motivation in school physical education classes, *European Journal of Psychology of Education, 2*, 241–250.

Goudas, M., Kolovelonis, A., & Dermitzaki, I. (2013). 'Implementation of self-regulation interventions in physical education and sports contexts.' In: H. Bembenutty, T. Cleary & A. Kitsantas (Eds.) *Applications of Self-Regulated Learning across Disciplines: A Tribute to Barry J. Zimmerman* (pp. 383–415). Greenwich, CT: Information Age.

Gray, S., MacIsaac, S., & Jess, M. (2015). Teaching 'health' in physical education in a 'healthy' way, *Retos, 28*, 26–33.

Gray, S. & Sproule, J. (2011). Developing pupils' performance in team invasion games: A comparative study within a Scottish context, *Physical Education and Sport Pedagogy, 16*(1), 15–32.

Gray, S., Sproule, J., & Morgan, K. (2009). Teaching team invasion games and motivational climate, *European Physical Education Review, 15*(1), 1–24.

Griffin, L.L., Mitchell, S.A., & Oslin, J.L. (1997). *Teaching Sport Concepts and Skill.* Illinois: Human Kinetics.

Harvey, S. & Jarrett, K. (2014). A review of the game-centred approaches to teaching and coaching literature since 2006, *Physical Education and Sport Pedagogy, 19*(3), 278–300.

Hassan, M. & Morgan, K. (2015). Effects of a mastery intervention programme on the motivational climate in sport coaching, *International Journal of Sport Science and Coaching, 10*, 487–503.

Hopper, T., Butler, J., & Storey, B. (2009). *TGfU: Simply Good Pedagogy: Understanding a Complex Challenge.* Ottawa, Ontario: PHE-Canada.

Hu, Y.-Y., Parker, S.H., Lipisitz, S.R., Arriaga, A.F., Peyre, S.E., Corso, K.A., Roth, E.M., Yule, S.J., & Greenberg, C.C. (2016). Surgeons' leadership styles and team behavior in the operating room, *Journal of the American College of Surgeons, 222*, 41–51.

Kaplan, A. (2008). Clarifying metacognition, self-regulation, and self-regulated learning: What's the purpose?, *Educational Psychology Review, 20*, 477–484.

Kavussanu, M. & Roberts, G.C. (2001). Moral functioning in sport: An achievement goal perspective, *Journal of Sport & Exercise Psychology, 23*, 37–54.

Kinchin, I. (2010). Solving Cordelia's dilemma: Threshold concepts within a punctuated model of learning, *Journal of Biological Education, 44*(2), 53–57.

Kirk, D. & MacPhail, A. (2002). Teaching games for understanding and situated learning: Re-thinking the Bunker-Thorpe model, *Journal of Teaching in Physical Education, 21*(4), 177–192.

Launder, A.G. (2001). *Play Practice: The Games Approach to Teaching and Coaching Sports.* Illinois: Human Kinetics.

Lave, J. & Wenger, E. (1991). *Situated Learning: Legitimate Peripheral Participation.* New York: Cambridge University Press.

Light, R. (2008). Complex learning theory-its epistemology and its assumptions about learning: Implications for physical education, *Journal of Teaching in Physical Education, 27*, 21–37.

Mandigo, J.L., Holt, N., Anderson, A., & Sheppard, J. (2008). Children's motivational experiences following autonomy-supportive games lessons, *European Physical Education Review, 14*(3), 407–425.

Mawer, M. (1999). 'Teaching styles and teaching approaches in physical education: Research developments.' In: C.A. Hardy & M. Mawer (Eds.) *Learning and Teaching in Physical Education* (pp. 83–104). New York: Routledge.

Metzler, M.W. (1989). A review of research on time in sport pedagogy, *Journal of Teaching in Physical Education, 8*, 87–103.

Miller, A., Christensen, E., Eather, N., Gray, S., Sproule, J., Keay, J., & Lubans, D. (2015). Can physical education and physical activity outcomes be developed simultaneously using a game-centered approach?, *European Physical Education Review*. Retrieved from http://epe.sagepub.com.ezproxy.is.ed.ac.uk/content/22/1/113.full.pdf+html.

Mitchell, F., Gray, S., & Inchley, J. (2015). 'This choice thing really works . . .': Changes in experiences and engagement of adolescent girls in physical education classes, during a school-based physical activity programme, *Physical Education and Sport Pedagogy, 20*(6), 593–611.

Moreno, J.A., González-Cutre, D., Sicilia, A., & Spray, C.M. (2010). Motivation in the exercise setting: Integrating constructs from the approach-avoidance achievement goal framework and self-determination theory, *Psychology of Sport and Exercise, 11*, 542–550.

Morgan, K. (2016). Reconceptualising motivational climate in physical education and sport coaching: An interdisciplinary perspective, *Quest*. Retrieved from http://dx.doi.org/10.1080/00336297.2016.1152984.

Morgan, K., Milton, D., & Longville, J. (2015). 'Motivating students for learning in PE.' In: S. Capel & M. Whitehead (Eds.) *Learning to Teach Physical Education in Secondary School* (pp. 107–120). London: Routledge.

Morgan, K., Sproule, J., & Kingston, K. (2005). Teaching styles, motivational climate and pupils' cognitive and affective responses in physical education, *European Physical Education Review, 11*(3), 1–27.

Mosston, M. & Ashworth, S. (2002). *Teaching Physical Education*. San Francisco: Benjamin Cummins.

Moy, B., Renshaw, I., & Davids, K. (2015). The impact of nonlinear pedagogy on physical education teacher education students' intrinsic motivation, *Physical Education and Sport Pedagogy*. Retrieved from http://dx.doi.org/10.1080/17408989.2015.1072506.

Nathan, S. & Haynes, J. (2013). A move to an innovative games teaching model: Style E Tactical (SET), *Asia-Pacific Journal of Health, Sport and Physical Education, 4*(3), 287–302.

Newell, K.M. (1986). 'Constraints on the development of coordination.' In: M.G. Wade & H.T.A Whiting (Eds.) *Motor Development in Children: Aspects of Coordination and Control* (pp. 341–361). Amsterdam: Martinus Nijhoff Publishers.

Newton, A. & Bowler, M. (2015). 'Assessment for and of learning in PE.' In: S. Capel & M. Whitehead (Eds.) *Learning to Teach Physical Education in the Secondary School* (pp. 140–155). London: Routledge.

Nicholls, J.G. (1984). Achievement motivation: Conceptions of ability, subjective experience, task choice, and performance, *Psychological Review, 91*, 328–346.

Nicholls, J.G. (1989). *The Competitive Ethos and Democratic Education*. Cambridge, MA: Harvard University Press.

Ommundsen, Y. & Kvalo, S.E. (2007). Autonomy-mastery supportive or performance focused? Different teacher behaviours and pupils' outcomes in physical education, *Scandinavian Journal of Educational Research, 51*(4), 385–413.

Perry, N.E., Hutchinson, L., & Thauberger, C. (2008). Talking about teaching self-regulated learning: Scaffolding student teachers' development and use of practices that promote self-regulated learning, *International Journal of Educational Research, 47*(2), 97–108.

Reeve, J. (2009). Why teachers adopt a controlling motivating style toward students and how they can become more autonomy supportive, *Educational Psychologist, 44,* 159–75.

Reeve, J., Ryan, R.M., Deci, E.L., & Jang, H. (2008). 'Understanding and promoting autonomous self-regulation.' In: D.H. Schunk & B.J. Zimmerman (Eds.) *Motivation and Self-Regulated Learning: Theory, Research and Applications* (pp. 223–244). New York: Erlbaum.

Ridgers, N.D., Fazey, D.M.A., & Fairclough, S.J. (2007). Perceptions of athletic competence and fear of negative evaluation during Physical Education, *British Journal of Educational Psychology, 77,* 339–349.

Roberts, G.C. (2001). 'Advances in motivation in sport and exercise: Conceptual constraints and convergence.' In: G.C. Roberts (Ed.) *Advances in Motivation in Sport and Exercise* (pp. 1–50). Champaign, IL: Human Kinetics.

Rosebrough, T.R. & Leverett, R.G. (2011). *Transformational Teaching in the Information Age: Making Why and How We Teach Relevant to Students.* Alexandria: Association for Supervision and Curriculum Development.

Slavich, G.M. & Zimbardo, P.G. (2012). Transformational teaching: Theoretical underpinnings, basic principles, and core methods, *Educational Psychology Review, 24*(4), 569–608.

Sproule, J., Martindale, R., Wang, J., Allison, P., Nash, C., & Gray, S. (2013). Investigating the experience of outdoor and adventurous project work in an educational setting using a self-determination framework, *European Physical Education Review, 19*(3), 315–328.

Standage, M., Duda, J.L., & Ntoumanis, N. (2005). A test of self-determination theory in school physical education, *British Journal of Educational Psychology, 75,* 411–433.

Stidder, G. & Hayes, S. (2013). *Equity and Inclusion in Physical Education and Sport.* London: Routledge.

Stolz, S. & Pill, S. (2014). Teaching games and sport for understanding: Exploring and reconsidering its relevance in physical education, *European Physical Education Review, 20*(1), 36–71.

Whitehead, S. & Biddle, S. (2008). Adolescent girls' perceptions of physical activity: A focus group study, *European Physical Education Review, 14*(2), 243–262.

Wright, J. (2004). 'Critical inquiry and problem-solving in physical education.' In: L. Burrows, D. Macdonald & J. Wright (Eds.) *Critical Inquiry and Problem-Solving in Physical Education* (pp. 3–15). London: Routledge.

Zimmerman, B.J. (1989). A social cognitive view of self-regulated academic learning, *Journal of Educational Psychology, 81,* 329–339.

Zimmerman, B.J. (2000). 'Attaining self-regulation: A social cognitive perspective.' In: M. Boekaerts, P.R. Pintrich & M. Zeider (Eds.) *Metacognition in Educational Theory and Practice* (pp. 13–39). San Diego, CA: Academic Press.

Zimmerman, B.J. & Schunk, D.H. (2011). *Handbook of Self-Regulation of Learning and Performance.* New York: Routledge.

10 Understanding physical education teachers' day-to-day practice

Challenging the 'unfair' picture

Paul McMillan

Introduction

The main thrust of this present textbook, and other recently published collections (see Ennis, 2016), is with the 'transformative' potential of physical education. Despite the challenges of defining transformative learning and teaching in physical education (Ovens, 2017; Tinning, 2017), it is difficult to argue that the theorising resulting from this perspective has not advanced the subject in many ways (see the Introduction by Thorburn, this volume). Generally, this transformative agenda has progressively brought 'critical' lenses to the subject with the intention of uncovering how inequalities and injustices come to operate in specific physical education contexts and to stimulate awareness of how to promote emancipation and change. I see the merit in this transformative agenda and also recognise there is further empirical research required in physical education in order to provide some concrete guidance on how to transform the status quo and promote a more equitable and democratic society (Fernández-Balboa, 2015).

While there is much research still to be done to sketch out what transformative pedagogies might look like in practice (Fernández-Balboa, 2015; Ovens, 2017; Tinning, 2017), this challenge will *not* be taken up in the present chapter. Instead, due to a string of limitations within the existing research literature, I argue that we have yet to capture a sufficiently detailed picture of teachers' day-to-day practice in physical education let alone interrogating these practices to instigate emancipation and change. I contend that the limitations within the existing research literature have skewed our conceptions of teachers' practice in schools. Accordingly, there is a need for research studies to start from scratch to (re)build a conceptualisation of teachers' practices from a bottom-up perspective.

The chapter begins by presenting a brief overview of the literature reporting physical education teachers' actions in schools. After acknowledging a number of studies reporting teachers' practices as over-reliant on forms of 'direct' teaching, an examination of three key research traditions is provided to demonstrate the ways in which contemporary research has never really managed to capture 'real-world' teaching (Rovegno, 2009). Thereafter, the chapter sets out the methodological stance for a study that looked to avoid the problems and pitfalls identified in the majority of the research literature. It reports two main findings following qualitative observation and teacher interviews: firstly, that teachers' construal of teacher–learner relationships as 'reciprocal' in nature provided latitude to interact with the learners in their classes in a variety of ways; secondly, the variation displayed in the practices of these teachers enabled five framing categories to be constructed as they represent the patterns of interaction identified in the study. These were teacher-directed, teacher-guided, learner-led, teacher–learner-negotiated, and learner-initiated practice. Given the range of teaching approaches captured by this study and the 'mismatch' with the accounts of teachers' practices reported in the literature, a closing 'future directions' section raises a number of implications for researchers, teacher educators, and student teachers.

Main findings
Physical education teachers' practices: What do we know?

Reviewing the physical education literature reveals teachers' practices across the Anglophone world are consistently reported as over-reliant on forms of 'direct' teaching. For example, large-scale international comparison surveys (Hardman & Marshall, 2005; Pühse & Gerber, 2005) suggest teachers themselves remain in control of the events that take place in physical education classes. Additionally, large-scale studies researching the styles of teaching favoured by participants (Curtner-Smith, Todorovich, Mccaughtry & Lacon, 2001; Kulinna & Cothran, 2003; Syrmpas, Digelidis & Watt, 2016) discovered that teachers prefer to take control of the decisions in regards to what happens before, during, and after the teaching episodes that comprise lessons. Concerns regarding the prevalence of 'direct' teaching have intensified in recent years as the possibility of, and expectations for, physical education lessons to address a wider range of learning experiences have emerged across the Anglophone world (Bailey et al., 2009). Thus, alongside supporting the skills and abilities associated with physical development, lessons should contribute to the cognitive, social, and emotional development of children. While physical education is capable of pursuing a wide range of educational outcomes, the likelihood of achieving these broad learning experiences through forms of direct teaching is scant (Kirk, 2013).

Shifting to include a broader repertoire of teaching approaches in physical education lessons has been a perennial challenge for the profession (Kirk, 2010; Tinning, 2010). While there are a number of possible options for reorienting practice – see, for example, Mosston and Ashworth's (2002) 11 'styles' of teaching and Metzler's (2011) eight instructional 'models' – scholars contend that physical education teachers rarely move away from 'direct' teaching with much criticism being levied against their professional capabilities (Kirk, 2010; Tinning, 2010). Recognising the enduring trend of 'direct' teaching in physical education, and the contemporary demands of addressing a wider range of learning experiences, Kirk (2010) warns of the challenges ahead for the profession. He foresees the subject becoming 'extinct' in the near future with 'radical change' as the only pathway to secure the 'survival' of physical education (Kirk, 2010). While open to the possibility of changing current practice, I am left wondering whether the claims about 'direct' teaching dominating the profession are robust enough for us to uncritically instigate *radical* change. For instance, are these claims a fair representation of physical education teachers' day-to-day practices? Are all teachers across the Anglophone world interacting with learners in a direct way? Might there be teachers with broad teaching repertoires that have not been captured and reported in the literature? The following paragraphs retain this sceptical stance and consider how research traditions and methods may have shaped our conceptions of 'teaching' in physical education.

Scrutinising physical education research methods

Interest in the empirical investigation of physical education teachers' practices has been a burgeoning area in the research literature over the past 60 years. In fact, Macdonald et al. (2002) identify several distinctly different theoretical perspectives explicitly informing research investigating physical education teachers' practice. However, as this section will demonstrate, not all theoretical perspectives carry an equal weighting in the physical education literature (Tinning, 2010). This section presents three chronologically-informed reviews of how developments of teachers' day-to-day practices in school settings have been distorted by the research literature.

Historical marker one: The rise of 'scientific tales' from the 1970s and 1980s

Lee (2003) and Macdonald et al. (2002) note that positivistic notions from the natural sciences informed much of the early research investigating physical education teachers' practice. Guided by the assumptions of the process-product model (Dunkin & Biddle, 1974), where researchers set out to measure objectively and establish causality between two or more research variables, one prominent stream of research was the systematic investigation of 'The Spectrum of Teaching Styles' (Mosston, 1966). This teaching styles research agenda emerged during the 1970s and *continues* to thrive in contemporary times (Goldberger, Ashworth & Byra, 2012).

While there was interest in researching various teaching methods prior to the arrival of Mosston's (1966) teaching styles, his work added a conceptual framework for process-product researchers to study systematically the teaching of physical education (Rovegno, 2009). However, Rovegno (2009) recognises a fundamental flaw in the research design of many teaching styles studies as the research protocols often demanded just *one* style to be operationalised in a unit of work to verify that the findings of a given study can be attributed to the particular style under investigation. Crucially, the 'mobility ability' potential of Mosston and Ashworth's (2002) later revisions of the spectrum, which encourages teachers to shift rapidly within and between different styles of teaching to more accurately reflect the realities of class settings, has been largely overlooked by researchers. Therefore, due to the incumbent demands of research methodology, scholars have constructed linear and straightforward interpretations in the literature by suggesting teachers only deploy one style of teaching across a lesson or series of lessons (Rovegno, 2009).

Despite a limitation with the extent to which this research reflects the realities of teaching in physical education, these studies continue to heavily influence the profession. For example, Tinning (2010) underscores the influence of this body of work:

> Most PE teachers learn about Mosston's Spectrum of Teaching Styles in their undergraduate teacher education and his framework . . . has had a central role in shaping the way in which many PE teachers think about their teaching activities.
>
> (p. 43)

In the light of Tinning's comments about the ubiquitous nature of Mosston's work, it can be challenging to discuss teaching in physical education without defaulting to the terminology and research findings associated with this framework. While the teaching styles research community has made helpful contributions to existing understanding, it appears that most of what we know about teaching in physical education classes through these studies has become crystalised over time and very difficult to challenge (Tinning, 2010).

Historical marker two: A broader research focus from the mid-1980s

Physical education research broadened in focus from the mid-1980s onwards (Lee, 2003; Macdonald, 2002; Pope, 2006). Pope (2006) claims that there was unease in the early 1980s relating to the 'restrictive nature' of research investigating teachers' practice. A number of alternative research agendas started to emerge that generally, but not exclusively, used qualitative research methods to capture interpretations of teachers' practices. Of particular interest for the present chapter are the studies that started to document teacher *and* learner behaviour in the classroom. The most relevant development were the studies inspired by Walter Doyle's original 'classroom ecology' model to investigate teacher–learner(s) interaction and the immediate constraints of the classroom environment. This research started to reconceptualise life in physical education classes by recasting teacher–learner behaviour as a more negotiated and unpredictable process (Hastie, 2009).

Despite the developments in classroom ecology, studies from the mid-1980s were largely framed by what Lee (2003) refers to as the 'wider angle' lens. In other words, a form of macro-level sociology increasingly informed the physical education research landscape and, accordingly, interests 'shifted away from [micro] classroom processes' to include 'the study of policy . . . issues of "difference", identity and the body' (Evans & Davies, 2006, pp. 113–114). Consequently, Hastie (2009) complains that:

there was a solid and extensive program of research using the classroom ecology model . . . now fast forward . . . to 2007 only eight papers [in prominent physical education journals] . . . identified observation [in classes] . . . as . . . critical.

(p. 156)

The comments of Hastie (2009) suggest there has been a progressive 'disappearance' of observation research reporting scenes from physical education classes in their present day form.

Historical marker three: The 1990s onwards and the preoccupation with 'what's broken'

Physical education research from the early–mid-1990s, while still broadening in scope, increasingly turned to interrogate the inequalities and injustices inherent within physical education (Macdonald et al., 2002). As I highlighted earlier, it is difficult to argue that these 'critical' perspectives have not advanced physical education in many ways. For instance, who would argue against research agendas based on fairness and equity? Well, Tinning (2002), one of the earliest physical education scholars identifying himself as being 'within the critical pedagogy big tent' (p. 224), argued for more 'modest' interpretations of this theoretical perspective. Tinning's (2002) view was that the language used by these scholars was overly forceful in describing the limitations of current practices and their visions for change were not always corroborated with empirical evidence.

More recently, in reviewing the findings of studies using a 'critical' lens to investigate physical education settings, Enright, Hill, Sanford and Gard (2014) observed that what is shared across this research is a 'preoccupation with failure'. In other words, rather than broadening our conceptions of teaching, there is a strong move to inform us of 'what's broken' (Enright et al., 2014). The concluding comments of Enright et al. (2014), in the same vein as Tinning (2002), encapsulate the impact of such a deficit-based perspective:

an unintended consequence of deficit thinking is that sometimes we end up seeking problems even where strengths are shouting at us . . . to insist only on these sorts of stories is to flatten our experience and to overlook the many other stories that form our field.

(p. 11)

This quotation illuminates how contemporary research agendas may have inadvertently obscured our conceptions of teachers' practice in physical education classes. These studies use sophisticated theoretical ideas to bring negative constraints into view but, in attempting to make the case for emancipation and change, there is a tendency to overemphasise these constraints as part of the critique (Enright et al., 2014; Tinning, 2002). While there will always be scope to improve and change physical education teachers' practices, the question remains whether people are repressed (and if current practices are as repressive) to the extent suggested by these 'critical' scholars.

In summary, the scrutiny of research traditions and methods in preceding paragraphs has revealed the ways in which key research developments have shaped contemporary thinking about physical education teachers' practice. It has shown how: teaching styles research studies employing a process-product design stripped the detail out of classroom life, but these continue to dominate present-day thinking and practice (Tinning, 2010); the broadening of research interests from the mid-1980s led to a progressive 'disappearance' of observation research documenting events in classes (Hastie, 2009); and the pre-occupation from the mid-1990s with 'what's broken' has obscured more 'appreciative' tales about physical education from surfacing (Enright et al., 2014).

Drawing these three 'markers' together and considering their collective impact, suggests there are profound issues for the physical education profession. In line with Rovegno (2009), there is a danger our contemporary 'conceptions of teaching have been largely determined by university scholars' (p. 53); this is due partly to the demands of research methodologies and partly to their allegiances to certain theoretical perspectives. Given the concerns raised in this section, it appears that the contemporary research literature no longer paints a faithful portrait of teachers' practices. It is time for 'fresh' interpretations to emerge. Accordingly, I present an overview of a research study that investigated this 'flawed' picture of teachers' practices.

Challenging the 'unfair' picture

Background

My research took up the challenge of capturing a 'fresh' interpretation of teachers' practices. It was inspired by Rovegno's (2009) call for more 'naturalistic' research to be conducted in physical education as few studies have adopted this perspective. This naturalistic account, where researchers use qualitative methods to document the practices that teachers themselves initiate and sustain in their school contexts, appeared to be a valuable way to review current conceptions of teaching in the physical education literature. It involved documenting teachers' thinking and actions in their daily working lives without relying on a highly restrictive, experimental research methodology or advancing a pre-existing theoretical agenda for how things 'ought to be'. Importantly, adopting a naturalistic stance presents a restricted account of the empirical world, but it is restricted in quite different ways from much of the existing research conducted in physical education (Rovegno, 2009).

Research design

The study tracked six teachers working in different secondary school contexts across Scotland. A pilot study and conversations with a number of key informants were crucial to ensure that the participants chosen were suited to the demands of the study. A key concern in sampling was the recruitment of highly competent practitioners. There were two main advantages in selecting highly competent teachers. Firstly, this approach to sampling minimised the possibility for differences in professional capabilities being a confounding influence on the different interactions performed by these teachers. Secondly, highly competent teachers could enhance the credibility of the findings and increase the overall potential for the study to impact physical education teachers' practices. A further, related, but equally important, concern in sampling was the desire to recruit teachers who individually displayed features in their practice that were distinct from those of other participants. Including diversity in the patterns of interaction across the sample was important so research observations could document a broad range of practices taking place in physical education.

Two main research methods were used to gather data: observations of lessons in schools and semi-structured interviews with teachers. These methods were employed during two distinct phases of the research study: the first phase involved visiting classrooms on 88 occasions to observe teachers in action, and, the second phase, involved interviewing each teacher on one occasion after all observations were complete. The observation work provided a fine-grained account of teachers' actions in classrooms together with insights into how various purposes and contextual influences shape their practices. The interviews provided an opportunity to explore insights from the observation work with these teachers in an interactive fashion and incorporate their views into the research findings.

Mapping teacher–learner relationships

In observations of, and interview discussion with, teachers about their practice, they all specifically mentioned the need to develop 'relationships' with the learners in their classes. Indeed, relationships appeared to be a key driver for the many decisions that teachers made about their practice. In the following interview exchange with a teacher (Gaynor), she confirmed the link between the relationships she has with learners and the 'conscious decision[s]' she makes about her classroom practice:

Paul: I've seen quite a lot of variation in the way that you're able to work with different groups of people, but would you say that's about right that you've got various ways that you can work quite comfortably?

Gaynor: Yeah, definitely, I think I make a conscious decision, based on the relationship I build up with the class. I mean I think the first lesson you came out to see me I'd only been at the school three months and by then I felt like I knew my classes even quite well to understand what the best approaches were for the different classes, and they [the classes] are different.

On Gaynor's account, it appears that teacher–learner relationships played a large part in deciding the 'best approaches . . . for the different classes' that were observed during this study. Indeed, all participants taking part identified a connection between these relationships and the ways in which they employed various teaching approaches.

Having established a link between teacher–learner relations and practice, interviews pursued the main factors that the teachers represented as informing these relationships. At the heart of a cluster of ideas associated with these teacher–learner relationships were 'respect', 'time', 'familiarity', and 'context'. Given the emphasis placed on documenting the varied nature of practice, 'respect' will be emphasised most in this chapter as the teachers recognised this factor as central to the deployment of a broad teaching repertoire.[1]

Respect and relationships: Generating scope for a broad range of teacher–learner interactions

In the next quotation, note how a teacher (Erika), in discussing relationships in her interview, encapsulates the value of respect very clearly:

Paul: You mentioned about a relationship there. What do you mean by that? What does that involve?

Erika: Well, I think when you first meet your class I think you need to be quite firm with them and they need to know what the boundaries are, and they need to know that you are like a human being as well, and you [the teacher] need to be respectful towards them [the learners].

These comments connect the idea of respect to the ways in which people are treated in classes. The essence of respect, according to the six teachers, appeared to involve being mindful of the rights, worth, and feelings of *all* people in the classroom: the teacher and the learners. In other words, while these teachers appeared to demand respect *from* the learners, evidence suggests they also showed a genuine regard and respect *for* the learners.

Comments made by teachers during their interviews also indicated how these relationships, founded upon a respect *for* the learners' rights, created conditions for the learners themselves to contribute meaningfully to the events that took place in classes. For example, the following comments by Gaynor support a view that these relationships were reciprocal in nature and provided the capacity for *interactive* exchanges to take place between the teacher and learners:

Gaynor: If I didn't have that relationship, if it was a strictly, I'm a teacher, you're my learners, you'll do what I say, I don't think I would have had that . . . I'm going to use a big word here . . . reciprocity!

Paul: It's not just teacher and learner but there's a two-way sort of exchange almost. Is that what you're saying, is it?

Gaynor: Yeah, and I thought it was quite a mature level for them [the learners] to be on.

Gaynor's preceding comments suggest that there are situations in classes where the teacher–learner interactions are *reciprocal* in nature and involve much more than 'I'm a teacher, you're my learners . . . do what I say'. The interpretation of respect outlined by all the teachers depicted an *unequal*, but not wholly asymmetric relationship with the learners in their classes. Therefore, the nature of these relationships appears to offer potential for teacher–learner interactions where with the learners, to a degree at least, have an active role in deciding what takes place in the classroom. Having established that these relationships involved a shared or mutual respect, and the scope this offers for the learners to play a relevant role in deciding what happens and does not happen in classes, the next section will present the patterns of interaction that were captured during my observation work.

Tracking teacher–learner interaction

Close analysis revealed the *different* ways in which the teachers interacted with learners during their day-to-day practice. For instance, there were moments where the teacher largely controlled situations, other moments where the teacher and learners collectively debated the direction of situations, and still other moments where a learner(s) took control of situations. The following five framing categories were constructed to delineate the variation in these interaction patterns: teacher-directed, teacher-guided, learner-led, teacher–learner-negotiated, and learner-initiated practice. These identifiable patterns of teacher–learner interaction *differed* in the degree of control in relation to what was said and done in the classroom. In other words, there is a shift in the degree of control in regards to who takes the initiative – the teacher or the learners – in classes as the categories progress from teacher-directed practice to learner-initiated practice.

Teacher-directed practice: The teacher 'in charge'

Working in a teacher-directed way for a section of a lesson was common across observations of all the teachers. Teacher-directed practice generally involved the teacher being explicitly 'in charge' in the sense that she or he led a series of acts relating to what, how, when, and where particular actions could happen. The teacher acted to set out the content for a section of a lesson by using a lot of explanation and often accompanying this with a teacher and/or learner demonstration. For the most part, the whole class or a smaller sub-group of learners listened to the opening explanation(s) from the teacher. Once the opening explanation was complete, the teacher often used some 'confirmation questions' to gauge if the learners were 'clear' on what was expected; learners could ask for further explanation and information. Thereafter, the learners were expected to follow these instructions while the teacher very often made the decisions regarding when to start, when to stop, and when to move on to a related or different task.

The following extract is from a teacher (Erika) while she acted in a teacher-directed way during a lesson. In this extract, she worked with an S1 (age 12–13 years) class in their second lesson of a Scottish Country Dancing unit:

> The boys and girls are brought together momentarily and are asked to sit on the floor so Erika can explain the focus and intentions of the lesson. The class will work on a Scottish Dance called 'The Gay Gordons'. To start the dance lesson, Erika asks the boys and girls to 'line up' separately along the length of the assembly hall. This arrangement has the boys standing side-by-side in one stretched out line and the girls standing immediately in front of the boys in a similar side-by-side formation. Erika stands in the middle of the hall and explains that the focus of the warm up will be the 'skip change of step'. This step sequence will be used to travel across the width of the hall with the girls' line working at the same time, followed by a boys' line working at the same time. Erika demonstrates what this step pattern should look like in front of the whole class and continually repeats the phrase 'right, right, left, left' to indicate the stepping sequence of her feet as she performs it. After this demonstration, the class are asked if they 'understand' and then they start to perform back and forth in these two lines. The step sequence is rehearsed for several minutes. Erika offers several pointers to the whole class in relation to working on the balls of the feet and taking short, sharp steps.

Teacher-guided practice: 'Setting up' situations

The form of teacher-guided practice presented in this section was common across all the participants' teaching repertoires. Teacher-guided practice generally involved the teacher 'setting up' situations in which the learners have to formulate some kind of response. In 'setting up' a situation, the teacher initially engaged in some explanation and discussion to make clear the boundaries of the task. For the most part, the whole class or a smaller sub-group of learners listened to the opening explanation(s) from the teacher. The teachers' use of questioning was a key part of setting up these situations; the teacher used questions that had a range of possible solutions or where the learners had to apply their knowledge to solve a problem within the situation. After a situation had been 'set up' by the teacher, the expectation was for learners to work as an individual or as part of a group to formulate a verbal or movement-related response.

For example, this extract shows a teacher (Seymour) working with an S3 athletics class in an open-ended situation where the class had to share ideas and experiment to formulate a response:

> Seymour explains that the girls should 'stay in the same [relay running] order' so that they can 'practice handing over the [relay] baton' and '. . . aim to get this thing [the baton] round the track as fast as possible'. He lets the girls know: 'first come up with a way of practising the relay change over in the space [a long thin section of the games hall] . . . running, recovery, and taking-off. Come up with a way to solve the organisational problem. How

you can organise the group and the space' so you can change-over the baton at full speed.

Seymour circulates round the class and listens to some of the discussions, but makes limited comments unless asked a direct question. The learners at one group set up a long circuit of cones where they would run up one side doing change overs, pass round the cone at the top end and start to run down the other side. The learners completed several practice runs where they could continually change over the relay baton. After practising for a few minutes the group stop and they start to slowly gather together.

Amber: 'Did that work?' Another learner, Redina, provides some comments for improvement.

Redina: 'it's too short [points her hands to one side of the circuit then the other] . . . the distance at the ends is too short' to get back up to full speed for the change-over immediately after the bend. Seymour arrives at this group as the learners are having this discussion. He listens to Redina's explanation.

Seymour: 'What do you have to do [after listening to Redina explaining]?' The learners suggest a few things like having fewer people performing at a time and changing the layout of the cones. Seymour listens to these suggestions and then moves off to another group as the girls continue to share ideas.

Learner-led practice: The learners 'taking on responsibility'

Analysis of observation data revealed that learner-led practice was a way in which four teachers worked with their classes. Learner-led practice generally involved learners 'taking on responsibility' for leading in a range of different ways during a class. The learners were considered to be 'leading' in a class when they were designated by the teacher to be a leader or the teacher specifically requested that a learner or group of learners take charge for a section(s) of a lesson. In general, the learners were supported in their performance of these leadership roles in the following ways: the teacher presented information or resources to the class; the learners recalled information from a previous lesson or series of lessons; the learners had time to plan ideas and liaise with the teacher in advance of a lesson. For the most part, teachers provided support to the learners taking on various forms of responsibility and, at times, this role demanded that the teacher had to respond to changing situations.

The following passage is taken from an S2 (age 13–14 years) mixed dance lesson where one learner led a task with the whole class. The teacher – Jessie – gathers the learners in briefly to set the scene at the start of the class before a learner called Ralph leads an extended section of the lesson.

Jessie: 'Once Ralph has done about 10–15 minutes of dance today we'll get into the same groups as last week and design a movement sequence with at least three movements . . . must include unison . . . cannon . . . levels . . . OK Ralph, over to you!'

Ralph quickly gets to his feet and steps behind the curtain to the music player. The class get to their feet and position themselves into two lines. A fast-paced, contemporary song starts to play loudly. Ralph appears from behind the curtain and jumps to a spot in front of the class. As soon as he lands, he is facing towards the class and immediately starts to perform a series of linked movements in time with the music. The rest of the class follow along as best as possible. The more able learners seem to be able to keep up with Ralph and have arranged themselves in the front row. The less able learners – who seem to be slightly out of time with Ralph's pace and verbal commands – are arranged towards the back of the class. The song is played a few times through and the same moves are rehearsed with Ralph taking the lead at the front. Jessie joins in with the learners in back row during the repeat performances and completes the whole routine.

In this example, Ralph was requested by Jessie to take on a leadership role. Ralph, a keen dancer, has choreographed this routine at home. Despite Jessie's minimal input to support the learner-led efforts in this extract, she has already liaised with Ralph in advance of the lesson to ensure the material he presents is appropriate for the learners.

Teacher–learner-negotiated practice: Finding the 'middle ground'

Working in a teacher–learner-negotiated way was an integral part of three teachers' practices. Teacher–learner-negotiated practice generally involved the teacher and the learners finding the 'middle ground' regarding the way ahead at various transition points in a lesson or series of lessons. These transition points could include: the start of a new unit of work; the start of a specific lesson; during a specific lesson; and at the end of a lesson or unit of work. In finding the middle ground, open discussion and debate helped to reach a compromise between the teacher and learners. Most often, the teacher instigated these discussions and debates and, in the early stages of these exchanges, there was much use of explanation and questioning to start a form of dialogue. By initiating a class debate in this way before, during, or after a lesson or unit of work, the teacher could elicit responses and suggestions from the learners. As part of this dialogue, there was an opportunity for the learners to suggest future directions and the specific focus for class content.

In the following example, Gaynor works with an S3 class that have recently finished an extended unit of creative dance. This class are at the start of a new unit of work and badminton and gymnastics are used simultaneously in the lesson. I select exchanges from the closing stages of this lesson to exemplify several features of teacher–learner-negotiated practice. In particular, note the way in which there is discussion and debate between the teacher and learners together with the potential use of learners' reflection on their experiences to inform their dialogue with the teacher:

> Gaynor is positioned at the entrance to the equipment cupboard and there is only the tall box to be put away and a gymnastics mat. Gaynor calls the girls over and they make their way towards her and gather tightly around the tall box. Gaynor leans on the box with her elbows and her forearms are resting on the top. Gaynor says 'So girls we can stay with the same format next week [using badminton and gymnastics simultaneously in a lesson] for the Wednesday and the Friday . . . you suggested [earlier in the week] that you might be interested in dodgeball, basketball, and indoor rounders'.[2] One learner gasps loudly at the indoor rounders suggestion. Gaynor responds that it may be dodgeball that is the preferred option. Many of the girls respond with a 'yeah' and this would be the preferred activity and one learner offers a low level explanation as to why this is the case. The conversation continues back and forth for a few minutes more and finishes with Gaynor offering a reminder that 'Alright so dodgeball next Wednesday' and an indication that more negotiation may be ahead at the end of the next class as 'we can see if we'll keep that [dodgeball] for the Friday'.

Learner-initiated practice: Using 'improvised moments'

Learner-initiated practice was observed during the lessons of three teachers. This form of practice generally involved the teacher *using* 'improvised moments' in a lesson. In terms of the teacher *using* improvised moments, this involved the way she or he can respond to, and be attentive of, changing situations in a lesson. These are the moments where a learner or group of learners asks a question, responds to a teacher's question or statement, suggests something they would like to do or continue doing, or raises an idea that is picked up by the teacher and this forms a major focus of a lesson. In other words, these are the spontaneous, ad hoc moments where a suggestion emerges from a learner(s) and then the teacher allows this to influence the direction of the lesson.

For example, as Jessie worked with an S3 athletics class she used an improvised moment that emerged from the learners and then responded by making sprint starts and sprint technique the focus of the lesson.

> Jessie let me know that she was moving back over to the timed sprint group and explained that this group would be working to complete a few more 100 metre sprints in the remaining time left before the end of the period. I decide to stay with a group working on a distance running task. However, as soon as Jessie arrived at these learners, I could see she was working with them on something other than the 100 metre sprint. These learners completed no more timed 100 metre sprints. Instead, they were now working across the track over a shorter distance; I could see Jessie continually speaking to these

learners as they worked across the track. I quickly approached Jessie as she was working with this group. I was interested in that Jessie was not necessarily working with the learners on what she intended to do only a few minutes previously i.e. more 100 metre sprints. As soon as I arrived, Jessie immediately came to chat with me as the learners continued to work on their sprinting in the background. Jessie immediately informs me that, 'the girls wanted to work a bit more on their starts and a bit more on their sprinting technique'.

Future directions

Based on these findings, it can be argued that existing research literature has presented an insufficient account of teachers' practices. The range of interaction patterns that this study has revealed, and the underpinning influence of teacher–learner relationships, appears to be at odds with the accounts reported in the research literature. However, before turning to highlight the implications of this 'mismatch', it seems important to acknowledge the limitations of this study. My decision to include six participants was crucial to ensure I could capture a fine-grained account of each teacher's practice, but this small sample size has restricted my study from making any bold claims about teaching in Scotland or other national contexts. Further, my decision to recruit highly competent teachers has also restricted this study from making sweeping generalisations about practice. It is quite possible that these highly competent teachers have a broader repertoire of teaching approaches, and a different approach to the decisions they make about their practice, in comparison to teachers with lower competency levels. However, while we must apply considerable caution in generalising these findings, I would argue there is much value in this study for future researchers, teacher educators, and student teachers.

Looking first at future researchers, it is striking to note that learner-led practice was a major part of four teachers' practices. These findings contrast markedly with existing literature reporting teachers' overuse of 'direct' teaching approaches. My research revealed that there are teachers (albeit highly competent ones in this case) capable of working beyond the realms of 'direct' teaching, yet I was unable to find research studies in the literature documenting learner-led approaches in *naturally* occurring situations. In fact, alongside teacher-directed and learner-led practices, this chapter noted that there were instances of teacher-guided, teacher–learner-negotiated and learner-initiated practices. Recognising the middle ground between the teacher 'in charge' and learners 'taking on responsibility' via teacher-guided, teacher–learner-negotiated, and learner-initiated practices, maps a crucial 'grey area' that exists between these two perspectives. Therefore, there is scope for future researchers to identify and track practitioners performing broad teaching repertoires not only to report novel practices that other teachers can pursue, but also to start building conceptions of teaching that transcend a deficit-based perspective.

Turning to teacher educators and student teachers, I suggest there is a requirement for both parties to critically appraise the research literature. With the teachers' practices in my study comprising three, four, or even five of these patterns of interaction, evidence suggests that these teachers have a broader teaching repertoire than is currently conveyed in the research literature. Seeking out studies employing a range of theoretical perspectives, coupled with scrutiny of their methodological design, could help deepen awareness of school settings and guide the decisions teacher educators make about the preparation of students for school-based teaching placements. Likewise, developing an awareness of the limitations of the research literature, together with an appreciation of the realities of physical education classes via the study reported in this current chapter, could give student teachers a clear sense of the practices they will need to bring to life during school-based teaching placements (and beyond).

Summary of key findings

- Teacher–learner relationships informed the decisions teachers made about their practice.
- Respect was at the 'core' of teacher–learner relationships.
- A mutual or shared form of respect provided scope for the learners to have a role, to a degree at least, in deciding what happens in classes.
- The teachers displayed a broad teaching repertoire.
- The following patterns of interaction comprised the repertoires of these teachers: teacher-directed practice; teacher-guided practice; learner-led practice; teacher–learner-negotiated practice; learner-initiated practice.

Reflective tasks

- Why should we be concerned with the conceptions of teaching presented in the literature?
- What are the challenges of capturing 'real-world' teaching?
- Is 'real-world' teaching distorted by the research literature?
- What is 'naturalistic' inquiry and how might this stance be a helpful (and limited) way to challenge existing conceptions of teachers' practices in the literature?
- Is there is a 'mismatch' between the literature and real-world' teaching and, if so, what are the implications for future researchers, teacher educators, and student teachers?

Further readings

Rovegno, I. (2009). 'Conceptions of teaching in the service of teacher education, theory, and research.' In: L. Housner, M. Metzler, P. Schempp & T. Templin (Eds.) *Historic Traditions and Future Directions of Research on Teaching and Teacher Education in Physical Education* (pp. 51–57). Morgantown, WV: Fitness Information Technology.

Tinning, R. (2010). *Pedagogy and Human Movement: Theory, Practice, Research.* London: Routledge.

Notes

1 Readers with an interest in reviewing a comprehensive account of these teacher–learner relationships can refer to McMillan (2016).
2 Rounders is a striking and fielding activity with similarities to softball and baseball.

References

Bailey, R., Armour, K., Kirk, D., Jess, M., Pickup, I., & Sandford, R. (2009). The educational benefits claimed for physical education and school sport: An academic review, *Research Papers in Education, 24*(1), 1–27.

Curtner-Smith, M.D., Todorovich, J.R., Mccaughtry, N.A., & Lacon, S.A. (2001). Urban teachers' use of productive and reproductive teaching styles within the confines of the national curriculum for physical education, *European Physical Education Review, 7*(2), 177–190.

Dunkin, M.J. & Biddle, B. (1974). *The Study of Teaching*. New York, NY: Holt, Rinehart and Winston.

Ennis, C.D. (Ed.). (2016). *Routledge Handbook of Physical Education Pedagogies*. London: Routledge.

Enright, E., Hill, J., Sanford, R., & Gard, M. (2014). Looking beyond what's broken: Towards an appreciative research agenda for physical education and sport pedagogy, *Sport, Education and Society, 19*(7), 912–926.

Evans, J. & Davies, B. (2006). 'The sociology of physical education.' In: D. Kirk, D. Macdonald & M. O'Sullivan (Eds.) *The Handbook of Physical Education* (pp. 109–122). London: Sage.

Fernández-Balboa, J.M. (2015). Imploding the boundaries of transformative/critical pedagogy and research in physical education and sport pedagogy: Looking inward for (self-) consciousness/knowledge and transformation, *Sport, Education and Society*. Retrieved from http://www.tandfonline.com/doi/full/10.1080/13573 322.2015.1050371.

Goldberger, M., Ashworth, S., & Byra, M. (2012). Spectrum of teaching styles retrospective 2012, *Quest, 64*, 268–282.

Hardman, K. & Marshall, J.J. (2005). 'Physical education in schools in European context: Charter principles, promises and implementation realities.' In: K. Green & K. Hardman (Eds.) *Physical Education: Essential Issues* (pp. 39–64). London: Sage.

Hastie, P.A. (2009). 'Who's watching the children? Current issues relating to the research agenda in physical education classrooms.' In: L. Housner, M. Metzler, P. Schempp & T. Templin (Eds.) *Historic Traditions and Future Directions of Research on Teaching and Teacher Education in Physical Education* (pp. 155–158). Morgantown, WV: Fitness Information Technology.

Kirk, D. (2010). *Physical Education Futures*. London: Routledge.

Kirk, D. (2013). Educational value and models-based practice in physical education, *Educational Philosophy and Theory, 45*(9), 973–986.

Kulinna, P.H. & Cothran, D.J. (2003). Physical education teachers' self-reported use and perceptions of various teaching styles, *Learning and Instruction, 31*(6), 597–609.

Lee, A. (2003). 'How the field evolved.' In: S. Silverman & C. Ennis (Eds.) *Student Learning in Physical Education: Applying Research to Enhance Instruction* (2nd ed., pp. 9–33). Champaign, IL: Human Kinetics.

Macdonald, D., Kirk, D., Metzler, M., Nilges, L.M., Schempp, P., & Wright, J. (2002). It's all very well, in theory: Theoretical perspectives and their applications in contemporary pedagogical research, *Quest, 54*, 133–156.

McMillan, P.J. (2016). *Weaving a pedagogical web: A qualitative investigation of secondary physical education teachers' practice.* (Unpublished doctoral thesis). The University of Edinburgh: Edinburgh.

Metzler, M.W. (2011). *Instructional Models for Physical Education* (3rd ed.). Scottsdale, AZ: Holcomb-Hathaway.

Mosston, M. (1966). *Teaching Physical Education.* Columbus, OH: Merrill.

Mosston, M. & Ashworth, S. (2002). *Teaching Physical Education* (5th ed.). Boston, MA: Benjamin Cummings.

Ovens, A. (2017). 'Transformative aspirations and realities in Physical Education Teacher Education (PETE).' In: C.D. Ennis (Ed.) *Routledge Handbook of Physical Education Pedagogies* (pp. 295–306). London: Routledge.

Pope, C. (2006). 'Interpretive perspectives in physical education.' In: D. Kirk, D. Macdonald & M. O'Sullivan (Eds.) *The Handbook of Physical Education* (pp. 21–36). London: Sage.

Pühse, U. & Gerber, M. (Eds.). (2005). *International Comparison of Physical Education: Concepts, Problems, Prospects.* Oxford: Meyer.

Rovegno, I. (2009). 'Conceptions of teaching in the service of teacher education, theory, and research.' In: L. Housner, M. Metzler, P. Schempp & T. Templin (Eds.) *Historic Traditions and Future Directions of Research on Teaching and Teacher Education in Physical Education* (pp. 51–57). Morgantown, WV: Fitness Information Technology.

Syrmpas, I., Digelidis, N., & Watt, A. (2016). An examination of Greek physical educators' implementation and perceptions of spectrum teaching styles, *European Physical Education Review, 22*(2), 201–214.

Tinning, R. (2002). Toward a 'modest pedagogy': Reflections on the problematics of critical pedagogy, *Quest, 54*(3), 224–240.

Tinning, R. (2010). *Pedagogy and Human Movement: Theory, Practice, Research.* London: Routledge.

Tinning, R. (2017). 'Transformative pedagogies and physical education: Exploring the possibilities for personal change and social change.' In: C.D. Ennis (Ed.) *Routledge Handbook of Physical Education Pedagogies* (pp. 281–294). London: Routledge.

11 The digitised future of physical education

Activity trackers, biosensors and algorithmic biopedagogies

Ben Williamson

Introduction

Digital technology has gained a prominent position in the curriculum and educational policy of most developed countries (Selwyn, 2016). Physical education has often been hesitant in comparison with other subject areas in embracing and implementing digital technology. However, recent technological advancement in mobile technologies (tablet PCs, smartphones and wearable devices) has meant that appliances and software applications are now available that better fit the subject (Gard, 2014). This chapter provides an analysis of the emergence of wearable and mobile activity trackers, biosensors and personal analytics apps in physical education, arguing that the algorithmic processes embedded in these devices and software have an increasingly powerful part to play in how people learn about their own bodies, fitness and health. In doing so, the chapter considers the possible digitised future of physical education, examining particularly how health-tracking technologies promote new 'biopedagogies' of bodily optimisation based on data-led and algorithmically-mediated understandings of the body. These developments and issues suggest the need for greater attention to how algorithmic systems are becoming embedded in emerging physical education technologies and pedagogical practices.

Software, algorithms and data

Recent social science studies of digital technology have begun to acknowledge the importance of studying the software, algorithms and data that enact any device or platform (Kitchin & Dodge, 2011; Mackenzie, 2005). A 'device' in this context refers to a piece of hardware, such as a mobile computing device or a wearable technology; a 'platform' refers to internet-based applications such as social media sites that process information, communication and news (Beer, 2013; van Dijck & Poell, 2013). Van Dijck and Poell (2013, p. 5) have defined the contemporary social media environment in terms of its 'programmability', describing the 'computer code, data, algorithms, protocols, interfaces and the platform organisations that are responsible for programming', which together 'steer user experiences, content and user relations via platforms'. As such, the programmed software running any device or platform is significant in shaping the user experience, how they access information, how they communicate, what media they encounter, which consumer products they are recommended and purchase, and so on.

All of this can happen because platforms have been programmed to continually collect data about their users, and the platform organisations behind them construct algorithms to process that data in order to make sense of it and then provide further recommendations and prompts.

In computer science terms, an algorithm is simply a precise, mechanical set of step-by-step instructions designed to complete a particular computing process in such a way that requires 'no human intuition or guesswork' (MacCormick, 2012, p. 3). However, social scientific studies of algorithms acknowledge that human intentions do structure the algorithms that are programmed into computers (Neyland, 2015). Software and data-processing algorithms are not just neutral objects. Rather, they reflect the particular goals of those that program them. For example, Gillespie (2016) claims that 'algorithms are full of people' -programmers, designers, project managers, business managers – who all define what the algorithm is supposed to do, what data it will collect and analyse, and how it will enact its goal.

The role of programmability and algorithms in education has grown dramatically in recent years. A new specialist field of 'education data science' has emerged that combines algorithm-driven techniques of data analysis with software application design (Williamson, 2016a). As devices such as computers, laptops, tablet PCs and other mobile technologies have proliferated, new kinds of web-based platforms such as online courses, behaviour-monitoring sites, learning analytics and adaptive learning systems have been developed, promoted, and put into use. Physical education is now becoming subject to new forms of digitisation and educational data science. The rest of this chapter refers to wearable and mobile devices and web platforms that enable the physical activities, fitness and healthiness of young people to be tracked, analysed and presented. It pays attention to how the software and algorithms have been programmed to quantify embodied physical activity and to enable particular kinds of user experiences and recommend activities that might enhance young people's fitness and healthy behaviours.

Quantifying fitness

The term 'quantified self' refers to the growing trend of using digital technologies designed to enable people to track, monitor and analyse their physical activity, health and fitness. The idea of a 'quantified self' first emerged through the launch of the Quantified Self web community in 2008. Focused on the ideal of a 'data-driven life' and 'self-knowledge through numbers', self-quantifiers use statistical data collected from self-tracking mobile devices, electronic biosensors and data analytics apps to understand their personal health and, on that basis, to modify and optimise their health behaviours (Wolf, 2010). The term quantified self has since been applied to the use of health-tracking devices for various practices of 'lifelogging', 'lifestreaming', 'self-science' and 'personal analytics'.

Digital health-tracking devices include a variety of smartwatches, wearable biosensors, accelerometers, pedometers, biometrics, GPS devices, and wi-fi or Bluetooth-enabled clothing and wearable body metric textiles, plus assorted smartphone applications and peripherals (Swan, 2012). Wrist-worn devices such as the FitBit have become popular recognisable everyday brands, while new products such as sensor-enabled training shoes are being marketed as consumer objects to promote healthy lifestyles. Wearable devices like the FitBit have been made possible by technical advances in the miniaturisation of biosensors. Biosensor devices combine a biological element (sweat, saliva, blood sample, or CO2) with a physiochemical detector that converts it into an electrical signal that can from there become part of a larger platform where it can be transformed into data and visualisations to be displayed on a screen (Nafus, 2016). Not all health-tracking devices rely on biosensors. Some require users to record their own information (such as what they eat), or on GPS and accelerometry technologies to sense movement and location. Twinned with these devices, a huge range of apps and web platforms to support user-led health data collection is available to track and analyse food and drink intake, mood and emotion, physical activity and workouts of all kinds, sleep, inactivity, reproductive health and more. These apps and web platforms allow users to interpret and visualise the health data collected through tracking devices, and to use these insights from the data to inform their health behaviour choices.

Health expertise

The quantified self has become a cultural phenomenon, not just a technical fad, and the practices, meanings, discourses and technologies associated with self-tracking are the product of broader social, cultural and political processes and the role of particular experts of the body and health (Lupton, 2016). Powerful commercial, governmental, cultural and scientific imperatives frame the design and use of these devices. Major computing and mobile technology companies have entered the field, including Apple and Google, and a lively entrepreneurial 'start-up' scene has emerged (Boessel, 2013a). Strong interest in self-quantification has been expressed by medical professionals and by governments too (Boessel, 2013b). For example, the use of wearable health monitors and associated algorithmic techniques of 'predictive analytics' has been promoted as 'a huge opportunity for an over-stretched healthcare system' (Nesta, 2015). In addition, a distinctive cultural discourse has emerged around these health-tracking devices. The emphasis is placed on personal goals and challenges, 'life projects', personal discovery, motivational prompts and nudges, being rewarded for meeting or beating goals, and on using insights gained from data to make healthy lifestyle choices. The expert language of social science is invoked through commitments to 'self-ethnography' and 'self-science'. Self-quantification is, in other words, a form of 'labour' that transforms physical exercise into a form of work upon the self (Till, 2014).

The practices of the quantified self are additionally embedded in particular scientific disciplines that provide the specialist knowledges as well as the data analytics techniques required for the devices to function as intended. In particular, the biomedical sciences have become the basis for the expert descriptions and explanations of the physiological body that are encoded in the devices and platforms used by self-trackers. Since the mid-nineteenth century biomedical science has helped to define health and fitness and intervened in debates about the relationship between the state and its citizens (Heggie, 2016). As biomedical knowledge is today encoded in health-tracking devices and platforms, it is becoming embodied in citizens' everyday maintenance of their health and fitness, in ways that sustain the health agendas of the state.

Biodigital life and biocitizens

The quantified self is an emerging hybrid assembled from science methods, public health agendas, digital tracking, social networking, and technology entrepreneurship. The hybrid mix of social processes, technological developments and scientific knowledges that are combined in practices and techniques of self-quantification raises significant conceptual challenges for education research, not least for understanding new digitised forms of physical education. Youdell (2016) has recently begun calling for educational research that is attentive to the interactions between biological and social process involved in learning, or what she terms 'critical biosocial' studies of education. Pykett and Disney (2015) too have sought to develop hybrid biosocial accounts of social life that give adequate attention to the biological, the technological, the material, and the biological aspects of life. Such biosocial studies acknowledge the reciprocal relations between biological and social processes, and seek to trace how social environments and experiences get 'under the skin' to influence the body (Pickersgill, 2013). According to such work, the biological body is influenced by the structures and environments that constitute society, that is, 'the body bears the inscriptions of its socially and materially situated milieu' (Meloni, Williams & Martin, 2016, p. 13).

To this we need to add technology as a specific aspect of contemporary biosocial processes. As environments are increasingly inhabited by digital technologies, they are becoming part of the experiential landscapes that can pierce beneath the skin to alter the body itself (Hayles, 2014). As a result of these technologically-mediated biosocial processes, new forms of 'biodigital life' are emerging, whereby bodies, technologies and social processes need to be understood as working reciprocally to produce new ways of living and learning (Williamson, 2016b).

Health-tracking devices and platforms can therefore be understood as prosthetic technologies that act as extensions of the body, augmenting it with data and motivational nudges that urge citizens to change their healthy behaviours. Lupton (2015) terms the idealised figure of such techniques a 'socially fit biocitizen' who accepts the duty of self-responsibility and the entrepreneurial management and optimisation of one's life, including promoting and maintaining good health and physical fitness. A socially fit biocitizen is therefore an individual who has been taught by health-tracking systems to comport his or her body according to the expert medical knowledge and normative moral codes of behaviour that have been coded into the devices. Drawing on these conceptual points of anchorage, the next section details a range of health and physical tracking devices and platforms for use in physical education. These technologies are intended to produce 'socially fit biocitizens' and also lead to new biosocial and biodigital configurations of healthy living for children and young people.

Main findings
Digital biopedagogical platforms

Though physical education has been hesitant to adopt digital technologies, Gard (2014) suggests that the future of health and physical education is likely to become increasingly digitised as new technologies of 'big data', surveillance, 'exergaming', and automation converge with political, economic and public health imperatives to make new pedagogic practices possible. One notable advocate of the use of digital technologies in physical education is the 'PE Geek', an Australian educator who maintains an extensive website of digital devices, apps and web platforms for use in PE pedagogy. The website (https://thepegeek.com/) contains blog postings, webinars and podcasts on different technologies, and also advertises consultation, workshops, professional development programmes, and an annual ConnectedPE Online conference for physical educators. The PE Geek endorses technologies such as video analysis, movement analysis and assessment tools, digital training websites, and wearable health and fitness trackers.

An emerging market in wearable physical activity monitors is now being promoted to schools that combine tracking and biosensing capacities with built-in algorithms for calculating and estimating health and fitness levels (Schaefer, Van Loan & German, 2014). These technologies combine smartphones, tablet and wearable computing devices with online platforms for health and fitness analysis, and are capable of collecting and disseminating large amounts of personal biophysical data. Many health-tracking apps for children are designed to encourage healthy lifestyles, aid dietary planning, and encourage physical activity. Popular features of health-related apps for children include the concept of caring for virtual creatures by fulfilling their dietary and fitness needs, often combined with various gaming and competition elements and online social media platforms (Hswen, Murti, Vormawor, Bhattacharjee & Naslund, 2013).

The emerging technologies of physical education are accurately captured in the term 'digitised biopedagogical platforms'. They constitute an emerging form of digitally enacted biopedagogy, or a body pedagogy, that conveys knowledge, competencies, skills and moral codes relating to what the body is and ought to be, whose and what bodies have status and value, and what 'body work' needs to be done to make it 'fit' both in terms of health and the social order (Evans & Rich, 2011). A biopedagogy in this sense is the product of a socially negotiated agreement about ways to measure, evaluate and act upon children's embodied health, fitness and activity, and can be understood as a key way in which the healthy social order of the wider society might be maintained or enhanced by intervening in the embodied lives and personal health of children and young people. As Vander Schee (2009, p. 558) phrases it, biopedagogies consist of 'particular knowledges and truths about the ways in which individuals should conduct their lives for the betterment of self and society'. They constitute key technologies for the production of socially fit biocitizens who have been enabled to conduct their lifestyles in ways that might support both personal and health and wider health of society at large.

Healthy bodies and healthy societies

The task of improving the health of both self and society is one of the animating aims of Fitnessgram, 'the most widely used youth physical fitness assessment, education and reporting tool in the world' (http://www.fitnessgram.net/). As a fitness software platform, Fitnessgram consists of a range of tests, instruments and data-presentation tools that enable schools to collect and aggregate data and generate reports on children's body composition, health and fitness. In its most recent iterations, Fitnessgram has been redesigned for use on mobile devices, and is able to supply educators and school administrators with immediate data on individual student activity, performance and fitness through a dynamic data dashboard interface:

> Based on Healthy Fitness Zone® standards, created by the FitnessGram Scientific Advisory Board, FitnessGram uses criterion-based standards, carefully established for each age and gender.
>
> FitnessGram assesses the five components of health-related fitness: Aerobic Capacity, Muscular Strength, Muscular Endurance, Flexibility, and Body Composition.
>
> Personalised reports provide objective, feedback and positive reinforcement which are vital to changing behaviour.

Fitnessgram consists of a combination of scientific standards, medical expertise, age-referenced norms, reinforcement techniques, the objective reporting of biophysical data on children's health and fitness, and a commitment to behaviour modification (Pluim & Gard, 2016).

Fitnessgram is also a key organisation in the Presidential Youth Fitness Program (http://www.pyfp.org/), launched by First Lady Michelle Obama in 2014 as a partnership with a number of high-level governmental bodies. The initiative provides a highly standardised instructional programme and assessment technologies as well as teacher guidance for 'developing young people who have the physical competence and cognitive understanding about physical activity and fitness to adopt healthy, active lifestyles'. As a biopedagogical strategy, the Presidential Youth Fitness Program and Fitnessgram demonstrate how the physical activity, fitness and the body of the young person have become the target of governmental interest and intervention, and are bound up in wider public health and wellbeing agendas. Specifically as a digital platform, Fitnessgram is a powerful technology to enact this agenda by recording information about children's health and fitness and translating it via programmed algorithms into data that can be used for purposes of evaluation, comparison and subsequent decision making. In other words, Fitnessgram combines numerical knowledge about the individual body with societal imperatives around wellbeing and the maintenance of a healthy social order, and has the capacity to structure and shape pedagogical decisions about how to intervene in young people's lives and health.

Measurable and manageable bodies

In addition to its enactment of governmental agendas, Pluim and Gard (2016) have suggested that Fitnessgram is an instantiation of emerging techniques associated with 'big data' in the domain of PE pedagogy, making it equivalent with a worldwide trend towards measurability, accountability, performativity and standardisation in other areas of education. For example, Zamzee (https://www.zamzee.com/), the 'game that gets kids moving', combines accelerometry technologies, game design and 'motivation science'. It consists of a wearable 'meter' device to 'measure the intensity and duration of physical activity'; an online 'motivational website' featuring challenges and lesson plans; and 'group analytics' to enable educators and school administrators to 'track individual and group progress with real-time data'. The strapline for the product is 'Motivate. Measure. Manage'. It proposes to 'motivate' physical activity, to 'measure' it, and also 'manage' it, and can be understood as entirely consistent with current governmental priorities around behaviour change and behaviour modification programmes that target people's unhealthy lifestyles for active intervention (Davies, 2015).

Zamzee makes physical education consonant with wider educational trends in the use of data and metrics of quantitative measurement and assessment to monitor students and teachers as well as the systematic public collection of data at local, state and federal levels. These data collection and analysis practices are managerialist, evaluative and performative, in that they 'underpin new forms of educational provision and organisation that are more measurable, calculable and perhaps even controllable' (Selwyn, 2016, p. 83).

Gamifying fitness

Health tracking is not just managerialist and metrics-focused; it is also playful and fun. Sqord (https://sqord.com/), 'your online world, powered by real world play', consists of a wearable data logger, an online social media environment and a personalisable onscreen avatar. Sqord is marketed as 'one part social media, one part game platform, and one part fitness tracker', and the blurb for the device and app claims it is 'Motivating real-world activity and building life-long healthy habits with an online world full of friends, challenges, characters, points and awards.' Competitive and avatar-based health devices, apps and platforms such as

Sqord represent the 'gamification' of digital health among children. Gamification refers to the adding of game mechanics, technologies and techniques to non-game activities to make real life more like a game and a form of pleasure (Whitson, 2013). Many mainstream self-tracking devices and apps feature gamified elements, such as competing with others on specific physical activity challenges or racing to complete goals. Sqord allows users to compete with one another on an online leaderboard through data produced during physical challenges, as measured by their activity trackers, and are able to win rewards for completion of goals, which can be used to purchase upgrades and personalised features.

These techniques of gamification promise to make health, fitness and physical education more rewarding, fulfilling and fun, using incentivisation and rewards to shape desirable behaviours such as physical exercise or healthy eating habits. One of the claims of Sqord is not only that it 'makes healthy, active play more fun for kids' but also that it helps 'establish healthy habits and keep long term costs low' for wider medical health systems. Gamification is the result of device and platform designers taking up the task of 'persuading' and 'nudging' their users toward the 'right' behaviours by using the psychology of game design, which is how technology providers have become enforcers of 'medical prescription' through techniques of 'persuasive computing' (Nafus, 2016). However, gamifying one's health can also result in anxiety as 'experts and expertise embedded in technology are positioned as authorities over the individual's body' and 'guide citizens to become ideal subjects' (Lanius, 2015).

Biosensor surveillance

The gamification of self-tracking can also enable enhanced surveillance (Whitson, 2013). Sqord, like Zamzee and Fitnessgram, provides a surveillant administrative reporting tool for educators to access metrics on the physical activity levels and participation of each child player. Likewise, Polar Active is a wristwatch device that twins with the online Polar GoFit environment (https://polargofit.com/) to allow teachers to view, analyse and evaluate their students' physical activity while simultaneously motivating them 'to live a healthy lifestyle'. It is marketed as providing 'lessons to remember – lessons for life', and can also be used to provide 'continuous feedback' to parents. These examples demonstrate how physical activity trackers and biosensors can enable educators to subject young people to a surveillant gaze through the enumeration and visualisation of their physical activities, using streams of observed student data to make decisions and shape specific pedagogic interventions.

By wearing the devices and being signed up to health-tracking platforms, students are being subjected to behaviour modification programmes that are full of algorithms programmed to do the work of governing societal health. The software and algorithms that make self-quantification possible are not neutral or objective; rather, they are rife with embedded value judgments that reward some activities and not others. Biosensor surveillance, in other words, like all algorithmic practices and processes, is full of human hands, eyes and minds, which have designed and programmed the algorithms to detect and reward certain healthy activities while evaluating others in deficit terms and prescribing remedial intervention. Nafus (2016), for example, describes how the design of biosensor devices has turned complex social phenomenon with deep-rooted structural causes into personal deficits to solve. Embedding techniques of biosensor surveillance in physical education in schools via platforms such as Polar GoFit is one way in which wider societal problems of health and fitness are being translated into the personal responsibilities – and the continuous evaluation – of children and young people.

Private bodies

Fitnessgram, Zamzee, Polar GoFit and Sqord are all commercial products, and are evidence of how a lucrative market in fitness tracking is being opened up through the availability of the devices to physical educators and schools. They are artefacts of the increasing prevalence of neoliberal-based privatisation reforms that involve both the importing of ideas and practices from the private sector within the public sector in order to make efficiency gains, and the opening up of public education provision to private sector involvement on a profit-making basis (see Thorburn, Chapter 1; Evans & Davies, 2014). These companies are therefore turning the private lives of young people into private sector profit-making potential.

Biosensor science

The potential of health-tracking platforms is also proving appealing to academic researchers and scientists. The Quantified Self Institute (http://www.qsinstitute. org/) manages a major research project, 'Wearable Technologies for Active Living', to develop wearable activity monitors for children and a data platform to analyse and present the results. Its planned wearable sensor device 'makes children and parents aware of their physical activity', while the analysis of the data gained from the overall users on the accompanying data analytics platform is intended to be 'used in scientific research in which awareness, behaviour and the prevention of obesity play an important role'. As an academic research programme, the Quantified Self Institute provides evidence of how the enumeration of children's physical activity and fitness is becoming a significant scientific enterprise.

   The biomedical scientific expertise and knowledge that underpins the design of wearable activity-monitoring devices is a major influence on what the devices measure, how they measure and present the data, and how the human subject that is the object of the measurement is understood and treated. In particular, researchers in the field of physiological sciences have sought to develop physiological analytics devices, based on physiological modelling practices that seek to analyse factors such as heart-rate variability, autonomous nervous functioning, and respiratory-rate variability as a way to quantify other underlying physiological processes. Health informatics, bioinformatics and digital medicine also provide the expert knowledges on which physical activity monitors are programmed. Other fields such as motivation science and the behavioural sciences are additional influences. These knowledges are then entwined with expertise in algorithms and data analytics in the design of healt-tracking devices, so that the devices can approximate or predict users' future health and automate prescriptive pedagogic recommendations on exercise and diet. Designed around algorithms and physiological models expressed in computer code, the devices are increasingly augmenting and mediating the ways in which individuals and social groups engage with their own bodies and health, and transforming how they undertake physical activity. Expert scientific forms of knowledge such as those of the medical profession and biomedical research have therefore become tools of social control by subjecting the body to quantification (Nafus, 2016), with 'self-mediation interfaces with health' now becoming 'inextricable from the manner in which people learn about health' (Rich & Miah, 2014, p. 301).

Global health

Self-tracking devices worn by children for physical education are also being linked to wider global agendas of social justice and citizenship. The children's charity UNICEF, for example, has promoted its initiative UNICEF Kid Power (http:// unicefkidpower.org/) as a way of linking mobile self-tracking with global citizenship and responsibility:

> UNICEF Kid Power gives you the power to save lives. By getting active with the UNICEF Kid Power Band, you can go on missions, earn points and unlock therapeutic food packets for severely malnourished children around the world.

Kid Power combines a wearable activity wristband and digital platform with issues of global citizenship and responsibility along with a competitive appeal inspired by motivation science and techniques of gamification inspired by the commercial quantified self-movement. As part of its marketing campaign, Kid Power has partnered with the *Star Wars* brand franchise, and many of the 'missions' that users can join are fronted by well-known sports personalities. Kid Power combines popular culture, gamification, and self-surveillance with the sciences of the body and data analytic technologies to produce a device and a platform that link personal health with global health. It makes physical fitness into a key indicator of responsible citizenship. UNICEF has also developed a 'Wearables for Good' competition to devise new designs for wearable technologies that can solve major global challenges in child health.

Anatomical analytics

Self-quantification encourages children to understand their bodies as 'personal laboratories', and in terms of 'objective' data and metrics rather than subjective, haptic and sensory embodied knowledge. It makes the body of the individual visible in terms of data, calculable as numbers, and on that basis amenable to enhancement, though as Nafus and Sherman (2014, p. 1793) caution, self-trackers 'interact with algorithms not as blind, mindless dupes, but as active participants in a dialogue that moves between data as an externalisation of self and internal, subjective, qualitative understandings of what the data means'. While there is certainly interpretive flexibility in how users engage with technologies, self-quantification algorithms also certainly do structure and shape possibilities for action. Ruckenstein (2014, p. 69) demonstrates how personal analytics make formerly 'unknown' aspects of bodies and lives more 'detectable', 'transparent' and 'visible', and therefore amenable to being better acted upon, controlled and improved.

Educational health apps like Unicef's Kid Power, Fitnessgram, Zamzee, Sqord, and Polar GoFit perform a digital anatomisation of the child's biophysiological body, a 'soulless abstraction of bodies into bits' (Nafus, 2016, p. 5), analysing and encoding it as data that can be compared by algorithms with expert physiological models held in a database. Their algorithms are powerful mechanisms for moulding and making health and physical activity data intelligible, combinable, comparable, amenable to data visualisation and representation, and the anatomical analytics of the body they perform can be used to shape decisions about practical action and intervention into individual's physical activities, health behaviours and fitness. As Lupton (2013, pp. 14–15) argues, 'the data themselves and the algorithms that interpret them and make predictions based on them' have a 'profound impact on how individuals view themselves and the world'. Health-tracking platforms do not just render the body as abstract graphs, tables and figures, but enforce particular social, governmental, medical, and commercial understandings of what 'health' and 'fitness' are and make them actionable for algorithmic optimisation. They treat the body in computational terms, as a system that might be analysed, debugged and reprogrammed to function optimally. Through 'the process of collecting, visualising, sharing and monitoring such data on one's body in a public space, users learn about the body in terms of appropriate forms of maintenance, development and repair' (Rich & Miah, 2014, pp. 305–306).

Future directions
Physically educating digital biocitizens

New kinds of activity trackers and health and fitness platforms for use in physical education pose a number of challenges for future research that might impact on practice. Devices and platforms such as UNICEF Kid Power, Polar GoFit, ZamZee and Sqord represent the child's body and health through numbers and visualisations in ways that are intelligible to children, and that touch them in very real corporeal ways by enforcing particular norms and values and attaching statistical measurements and evaluations of bodily health and physical activity to them. Moral codes relating to fitness and physiological codes that represent the health of the body are inscribed into the lines of code that enact health-tracking devices. As Rich and Miah (2014, p. 305) have argued, 'increasingly, younger people engage with these technologies as pedagogical devices through which they learn to recognise themselves and/or others as good, healthy, active and/or having desirable bodies in the pursuit of healthiness'. Unpacking the hidden work of algorithms – and the human hands that produce them – in the digital platforms and practices of PE remains an urgent task for future research.

As digitised biopedagogies, health-tracking devices and platforms act as normalising technologies that induct children into habits of self-quantification, behaviour change and self-care, not just for the purposes of better self-management but to support a governmental and economic ideology of individualised 'wellness' (Cederstrom & Spicer, 2015). They are exhorted to turn their lives 'into an exercise in wellness optimisation' as part of a new 'biomorality' that demands individuals act to become more healthy even as governmental austerity cuts into education, health, welfare and social services provision (Cederstrom & Spicer, 2015, p. 3). These technologies are prototypical of how digital biocitizens may be physically educated in the future, their bodies 'touched' by wearable devices and linked to networked online platforms that enforce and prompt people to conform to particular social and politicised norms of bodily comportment, healthiness and fitness. Techniques of health and wellness optimisation are part of wider state strategies that in recent years have employed scientific knowledge about the bodies and behaviours of individuals to develop targeted public policy interventions that might 'nudge' them to change their behaviours (Friedli & Stearn, 2015; Jones, Pykett & Whitehead, 2013). With data-driven techniques such as health-tracking platforms, new kinds of data analytic 'hypernudges' are becoming extremely powerful due to their networked, continuously updated, dynamic and pervasive nature (Yeung, 2016). In this sense, future research in PE needs to engage with emerging aspirations of government and their enactment through persuasive digital devices and platforms.

Moreover, these devices may even be reconfiguring the interactions between bodies and machines. Rich and Miah (2014, p. 308) for example, describe a condition of 'posthuman technological mediation and prostheticisation' in which 'new sensorial experiences, such as the wearing of fitbit health bands, which vibrate when you achieve your activity goals, combine different pedagogical forces to produce embodied ways of knowing'. Through self-quantification, people are represented merely as 'nodes' in the 'Internet of Things', exchanging data with other people as well as with other objects and devices through networked communication and informational systems:

> The body in this discourse becomes positioned as a 'smart machine' linked with other 'smart machines.' Bodily sensations become phenomena that are mediated and augmented through machines, transformed into data and then communicated back to the user. This vision of the body as augmented via self-tracking devices present a digital cyborg, in which such devices not only become prosthetics of the body but extend the body into a network with other bodies and with objects.
>
> (Lupton, 2013, p. 27)

The body in such imagery is conceived as a biological core, a skeletal, muscular and nervous system, which is increasingly surrounded and augmented by technical and information infrastructures, a range of 'artificial skins', and a 'networked cognitive system' (Beer, 2013, p. 131). Wearable activity monitors are perhaps the most prominent contemporary examples of such devices that touch people literally – by being worn on the skin – and also by modulating their lives with their insistent demands for them to alter their behaviours and adjust their bodily comportment to fit the moral, medical and computational codes that animate the devices. The digital application of 'artificial skins' and 'posthuman prosthetisation' – and the entangled medical, moral and computer codes that enact them – enabled by tracking devices in physical education remains an urgent area for further research.

Emerging biosocial studies are now increasingly taking seriously the reciprocal connections between biological processes and social, environmental, technological and other material influences. What lies beyond the body is now understood to be able to get 'under the skin' as environmental stimuli actually activate specific biological processes (Meloni et al., 2016). Wearable health monitors and physical activity devices, connected to networked and algorithmic analytics platforms, need to be understood from this kind of biosocial perspective as digitised biopedagogical platforms that bear the potential to prompt actual biological changes in the bodies of young people, and to activate their behaviours as socially fit biocitizens. From a sociological perspective, Fitzgerald, Rose & Singh (2016, p. 16) therefore urge for 'greater attention to the ways in which social experience is lived biologically', and to 'biological forms of human life that emerge within, and are reproduced by, specific kinds of social, political, and economic relations'.

As young learners increasingly find themselves touched by the artificial skins of technical systems via wearable activity monitors and personal analytics platforms and the like, new ways of accounting for their biologically lived and techno-logically-mediated experience are becoming necessary. The process of shaping a socially fit biocitizen is something to be lived biologically as devices increasingly touch and measure the body, and – programmed to life according to particular physiological, political, commercial and medical norms and values – seek to manoeuvre, prompt and optimise it to perform better than it could before. A critical biosocial approach that takes account of the dynamic interaction of the biological, the social, the environment, and the technological determinants of learning might provide an adequate conceptual and methodological toolkit for future directions in the study of physical education.

Summary of key findings

- Digital devices and platforms to track health, fitness and physical activity are being recognised by physical educators for their transformative pedagogic potential, while commercial, medical, governmental and charitable priorities around child health and wellbeing are animating new digital initiatives and projects that are reshaping the available pedagogies of physical education.

- Health and fitness devices and platforms hold potential for lively, digitised and data-enhanced practices that might enable children and their teachers to better see, examine, interpret and act upon health and physical activity data in playful and engaging ways.
- Digitally-mediated practices of health and fitness tracking also carry particular norms and values of health behaviour and bodily comportment that combine governmental, commercial and medical aspirations and forms of expert knowledge that are encoded in the functioning of the devices.
- Young people stand to be educated by these potentially transformative digital biopedagogies as both 'socially fit biocitizens' and as hybridised 'biodigital beings' whose behaviours and bodies have been 'hypernudged' to conform to emerging social orders pertaining to embodied fitness and health.
- Future research in digitised physical education will need to engage with the biosocial dynamics of physical and digitised environments – and the moral, medical and computer codes that enact them – with embodied biological and behavioural processes involved in learning.

Reflective tasks

- Using a notebook, keep a written personal log of your physical activities for a day or a week. Do you notice any patterns or connections, such as between the amount of activity and sleep?
- If you have a wearable or mobile fitness device, look for any patterns in your digital data. Does it tell you anything about your physical activities that you don't know? Does it reveal any hidden insights that you cannot get from keeping personal notes? Consider the following questions:
    - Does the device help you to feel like you are achieving new goals, and does it make you feel a sense of happiness and wellbeing?
    - Does it make you feel anxious that you are not achieving these goals?
    - Do the numbers and visualisations make you feel any differently about physical activity?
- What can numbers and visualisations not capture about physical activity, such as your emotions and feelings about it?
- What do you think you have learned about your own body, fitness and health from developing 'self-knowledge through numbers'?
- Consider any classroom experiences in physical education (either as a student or a teacher) where a health and fitness device could have been used to enhance the learning experience. What could these devices add to existing pedagogies?

Further reading

Gard, M. (2014). eHPE: A history of the future. *Sport, Education & Society, 19*(4), 827–845.

Lupton, D. (2016). *The Quantified Self: A Sociology of Self-Tracking Cultures.* London: Routledge.

Rich, E. & Miah, A. (2014). Understanding digital health as public pedagogy: A critical framework. *Societies, 4*(2), 296–315.

References

Beer, D. (2013). *Popular Culture and New Media: The Politics of Circulation.* London: Palgrave Macmillan.

Boessel, W.E. (2013a). Return of the quantrepreneurs, *The Society Pages: Cyborgology,* 26 September 2013. Retrieved from http://thesocietypages.org/cyborgology/2013/09/26/return-of-the-quantrepreneurs/#more-17136.

Boessel, W.E. (2013b). By whom, for whom? Science, startups, the quantified self, *The Society Pages: Cyborgology,* 17 October 2013. Retrieved from http://thesocietypages.org/cyborgology/2013/10/17/by-whom-for-whom-science-startups-and-quantified-self/.

Cederstrom, C. & Spicer, A. (2015). *The Wellness Syndrome.* Cambridge: Polity.

Davies, W. (2015). *The Happiness Industry: How Business and Government Sold Us Well-Being.* London: Verso.

Evans, J. & Davies, B. (2014). Physical education PLC: Neoliberalism, curriculum and governance: New directions for PESP research, *Sport, Education and Society, 19*(7), 869–884.

Evans, J. & Rich, E. (2011). Body policies and body pedagogies: Every child matters in totally pedagogised schools?, *Journal of Education Policy, 26*(3), 361–379.

Fitzgerald, D., Rose, N., & Singh, I. (2016). Revitalizing sociology: Urban life and mental illness between history and the present, *British Journal of Sociology, 67*(1), 138–160.

Friedli, L. & Stearn, R. (2015). Positive affect as coercive strategy: Conditionality, activation and the role of psychology in UK government workfare programmes, *Medical Humanities, 41*(1), 40–47.

Gard, M. (2014). eHPE: A history of the future, *Sport, Education & Society, 19*(4), 827–845.

Gillespie, T. (2016). Algorithms, clickworkers, and the befuddled fury around Facebook trends, *Social Media Collective,* 18 May 2016. Retrieved from https://socialmediacollective.org/2016/05/18/facebook-trends/.

Hayles, N.K. (2014). Cognition everywhere: The rise of the cognitive nonconscious and the costs of consciousness, *New Literary History, 45*(2), 199–220.

Heggie, V. (2016). Bodies, sport and science in the nineteenth century, *Past & Present.* Retrieved from http://dx.doi.org/10.1093/pastj/gtw004.

Hswen, Y., Murti, V., Vormawor, A.A., Bhattacharjee, R., & Naslund, J.A. (2013). Virtual avatars, gaming, and social media: Designing a mobile health app to help children choose healthier food options, *Journal of Mobile Technologies in Medicine, 2*(2), 8–14.

Jones, R., Pykett, J., & Whitehead, M. (2013). *Changing Behaviours: On the Rise of the Psychological State.* Cheltenham: Edward Elgar.

Kitchin, R. & Dodge, M. (2011). *Code/Space: Software and Everyday Life.* London: MIT Press.

Lanius, C. (2015). The hidden anxieties of the quantified self movement, *Cyborgology,* 5 May 2015. Retrieved from https://thesocietypages.org/cyborgology/2015/05/05/the-hidden-anxieties-of-the-quantified-self-movement/.

Lupton, D. (2013). Understanding the Human Machine, *IEEE Technology & Society*, Winter 2013, 25–30.

Lupton, D. (2015). Lively data, social fitness and biovalue: The intersections of health self-tracking and social media. Retrieved from SSRN http://ssrn.com/abstract=2666324.

Lupton, D. (2016). *The Quantified Self: A Sociology of Self-Tracking Cultures.* London: Routledge.

MacCormick, J. (2012). *9 Algorithms That Changed the Future: The Ingenious Ideas That Drive Today's Computers.* Oxford: Princeton University Press.

Mackenzie, A. (2005). *Cutting Code: Software and Sociality.* Oxford: Peter Lang.

Meloni, M., Williams, S., & Martin, P. (2016). The biosocial: Sociological themes and issues, *Biosocial Matters: Rethinking Sociology-Biology Relations in the Twenty-First Century.* Sociological Review Monograph Series, *64*(1), 7–25.

Nafus, D. (2016). 'Introduction.' In: D. Nafus (Ed.) *Quantified: Biosensing Technologies in Everyday Life* (pp. ix–xxxi). Cambridge, MA: MIT Press.

Nafus, D. & Sherman, J. (2014). This one does not go up to 11: The quantified self movement as an alternative big data practice, *International Journal of Communication, 8,* 1784–1794.

Nesta. (2015). Digital health. Nesta website. Retrieved from http://www.nesta.org.uk/project/digital-health.

Neyland, D. (2015). On organizing algorithms, *Theory, Culture & Society, 32*(1), 119–132.

Pickersgill, M. (2013). The social life of the brain: Neuroscience in society, *Current Sociology, 61*(3), 322–340.

Pluim, C. & Gard, M. (2016). Physical education's grand convergence: Fitnessgram®, big-data and the digital commerce of children's health, *Critical Studies in Education.* Retrieved from http://dx.doi.org/10.1080/17508487.2016.1194303.

Pykett, J. & Disney, T. (2015). Brain-targeted teaching and the biopolitical child, *Politics, Citizenship and Rights.* Retrieved from http://dx.doi.org/10.1007/978-981-4585-94-1_22-1.

Rich, E. & Miah, A. (2014). Understanding digital health as public pedagogy: A critical framework, *Societies, 4*(2), 296–315.

Ruckenstein, M. (2014). Visualized and interacted life: Personal analytics and engagements with data doubles, *Societies, 4,* 68–84.

Schaefer, S.E., Van Loan, M., & German, J.B. (2014). A feasibility study of wearable activity monitors for pre-adolescent school-age children, *Preventing Chronic Disease, 11,* 130262.

Selwyn, N. (2016). *Is Technology Good for Education?* Cambridge: Polity.

Swan, M. (2012). Sensor mania! The internet of things, wearable computing, objective metrics, and the quantified self 2.0, *Journal of Sensor and Actuator Networks, 1,* 217–253.

Till, C. (2014). Exercise as labour: Quantified self and the transformation of exercise into labour, *Societies, 4*(3), 446–462.

Vander Schee, C. (2009). Fruit, vegetables, fatness, and Foucault: Governing students and their families through school health policy, *Journal of Education Policy, 24*(5), 557–574.

van Dijck, J. & Poell, T. (2013). Understanding social media logic. *Media & Communication, 1*(1), 2–14.

Whitson, J.R. (2013). Gaming the quantified self, *Surveillance & Society, 11*(1), 163–176.

Williamson, B. (2016a). Digital methodologies of education governance: Pearson plc and the remediation of methods, *European Educational Research Journal, 15*(1), 34–53.

Williamson, B. (2016b). Coding the biodigital child: The biopolitics and pedagogic strategies of educational data science, *Pedagogy, Culture & Society*. Retrieved from http://dx.doi.org/10.1080/14681366.2016.1175499.

Wolf, G. (2010). The data-driven life, *New York Times*, 28 April 2010. Retrieved from http://www.nytimes.com/2010/05/02/magazine/02self-measurement-t.html.

Yeung, K. (2016). 'Hypernudge': Big data as a mode of regulation by design, *Information, Communication & Society*. Retrieved from http://www.tandfonline.com/doi/full/10.1080/1369118X.2016.1186713.

Youdell, D. (2016). What happens when we learn? 26 April 2016. Retrieved from https://deborahyoudell.wordpress.com/2016/04/25/what-happens-when-we-learn/.

Part V
A futures perspective

12 Past, present, and possible futures

Steven A. Stolz

Introduction

My aim in this chapter is to briefly revisit the past, critically discuss the present, and offer some thoughts on possible futures for physical education.[1] In relation to the latter, *Physical Education Futures* immediately comes to mind because it outlines three possible futures: more of the same, radical reform or extinction (Kirk, 2010). From the outset, it is worth noting the third possible future (extinction). To some within the discipline area of physical education, such a view is not only confronting, but controversial and unnecessarily alarmist (Thorpe, 2003). Irrespective whether we agree, disagree or are ambivalent towards any of the proposed futures put forward, there is much that can be gained from a close reading of this seminal book and subsequent interviews that contextualise the historical narrative employed (Stolz & Kirk, 2015a, 2015b). I am also cognisant of Kirk's (Stolz & Kirk, 2015a) cautionary comment about being 'careful what we wish for' in relation to hypothesising physical education futures. In one sense, this is a self-evident truism that there is an inherent risk that comes from making any prediction that may directly or indirectly become actualised at some time in the future, and of course may or may not necessarily be desired. In another sense, it highlights how those who are *in* the situation perceive and ascribe meaning to what it is they are experiencing at the time. This is made evident and reinforced by Kirk's comment that at the time of writing *Physical Education Futures* 'I saw it very much as telling it as I saw it – and in some respects it's one of those situations of – don't shoot the messenger folks' (Stolz & Kirk, 2015a, p. 79). It also brings to our attention deep ideological differences masqueraded as methodological divergences within the discipline area of physical education. For instance, Tinning (2015) laments what he perceives to be two 'positions' or 'camps' found in academic discourse that explicitly privileges knowledge generated by empirical-scientific research over interdisciplinary knowledge that is dismissed and discredited as 'fiction'.[2] The reason why I mention this here is due to the same type of criticisms being levelled against *Physical Education Futures*. What this demonstrates – at least to me – are some of the more noticeable incommensurable differences that exist between rival traditions found in physical education that is explored in *The Philosophy of Physical Education* (Stolz, 2014). Take for example the earlier case of methodological divergence and the ideological dogmatism driving these matters of subjective opinion. Here is a paradigm case of incommensurability between closed systems that are bound by scientific laws and open systems that have an infinite array of possibilities. In this case, the former implies a causal relationship that can predict a range of phenomena in nature that is supported by empirical evidence with a certain degree of accuracy; whereas, the latter may or may not be actualised at some point in the future, and hence is unpredictable because it is not bound by empirical evidence. Indeed, this should not be viewed as a deterrent for the kind of research methodology, but more a case of a strong rejoinder to those who may be dismissive and closed minded about the role of social science and/or interdisciplinary research in understanding human beings in social and cultural contexts. Of course, I could say more about how each view truth, but this would take me too far afield. Therefore, my intention is to commence with an historical analysis of physical education as a means to make sense of where present practices have emerged from, and why they may change in the future. Of course, the caveat being that by employing historicism there are certain limitations – which I have already briefly alluded to – in making any prediction about possible futures. As a result, it is unfair to judge historicism with the same level of accuracy found in closed systems, particularly when we can never expect more precision in the treatment of any subject than the nature of the subject permits.[3]

Due to my knowledge of MacIntyre's oeuvre, my critique will adopt a similar methodology of historicism and rational vindication.[4] MacIntyre's account of traditions demonstrates how histories develop and change over time, and hence why they are in a state of flux due to rival traditions of enquiry vying and competing for dominance. In fact, I was, and still am convinced that MacIntyre's account of traditions and conflict between traditions has meaningful utility across a wide spectrum of discipline areas and practices, and hence why in *The Philosophy of Physical Education* (Stolz, 2014) I draw on his account of rival traditions as a means to both make sense of rival and competing traditions in physical education, and to argue for a new tradition of physical education, which I refer to as embodied learning (Stolz, 2014, 2015a; Thorburn & Stolz, 2015). Consequently, for the purposes of this chapter, I will be concerned with three issues: first, I provide a brief historical narrative of physical education in order to both ground and contextualise how the *past* can help us make sense of where present practices have emerged from; second, I sketch out some *present* and prevalent practices found in contemporary forms of physical education and critically discuss each in turn; and, lastly, I outline what I perceive as *possible futures* for physical education, and at the same time consider any potential problems or benefits if they are to be realised and actualised.

Main findings
The past

My historical narrative will selectively focus on three well-known historical periods: Ancient Athens; the Middle Ages and the Reformation; and the twentieth century. This broad conceptual approach is concerned with identifying themes that have prevailed throughout the history of physical education. This critique should not be viewed as an exhaustive exploration of the history of physical education, nor is it meant to be, as my intention in this section is to elucidate themes that have been retained in some form or another in the present practice and practices of physical education.

Ancient Athens

A classical starting point in my historical narrative is the sophists who understood that the inculcation of the good mind and character was contingent upon the body being in harmony with the mind, and vice versa. The origins of these ideas are located in both the *Republic* and *Law*, which outline the key features of Greek education during Plato's time. Although the term 'physical education' is used in some translations, the term should be understand literally as a form of physical training that ranged from military-type exercises in archery, throwing of various missiles, skirmishes and so on, to physical training for athletic contests, such as gymnastics, boxing and so on, to physical culture in dance and wrestling for reinforcing cultural customs. Since the role of education was to produce Athenians who were virtuous before they became doctors, lawyers and so on, much was made of the mixed goods found in the various activities used to educate the Athenian of the importance of balance and harmony, particularly between the mind and body. Indeed, a special role was assigned to the role of physical culture within education because it was specifically concerned with both coming to know the body and the mind through certain cultural activities of importance. Consequently, the position of 'physical education' was viewed instrumentally as a means in education to demonstrate how an unhealthy body interferes with the cultivation of the mind, or vice versa. Accordingly, a healthy balance between body and mind is crucial because it is not possible to cultivate one without the other. Combined with this naturalistic attitude toward the mind and body, the celebration of the body in various forms, and the importance of aesthetic ideals, provide an early blueprint of a liberal education, which has been repeated in some form or another throughout history.

The Middle Ages and the Reformation

The trend of physical activity continues through the Middle Ages and Reformation periods, with a particular focus on military-type activities and certain ball games that were popular. Anti-naturalistic attitudes toward the body leading up to and after the Reformation meant that physical activities were grudgingly tolerated due to their instrumental benefit. Most historical narratives are critical of the role of the Catholic Church in anti-naturalistic attitudes toward the body, which in turn is claimed to have either directly and/or indirectly hindered the development of physical education in education (see, for example, Mechikoff, 2010). Such an account is overly simplistic as St Thomas Aquinas and Benedict bring to our attention the importance of the body, particularly physical activity in the education of the whole person (Ozolins, 2013). The irony is that Plato in the *Phaedo* influenced some of the anti-naturalistic views of this period by demarcating the soul as superior and the body as inferior in a hierarchal order of importance, particularly in relation to cultivating the intellect. Taking into consideration what was mentioned earlier, it would appear that Plato holds contradictory views on the body; however, this does not mean that the body is not important to Plato. In fact, as mentioned briefly above, to Plato education is not possible without physical education or physical training due to its role in the cultivation of the human person. That said, what may have contributed to a perception of a diminished or absent role of physical education, particularly within educational institutions from this period of time may be attributed to a range of factors, such as limited to no opportunities to pursue physical activities due to limited leisure time, the perceived value of game-orientated activities, and the influence of strict Protestant forms of religion that emphasised ascetic ideals, to name a few.

The twentieth century

Lastly, I turn my attention to the twentieth century, with a particular focus on Great Britain and Australia, for three reasons: (1) it is the historical period closest to present-day practice and practices in physical education; (2) there exists extensive literature on this topic; and, (3) there are notable similarities and parallels between these two countries in the history of physical education, but more importantly an historical understanding of the conflicts and tensions from this period is crucial if we are to understand the prevailing practice and practices of physical education today. Kirk's (1990, 1992, 1998a, 1998b, 2010)[5] socio-historical accounts of physical education are interesting due to the emphasis placed on 'crisis', 'conflict', 'problems', various forms of 'physical education discourse', and the conceptual account of 'social construction'. Certainly, the so-called demise of physical education-as-gymnastics around the mid-twentieth century and the prevailing rise of physical education-as-sport-techniques is significant and worth noting. The conditions that contributed to the demise of physical education-as-gymnastics are of course conflicts over particular practice or practices, about method or methods, issues concerned with which concepts should be assigned a central place in theory and practice, and so on. This is why the socio-historical account of physical education-as-sport-techniques is so important because the prevailing practice oppressed and defeated what it was threatened by in the various versions of gymnastics. In a sense, this is to state the obvious, but unless we understand the reasons why, their significance will be obscured. Likewise, I would argue that these socio-historical accounts do not go far enough in terms of highlighting the rational standards and justifications used by the prevailing practice for why their practice is superior. Alternatively, if for some reason this is not possible, then an account of the cause or causes of the ideological blindness on the part of the prevailing practice is crucial to elucidating the unresolvable character of these conflicts. In addition, I would argue that physical education-as-gymnastics was subsumed and transformed into physical education-as-sport-techniques as opposed to becoming extinct due to constituent features of 'child-centred progressivism' being evident in some practice and practices today. Though nothing is mentioned in a sustained fashion about the specific debates about 'child-centred progressivism', I suspect some of the conflict concerned age-old and perennial issues relating to traditionalism and progressivism in educational practice, and when deconstructed we are left with debates about how we view children's human nature from the point of view of psychology, sociology, philosophy and so on as it relates to educational contexts.

What my historical narrative reveals are the constant and recurring themes of the following: various forms of anthropological study of the body, particularly philosophical anthropology; and, physical activity that is pursued for a range of ends. Even though the nomenclature has evolved from physical training to physical education, and from around the mid-twentieth century onwards becomes more formalised within school curricula, it is hard to deny the retained themes of contemporary physical education that revolve around both physical activity through more codified versions of games, such as sport, and the study of the human body through physical activity (predominantly a scientific form of anthropological study of the body) with the intention of maximising sporting performance, increasing participation, and so on.

The present

My aim now is to succinctly outline three present and prevalent practices found in contemporary forms of physical education, and to critically discuss each in turn, starting with plural aims, approaches to teaching and curriculum frameworks, and the scientific and technological paradigm.

Plural aims

In Chapter 2 of this edited book, Stolz & Thorburn identify four aims – physical (or psychomotor), cognitive, affective and socio-moral – in the literature of contemporary physical education. As per my historical narrative, the mixed goods found in physical education from Ancient Athens is highly apt in making sense of the plurality of aims present in contemporary physical education. Just like there was a mix of instrumental and/or non-instrumental activities that were the means to bring about specific ends, it is questionable whether the same can be said of present aims. The issue is not that there are plural aims, but whether contemporary physical education can provide shared rational standards to justify how and on what criteria they have been successfully achieved. Indeed, what is missing is any notion of what an end-state may look like, and the methods by which they can be developed and successfully achieved. Unfortunately, the present aims would appear to have contributed to the conceptual confusion. Take for instance the health tradition of physical education (see Stolz, 2014). Where would this tradition reside? I am sure quite sophisticated arguments can be made for health to be a part of each aim, but then you would be left with a rather odd situation, as in Australia where the 'H' (Health) in 'HPE' (Foundation to Year 10) is disconnected from physical education ('PE') due to the content ('focus areas') that is mandated in the Australian curriculum (ACARA, 2016). This is not an argument to say that integration is not possible, but in practice it is unlikely for a range complicated reasons. In saying all of this, there is still the significant issue of how to resolve the non-educative practices that still persist in the name of physical education, and that do it such damage. Of course, schools exist for a range of reasons, and many of the practices found within are strictly speaking not educational, and this no doubt temporarily insulates physical education from confronting this issue. Certainly, physical education clearly has an important role to play in any education, particularly in the development of the whole person (see, for example, Stolz, 2014). Likewise, I would argue quite strongly that physical education has the potential to be *transformative* in an educative sense (Stolz, 2013a, 2013b, 2014, 2015a; Thorburn, 2008; Thorburn & Stolz, 2015), however, it is doubtful that by studying the body this will happen, and hence why greater emphasis needs to be placed on exploring our embodiment. The former only reinforces dualisms of the mind and body, whereas the latter has the potential to be truly transformative in the sense of coming to realise and know that the mind and body are intimately intertwined. Without a doubt this is no easy undertaking, and I am the first person to acknowledge that more research needs to be done of an interdisciplinary nature that can bring together embodied cognition, phenomenology, existentialism, and educational practice.

Approaches to teaching and curriculum frameworks

As we have already seen from my historical narrative, sports-orientated games or activities, particularly traditional team games, became an integral feature of contemporary physical education curricula from the 1950s onwards. Not only does there exist a plethora of literature in this area, but it has morphed into a sophisticated area that approaches the teaching of sports-related skills from a scientific point of view by attempting to codify certain variables as if teaching is a science or closed systems governed by natural laws (Stolz & Pill, 2014). The problem is that there is significant tension between physical education teachers who are concerned with educational practice, and who do not necessarily see or want to see the discrete boundaries placed around pedagogical models (see, for example, Stolz & Pill, 2016a, 2016b). Recently, 'models' of teaching or 'models-based practice' have been rejuvenated as an alternative to the claimed over-reliance and over-use of the 'direct method' or 'traditional approach' to teaching physical education that has been so widely criticised by academics (Kirk, 2010, 2013; Tinning, 2010). It is interesting to note that McMillan in Chapter 10 argues that these criticisms are an 'unfair picture' of the actual practices of many physical education teachers in the secondary school setting in Scotland. McMillan's findings are contrary to the literature, and hence should be noted as they highlight how teachers in the research project demonstrated a broad range of approaches or 'patterns of interaction' that was contingent upon the student–teacher relationship. I cannot say I am too surprised by the findings, taking into consideration the dynamic nature of teaching and its relational grounding with students in the learning process. In a way, some academics in the physical education space view teaching as if it is a discrete technical skill that can be learnt from practice in the same way as learning to ride a bike. To be fair this is a criticism that can be extended to most teacher education courses (see for example, Carr, 2000a, 2000b, 2003). That said, these themes seem to be more pronounced in physical education, in part due to strong anti-intellectual sentiments that basically infer that teachers cannot be trusted to think for themselves and/or be creative. This is reinforced in various ways in the literature, and clearly evident in the use of the terms 'non-negotiables' (Kirk, 2013) and 'immutable' (Hastie & Casey, 2014) features of models. In the interest of being balanced, each are attempting to control the implementation of the theoretical principles of the model into practice or research by building 'broad parameters' around the 'non-negotiables' of the model (see for example, Stolz & Kirk, 2015a). I need to stress that I understand the intent of what is basically a form of essentialism in order to try and capture the necessary properties of certain models. However, I question what appear to be a desire for doctrinal purity and another example of the slow erosion of teachers' professional autonomy and judgment. Similarly, I am troubled by the whole concept of models of teaching as if they are discrete entities or packages, as if I am choosing model A from the menu or smorgasbord for situation X, model B for situation Y, and so on. It begs the question: To what end or what are the aim or aims of each model? Furthermore, there is also the issue of, say for example, model A competing with model B or vice versa. Here we have the conditions ripe for rivalry between advocates of each model. In fact, this already happens and a precursory survey of the literature and/ or attendance at a conference will make this evidently clear due to the zeal of these advocates and blind allegiance to their model as if nothing else matters.

It is this blind allegiance that was the catalyst of a critique by Stolz and Thorburn (2015) of Arnold's (1979) account of meaning in movement, sport and physical education, particularly the concepts of learning 'about', 'through', and 'in' movement, which has gained prominence in curriculum documents in Australia. From a theory of curriculum point of view, the idea of integration is a rather attractive proposition; however, the theoretical origins or foundations of Arnold's concepts are at best an amalgam and reinterpretation of old physical training literature (the '*in*' dimension), the child-centred progressive movement (the '*through*' dimension), and the influence of both exercise science and sport in academicisation of the discipline area (the '*about*' dimension). To some this may not matter for a range of reasons, but what does matter is how Arnold's work has been variously interpreted and mostly misunderstood, particularly when implemented in curriculum documents. What is probably the most disconcerting thing to consider and ponder is the observation by Stolz and Thorburn (2015, p. 8), who state:

> Part of the problem as we see it concerns a lack of ideas within the physical education space for contrasting ideas to be conceived and trialled, and as a result this has led to Arnold's conceptual framework being taken forward uncritically both by policy-makers or tweaked by academics for their own purposes.

This observation speaks volumes about physical education and is best viewed as a challenge to those in the discipline area. In addition, for those who may not have been concerned about the theoretical origins of Arnold's ideas, then they should be because these ideas have been taken forward in ways that are deeply problematic and in a sense have aided the reinforcement of the scientific paradigm, which in itself is rather ironic taking into consideration the noticeable absence of the 'through' and 'in' dimensions, particularly the latter.

Scientific and technological paradigm

By the late twentieth century, physical education-as-sport-techniques have become so entrenched by the hegemonic forces of 'scientisation' in physical education that privileges the scientific paradigm over other forms of knowledge that it is quite difficult to qualify this influence (McKay, Gore & Kirk, 1990; Whitson & MacIntosh, 1990). Combined with the 'reconfiguration' or what is often perceived as 'social construction' of physical education in educational institutions, this demonstrates how the discipline area has been quick to change and align itself with popular trends of the time – such as sporting performance – in an attempt to remain relevant to stakeholders, such as policymakers, educators, the public, students, and so on (Kirk, 2000; Kirk, Mcdonald & Tinning, 1997; Macdonald, Kirk & Baraiuka, 1999). One obvious example of a disproportionate privileging of scientific-orientated content knowledge is most evident in the *Victorian Certificate of Education Study Design for Physical Education* (VCAA, 2010) in Australia. Even though the rationale aims to 'integrate theoretical knowledge with practical application through participation in physical activities' (VCAA, 2010, p. 7), this 'participation in practical activities' are basically laboratory activities to collect various data in order for students to analyse and write reports for assessment tasks. If this was not problematic enough, the high-stakes assessment of an end-of-year written examination worth 50% and two prescribed school-based pieces of assessment worth 25% excludes all forms of practical knowledge that could, and I would argue should, be assessed. As I have already argued elsewhere, the academicisation of the discipline area of physical education reinforces false dualisms; and probably more troubling is the intention to disconnect it from its central concerns, which are associated with using physical means to develop the whole person (see, for example, Stolz, 2013a, 2014). Whether the intent is to purposely separate academic learning from physical education is something worth debating; however, I have no doubts that privileging theoretically orientated knowledge through the various sub-disciplines of biomechanics, exercise physiology and so on, over practically orientated knowledge sends quite a clear message about what is valued. Equally troubling is the inability or inclination to actually 'integrate theoretical knowledge' with practical knowledge. Not only could this be easily accomplished by assessing physical performance in a range of different contexts, but it could and should contribute to students' overall marks for the subject, such as Queensland's *Physical Education Senior Syllabus* in Australia (QSA, 2010). In fact, I have and continue to argue that practical knowledge is a central feature of physical education and should be assessed accordingly (see, for example, Stolz, 2013b, 2014).

With the hegemonic influence of science within Western culture, it is not unusual to find technology often underpinning its rapid expansion and omnipresent acceptance to the point they sometimes go hand in hand. In Chapter 11, Williamson reminds us of the ubiquitous nature of digital technology in our lives and how emerging health-tracking technologies are promoting new 'biopedagogies' in physical education. Quite rightly he reminds us that the adoption of these digital technologies have the potential to be pedagogically transformative for physical education teachers, but at the same time greater thought needs to be given about the covert messages that are being portrayed from a 'biosocial perspective' because their use aims to produce a hybrid of 'socially fit biocitizens' and 'biodigital beings' that conform to socio-cultural norms of fitness and health. Furthermore, we should heed Gard's (2014) comments on 'eHPE' that the discipline area of physical education have ignored the function of digital technology in the world is, and will continue to be concerned with commerce, automation of work environments, and the monitoring and surveillance of populations. Whether these influences will be negative or not, time will tell; nonetheless, when it comes to business the sole purpose of which is to maximise profitability, it seems obvious that digital technologies at some point in the future may replace teachers and schools because it is more cost-effective to do so. In actual fact, it is already taking place in most higher education institutions through the blending of online education and various forms of face-to-face education, such as MOOCs (massive online open courses) that are offered for free. It is not coincidental that the so-called online revolution in education will benefit STEM (science, technology, engineering and mathematics) education and the literature is already claiming that when you compare the cost of online with face-to-face costs, online wins based on economic rationalist principles (see for example, Bonvillian & Singer, 2013).

Possible futures

In the last section of my chapter, I turn my attention to what I perceive as possible futures for physical education, and at the same time consider their relative strengths and limitations.

Outsourcing

One possible future for physical education is the continuation and the ascendancy of physical education programmes being outsourced to external providers. As Thorburn mentions in Chapter 1, neoliberal market influences are increasingly forcing teachers and schooling systems to negotiate a complex mix of public and/or private arrangements. Put simply, if schools can gain significantly reduced costs and, in turn, free up resources for other priorities, it is inevitable that these practices will flourish. We should not be so naïve to think that the discipline area of physical education is somehow immune from economic rationalism, fiscal austerity, free market forces, as external or private providers are competing with the profession for market share. Clearly, the discipline area of physical education is taking this all-pervasive trend of neoliberalism seriously with *Physical Education and Sport Pedagogy* and *Sport, Education and Society* each devoting special issues on the topic, with the former titled, 'School physical education curricula for future generations: Global neo-liberalism? Global lessons?' (Macdonald, 2014a), and the latter titled, 'Neoliberalism, privatisation and the future of physical education' (Evans & Davies, 2015).

The notion of 'choice' is misleading (see, for example, Macdonald, 2011, 2014b) because sometimes there is no 'choice', particularly in primary school contexts where generalist classroom teachers do not feel confident and so opt to outsource to external providers (Whipp, Hutton, Grove & Jackson, 2011). These causes are reinforced by Williams, Hay and Macdonald (2011) and are extended upon when they outline other reasons why outsourcing takes place, such as: access to expertise and physical resources, capability to provide variety and diversity, accreditation requirements, and their lack of sufficient professional development. However, it is only lately that Williams and Macdonald (2015) reviewed why this may be a problem due to the blurring of the boundaries of what a school is, who is a physical education teacher, who is an expert physical education teacher, what is quality physical education, and whether free markets should interfere with public goods such as education. In the same work, they ponder what they consider to be an 'ethical question' of whether physical education 'ought' to be outsourced. In this case, the authors, and possibly others from the discipline area have missed the point: this is not an 'ethical question' to ponder because economic ideologies do not deal with ethical or moral propositions, nor would they ever claim to. Likewise, the use of the 'ought' fallacy should be jettisoned because it is nonsensical to ask a question knowing the answer to the question before asking it. In the risk of stating the obvious, the discipline area of physical education at various levels is already being outsourced at such a rate that most physical education teachers and/or physical education teacher educators have or will take on the role of sports administrators and managers with reduced teaching load or no teaching at all. Over time, due to cost, these physical education teachers will be replaced with someone with a sports administration and/or management background with a diploma or certificate on a fixed contract, because they are cheaper to employ, there is no need for them to teach and, if things do not work out after the fixed period, they can be replaced with someone else or a cheaper option sourced through a competitive tender process. Due to the fierce competition from the tender process, an external provider has offered to manage and implement a physical education programme and provide human and physical resources for free, with the caveat that their major sponsor's merchandise is sold in the school to the students, students who participate in the sports classes are mandated to buy and wear clothing with the sponsor's logo, use the sponsor's products wherever possible during school hours, plus other conditions.

Although, I have intentionally painted a rather grim hypothetical scenario, it is not too fictional or outlandish that it may never ever happen (see for example, Burch, 2009; Hursch, 2015). As I see it at the moment, the discipline area will survive in some form or another as it always has, but the physical education teacher may become extinct or be replaced with a significantly different version than we know today, in part due to the noticeable absence of any educational intent. It may also be unavoidable for the discipline area of physical education to become more commoditised in order to compete with other or similar products. I hope I am wrong, but time will tell.

Evidence-based educational practice

The trend in education towards evidence-based educational practice is not surprising, taking into consideration the rise of accountability and surveillance that already exists through large-scale public testing in education (Thomas & Pring, 2004). In Australia, the obvious example is the National Assessment Programme – Literacy and Numeracy (NAPLAN) annual assessment of Years 3, 5, 7 and 9 students. At an international level, one notable case is the Programme for International Student Assessment (PISA), which tests 15-year-olds' mathematics, science and reading literacy levels. Each respective organisation that is responsible for the large-scale public testing subsequently publishes this data periodically for the public to access, with the former via the 'My School' website (www.myschool.edu.au), and the latter via the PISA section of the Organization for Economic Cooperation and Development (OECD) website (www.oecd.org/pisa). The idea of capturing this data and making it accessible to the public is in part due to powerful neoliberal influences that view consumer choice as crucial to improving the quality of the educational product through competition. Combined with economic rationalist concerns about public money being used effectively by schools, it is not too hard to see how the trend in evidence-based educational practice has come to be equated with improving the effectiveness and quality of student outcomes on NAPLAN or PISA tests. Central to this argument is the view that teaching should radically change and that progress can be made if it was viewed as a research-based profession that is based on a medical model with the scientific method pivotal to decision-making processes and practices (Hammersley, 1997). As Hargreaves (1997, p. 410) states, evidence-based teaching is 'primarily interested in *what works in what circumstances* and only secondarily in *why* it works'.

The implications for the discipline area of physical education could not be clearer, particularly if '*what works*' and '*why* it works' cannot be provided by evidence that a specific aim or set of aims have been satisfactorily achieved according to predetermined criteria of success. In this case, we should heed Hammersley's (2004) suggestion that we should be asking poignant questions, such as: What counts as evidence? Why is quantitative research privileged over qualitative research? Is the medical model applicable in teaching? Do teachers want to be viewed as researchers or engaged in this enterprise? Which research method or methods would teachers use to conduct their research on teaching? How would this research be scrutinised, particularly when data is generated? In a way, this is only a glimpse into the world of metrics and big data that may be used in education systems, and so it is only a matter of time before longitudinal data on a range of variables will be used to measure, store, analyse, evaluate and so on, which in turn will be made accessible to key stakeholders via databases, so that students' educational progress can be monitored in a whole suite of curriculum areas. If this sounds like a version of George Orwell's Big Brother from *Nineteen Eighty-Four*, then you are not mistaken.

Rival traditions of physical education

When I wrote *The Philosophy of Physical Education* I outlined what I considered to be the traditions of physical education. In one sense, I was responding to the 'physical-education-in-crisis' discourse that was, and to some extent still is, prevalent in the literature. The reasons for this 'crisis' discourse is complex, and this is not meant to be a criticism of those academics who had a major role in responding to what they considered to be a threat to the discipline area (Stolz & Kirk, 2015a). In another sense, I have come to the realisation that conflict within traditions, particularly its point and purpose, is normal and a sign of vibrancy. As such, conflict, disagreement and so on should not be viewed as something to be avoided or ignored. In fact, this is something that should be openly fostered beyond the academic literature, and encouraged at conferences, professional associations and societies, and so on. I need to stress that this is not to say this this does not happen already, but is more a case of comparing what I know it is like in other academic traditions. The reality is that the discipline area has much ground to make up. If progress is to be made, then dialectical engagement between two antagonistic and rival traditions needs to be fostered in such a way that there is a willingness and openness by adherents of each tradition to learn the language of the other in the hope of coming to understand what exactly it is they disagree about. Only when agreement about matters of disagreement have been reached is dialectical engagement between rival traditions possible. Such a view should not be seen as an academic exercise, but needs to be opened up to include its practitioners. In this case, what immediately comes to mind is my earlier example of Tinning's (2015) account of what he considered to be two 'positions' or 'camps' found in academic discourse of 'health' (H) and 'physical education' (PE) in 'HPE'. As I have already mentioned, central to this rational impasse are methodological divergences and the ideological dogmatism that blindly believes that empirical-scientific generated knowledge is essentially irrefutable truth. Of course, this is simply not the case, and is at best provisional until a superior theory or evidence is established that supersedes it. It also needs to be pointed out that knowledge and truth are highly contentious concepts that are not necessarily understood from a scientific point of view. In a way, what we have here is an issue of translatability, where each does not understand the other due to the particularities of the language, concepts, terminology and so on employed by each tradition. Unless each are prepared to engage with the other in order to first understand each other and possibly find a common language, it is only inevitable that at some point, either a tradition divides into two or more warring constituents, and become critics of each other, or one of the rival traditions becomes extinct (Stolz, 2015b). The obvious example of the latter is physical education-as-gymnastics, which was surpassed by physical education-as-sport-techniques in part due to both failing to understand the other and finding common ground (and vice versa). Unless we learn from the *past*, history will continue to repeat itself, and *possible futures* will become our *present* in ways we may not necessarily want or desire.

Conclusion

In this chapter, I started out with an historical narrative of physical education in order to make sense of where *present* practices have emerged. After broadly traversing three well-known periods (Ancient Athens, the Middle-Ages and the Reformation, and the twentieth century) two prevailing themes were identified: anthropological study of the body; and physical activity pursued for a range of ends.

In the second section of this chapter, I then turned my attention to three *present* and dominant practices in contemporary physical education. These being: plural aims, approaches to teaching and curriculum frameworks, and the scientific and technological paradigm. In relation to the first practice, I briefly revised the perennial issue of aims in contemporary physical education. It was argued that physical education has a long history of pursuing a range of ends (plural aims), which is not necessarily problematic; however, if there are no standards to justify how and on what criteria they have been successfully achieved it presents a number of significant issues. Until there is a shared understanding of what these ends or end-states are, this will not be possible. In the second practice, I provided an account of well-known models of teaching and curricula. During my critique, I pointed out some inconsistencies and, at the same time, asked some probing questions. Lastly, the hegemonic influence of science type knowledge in physical education was examined. Unfortunately, the academicisation of the discipline area of physical education would appear to have created false dualisms that do not exist. In particular, I drew attention to the disconnection with the historical core of physical education that is concerned with using physical means to develop the whole person. Along with the influence of science in contemporary physical education has been technology. The integration of technology in our lives has become so normalised that we tend to be complacent about its possible misuse and abuse, particularly in physical education. If we ignore the function of digital technologies and how they are used in physical education, and educational systems, there is a real risk that neoliberal agendas will take hold of the future direction of physical education.

In the last section, I outlined three *possible futures* for physical education based on *past* and *present* practices. The first possible future put forward engages with the trend of outsourcing that I see continuing in some form or another due to neoliberal forces. I put forward a hypothetical scenario to highlight how the practice of outsourcing is underpinned by economic ideologies that cannot be predicted in ways we think they can. In essence, this is the inherent danger of out-sourcing, and hence the need for caution and vigilance at all times. The second possible future discussed was the trend towards evidence-based teaching, which has significant implications for physical education because the plural aims that the discipline area claims to achieve will need to be verified according to predeter-mined criteria of success. How the discipline area responds and overcomes this challenge will in a way determine its future. In the last possible future, I argue that if progress is to be made in physical education, then dialectical engagement between rival traditions needs to be fostered in such a way that each is prepared to engage with the other to both come to understand the other and attempt to find a common language. I concluded that if this is not possible, then past history tells us what is likely to happen.

Summary of key findings

- An understanding of history and the history of physical education can both ground and contextualise how the *past* can help us make sense of where pres-ent practices have emerged from and why plural aims exist in contemporary physical education.
- Although plural aims *present* in contemporary physical education appear to have contributed to conceptual confusion, it was argued that the underlying issue is whether contemporary physical education can provide shared rational standards to justify how and on what criteria success can be achieved.
- Even though the *possible futures* for physical education outlined are predic-tions, *past* and *present* practices tells us what will happen if rival traditions are not prepared to understand what exactly it is they disagree about.
- If progress is to be made in physical education, then dialectical engagement between rival traditions needs to foster a willingness and openness of spirit. This is necessary before dialectical engagement between rival traditions is even possible.
- Unless the discipline area of physical education overcomes certain chal-lenges, *past* history tells what is likely to happen in the *present* and in possible *futures*.

Reflective tasks

- Why is an historical understanding of physical education important?
- What are the traditions of physical education that the author refers to, and are they useful in enhancing your understanding of physical education as a discipline area?
- To what extent do you agree with the author's central argument concerning plural aims in physical education?
- What are the 'pros' and 'cons' of the three models of teaching physical edu-cation outlined?

- What is practical knowledge and how could you assess it?
- What are the 'pros' and 'cons' of using digital technologies in physical education?
- To what extent do you agree with the *possible futures* proposed by the author?

Further reading

Biesta, G.J.J. (2010). *Good Education in an Age of Measurement: Ethics, Politics, Democracy*. Boulder, CO: Paradigm Publishers.

Burch, P. (2009). *Hidden Markets: The New Education Privatization*. London & New York: Routledge.

Dixon, J., McIntosh, P., Munrow, A., & Willetts, R. (1957). *Landmarks in the History of Physical Education*. London: Routledge & Kegan Paul.

Hursch, D. (2015). *The End of Public Schools: The Corporate Reform Agenda to Privatize Education*. London & New York: Routledge.

Kirk, D. (2010). *Physical Education Futures*. London & New York: Routledge.

Peters, M. (2011). *Neoliberalism and after?: Education, Social Policy, and the Crisis of Western Capitalism* (2nd ed.). New York: Peter Lang.

Phillips, M.G. & Roper, A.P. (2006). 'History of physical education.' In: D. Kirk, D. MacDonald & M. O'Sullivan (Eds.) *The Handbook of Physical Education* (pp. 123–140). London: Sage.

Stolz, S.A. (2014). *The Philosophy of Physical Education: A New Perspective*. London & New York: Routledge.

Van Dalen, D., Mitchell, E., & Bennett, B. (1953). *A World History of Physical Education: Cultural, Philosophical, Comparative*. Englewood Cliffs, NJ: Prentice Hall.

Notes

1 I would like to take this opportunity to thank Malcolm Thorburn for inviting me to pen the final chapter of this edited book. I have benefitted greatly from reading and thinking about my colleagues' work in this edited book. Regrettably, I have engaged with some of the preceding chapters at the expense of others. Unfortunately, space restrictions have limited my reply to my colleagues' work and, in some instances, I have had to put to one side those chapters that may not support my central theses of this chapter.

2 Tinning's (2015) response to the antagonism he experienced, or what he refers to as 'agnostic discourse', is surprising, particularly when he has been a leading academic in the discipline area for many years and was involved with Kirk in responding to what they saw as a crisis in physical education around the 1990s in Australia (see for example, Kirk & Tinning, 1990; Stolz & Kirk, 2015a). Unfortunately, an opportunity was missed in this paper to point out the closed-mindedness and blind allegiance to the empirical-scientific paradigm.

3 I have employed a similar type of argument in relation to assessment, see Stolz (2015c).

4 MacIntyre's (1981/2007, 1988, 1990) trilogy of *After Virtue, Whose Justice? Which Rationality?*, and *Three Rival Version of Moral Enquiry* are paradigmatic examples of the methodology I intend to employ.

5 I have listed what I consider to be the key works from Kirk's corpus on the history of physical education for the purposes of this chapter.

References

Arnold, P. (1979). *Meaning in Movement, Sport and Physical Education*. London: Heinemann.

Australian Curriculum, Assessment and Reporting Authority (ACARA). (2016). The Australian curriculum F-10: Health and physical education. Retrieved from http://www.australiancurriculum.edu.au/health-and-physical-education/structure.

Bonvillian, W. & Singer, S. (2013). The online challenge to higher education, *Issues in Science and Technology, 29*(4), 23–30.

Burch, P. (2009). *Hidden Markets: The New Education Privatization*. London & New York: Routledge.

Carr, D. (2000a). 'Is teaching a skill?' In: R. Curren (Ed.) *Philosophy of Education 1999* (pp. 204–212). Urbana, IL: Philosophy of Education Society.

Carr, D. (2000b). *Professionalism and Ethics in Teaching*. London & New York: Routledge.

Carr, D. (2003). *Making Sense of Education: An Introduction to the Philosophy and Theory of Education and Teaching*. London & New York: Routledge.

Evans, J. & Davies, B. (Ed.). (2014). Neoliberalism, privatisation and the future of physical education [Special issue], *Sport, Education and Society, 20*(1), 1–9.

Gard, M. (2014). eHPE: A history of the future, *Sport, Education & Society, 19*(6), 827–845.

Hammersley, M. (1997). Educational research and teaching: A response to David Hargreaves' TTA lecture, *British Educational Research Journal, 23*(2), 141–161.

Hammersley, M. (2004). 'Some questions about evidence-based practice in education.' In: G. Thomas & R. Pring (Eds.) *Evidence-Based Educational Practice* (pp. 133–149). Milton Keynes: Open University Press.

Hargreaves, D. (1997). In defence of research for evidence-based teaching: A rejoinder to Martyn Hammersley, *British Educational Research Journal, 23*(4), 405–419.

Hastie, P. & Casey, A. (2014). Fidelity in models-practice research in sport pedagogy: A guide for future investigations, *Journal of Teaching Physical Education, 33*, 422–431.

Hursch, D. (2015). *The End of Public Schools: The Corporate Reform Agenda to Privatize Education*. London & New York: Routledge.

Kirk, D. (1990). 'Defining the subject: Gymnastics and gender in British physical education.' In: D. Kirk & R. Tinning (Eds.) *Physical Education, Curriculum and Culture: Critical Issues in the Contemporary Crisis* (pp. 43–66). London, UK: The Falmer Press.

Kirk, D. (1992). *Defining Physical Education: The Social Construction of a School Subject in Postwar Britain*. London, UK: The Falmer Press.

Kirk, D. (1998a). *Physical Education and Curriculum Study: A Critical Introduction*. London: Croom Helm.

Kirk, D. (1998b). *Schooling Bodies: School Practice and Public Discourse 1880–1950*. London: Leicester University Press.

Kirk, D. (2000). The reconfiguration of the physical activity field in Australian higher education, 1970–1986, *Sporting Traditions: Journal of the Australian Society for Sports History, 16*(2), 17–38.

Kirk, D. (2010). *Physical Education Futures*. London & New York: Routledge.

Kirk, D. (2013). Educational values and models-based practice in physical education, *Educational Philosophy and Theory, 45*(9), 973–986.

Kirk, D., Macdonald, D., & Tinning, R. (1997). The social construction of peda-gogic discourse in physical education teacher education in Australia, *The Curriculum Journal, 8*(2), 27–298.

Kirk, D. & Tinning, R. (Eds.). (1990). *Physical Education, Curriculum and Culture: Critical Issues in the Contemporary Crisis*. London: The Falmer Press.

Macdonald, D. (2011). Like a fish in water: Physical education policy and practice in the era of neoliberal globalization, *Quest, 63*(1), 36–45.

Macdonald, D. (Ed.). (2014a). School physical education curricula for future gen-erations: Global neo-liberalism? Global lessons? [Special Issue], *Physical Education and Sport Pedagogy, 19*(5).

Macdonald, D. (2014b). Is global neo-liberalism shaping the future of physical edu-cation?, *Physical Education and Sport Pedagogy, 19*(5), 494–499.

Macdonald, D., Kirk, D., & Braiuka, S. (1999). The social construction of the physi-cal activity field at the school/university interface, *European Physical Education Review, 5*(31), 31–52.

MacIntyre, A. (1988). *Whose Justice? Which Rationality?* London, UK: Duckworth.

MacIntyre, A. (1990). *Three Rival Versions of Moral Enquiry: Encyclopaedia, Geneal-ogy, and Tradition*. Notre Dame, IN: Notre Dame University Press. (Gifford Lec-tures delivered at the University of Edinburgh in 1988)

MacIntyre, A. (1981/2007). *After Virtue: A Study in Moral Theory* (3rd edn.). Notre Dame, IN: Notre Dame University Press.

McKay, J., Gore, J., & Kirk, D. (1990). Beyond the limits of technocratic physical education, *Quest, 42*, 52–76.

Mechikoff, R. (2010). *History and Philosophy of Sport and Physical Education: From Ancient Civilizations to the Modern World* (5th ed.). New York, NY: McGraw-Hill.

Ozolins, J.T. (2013). The body and the place of physical activity in education: Some classical perspectives, *Educational Philosophy and Theory, 45*(9), 892–907.

Queensland Studies Authority (QSA). (2010). *Physical Education Senior Syllabus*. Brisbane, Queensland: QSA.

Stolz, S.A. (2013a). Phenomenology and physical education, *Educational Philosophy and Theory, 45*(9), 949–962.

Stolz, S.A. (2013b). The philosophy of G. Ryle and its significance for physical educa-tion: Some thoughts and reflections, *European Physical Education Review, 19*(3), 381–396.

Stolz, S.A. (2014). *The Philosophy of Physical Education: A New Perspective*. London & New York: Routledge.

Stolz, S.A. (2015a). Embodied learning, *Educational Philosophy and Theory, 47*(5), 474–487.

Stolz, S.A. (2015b). MacIntyre, rival traditions and education, *Discourse: Studies in the Cultural Politics of Education, 37*(3), 358–368.

Stolz, S.A. (2015c). Can educationally significant learning be assessed?, *Educational Philosophy and Theory*. Retrieved from http://dx.doi.org/10.1080/00131857.2015.1048664.

Stolz, S.A. & Kirk, D. (2015a). David Kirk on physical education and sport peda-gogy: In dialogue with Steven Stolz (part 1), *Asia-Pacific Journal of Health, Sport and Physical Education, 6*(1), 77–91.

Stolz, S.A. & Kirk, D. (2015b). David Kirk on physical education and sport peda-gogy: In dialogue with Steven Stolz (part 2), *Asia-Pacific Journal of Health, Sport and Physical Education, 6*(2), 127–142.

Stolz, S.A. & Pill, S. (2014). Teaching games and sport for understanding: Exploring and reconsidering its relevance in physical education, *European Physical Education Review, 20*(1), 36–71.

Stolz, S.A. & Pill, S. (2016a). A narrative approach to exploring TGfU-GS, *Sport, Education and Society, 21*(2), 239–261.

Stolz, S.A. & Pill, S. (2016b). Telling physical education teacher education tales through pedagogical case studies, *Sport, Education and Society, 21*(6), 868–887.

Stolz, S.A. & Thorburn, M. (2015). A genealogical analysis of Peter Arnold's conceptual account of meaning in movement, sport and physical education, *Sport, Education and Society*. Retrieved from http://dx.doi.org/10.1080/13573322.2015.1032923.

Thomas, G. & Pring, R. (Eds.). (2004). *Evidence-Based Educational Practice*. Milton Keynes: Open University Press.

Thorburn, M. (2008). Articulating a Merleau-Pontian phenomenology of physical education: The quest for active learner engagement and authentic assessment in high-stakes examination awards, *European Physical Education Review, 14*(2), 263–280.

Thorburn, M. & Stolz, S.A. (2015). Embodied learning and school-based physical culture: Implications for professionalism and practice in physical education, *Sport, Education and Society*. Retrieved from http://doi/full/10.1080/13573322.2015.1063993.

Thorpe, S. (2003). Crisis discourse in physical education and the laugh of the Michel Foucault, *Sport, Education and Society, 8*(2), 131–151.

Tinning, R. (2010). *Pedagogy and Human Movement: Theory, Practice, Research*. London & New York: Routledge.

Tinning, R. (2015). 'I don't read fiction': Academic discourse and the relationship between health and physical education, *Sport, Education and Society, 20*(6), 710–721.

Victorian Curriculum and Assessment Authority (VCAA). (2010). *Victorian Certificate of Education Study Design: Physical Education*. Melbourne, Victoria: VCAA.

Whipp, P., Hutton, H., Grove, J., & Jackson, B. (2011). Outsourcing physical education in primary schools: Evaluating the impact of externally provided programmes on generalist teachers, *Asia-Pacific Journal of Health, Sport and Physical Education, 2*(2), 67–77.

Whitson, D. & MacIntosh, D. (1990). The scientization of physical education: Discourses in performance, *Quest, 42*(1), 40–51.

Williams, B. & Macdonald, D. (2015). Explaining outsourcing in health, sport and physical education, *Sport, Education and Society, 20*(1), 57–72.

Williams, B., Hay, P., & Macdonald, D. (2011). The outsourcing of health, sport and physical educational work: A state of play, *Physical Education and Sport Pedagogy, 16*(4), 399–415.

13 Conclusion

Malcolm Thorburn

The preceding 12 chapters have tried to engage readers in reflection and review on the part *Transformative Learning and Teaching in Physical Education* can play in becoming a meaningful component of young people's lives. The elaboration and examples of practice outlined in the various chapters have often challenged hierarchical and behaviourist notions of learning, which have long had a strong foothold in the field of physical education. We have provided these elaborations and examples not in order to be deliberately provocative but to challenge readers to fully engage with the complexities of learning and teaching and to move beyond an uncritical acceptance of existing bodies of knowledge. Making progress on this basis has the potential to challenge existing beliefs, attitudes and understandings and encourage an activist view of teaching, where aiming to be a transformative teacher is a key part of teacher agency.

Therefore, we have written as authors who believe that creating the conditions for transformational learning requires *active* readers prepared to make an *inward* and *outward* turn. The inward turn happens when readers begin to critically reflect on particular experiences and moments in physical education. The outward turn 'involves the changed outlook on the world that arises out of coming to understand oneself – one's wishes, one's capabilities, one's questions, one's needs, one's feelings and one's failures' (English, 2010, p. 88). The merger of the inward and outward turns enables *new* understanding and a different way of viewing learning and teaching and of being in the world.

In this light, we hope that the chapters in *Transformative Learning and Teaching in Physical Education* have made sense not just as a review of current perspectives on physical education but as a connected series of chapters that relate to the reflections readers are having on their experiences of physical education, from wherever these might be arising. For we have argued that the closer the match between reflections on experience and engagement and perspectives-based enquiry, the greater the potential there is for physical education to make a constructive difference to the lives of young people and for ongoing reviews to take place on how gains in practice can be further enhanced and sustained over time.

In making progress in this way the chapter authors have engaged with four key transformative perspectives: a *societal perspective*, which connects with many of the main points of contestation surrounding physical education as part of contemporary schooling; a *theoretical perspective*, which presents an historical and contemporary-informed overview of the varied ways in which physical education can plausibly be conceptualised and supported; a *school perspective*, which helps identify and review many of the diverse ways in which physical education can be a key component in realising whole-school aims; and a *practice perspective*, which critically analyses how teachers' pedagogical practices can enhance high quality learning in physical education.

Societal perspective: The two chapters in this section contrasted some of the main points of contestation surrounding physical education as part of contemporary schooling. Chapter 1 by Malcolm Thorburn focused on 'Physical Education, economic liberalism and the free market' and analysed recent neoliberal changes in professionalism and the influence these may have for the governance of physical education. It was argued that educators could be rather dejected by neoliberalism; indeed, this has almost become the default position within physical education. And, it needs to be recognised that neoliberalism free market imperatives for choice and freedom may well raise professional-related concerns about control and autonomy, and social concerns about increasing inequalities. Furthermore, there may be concerns over the modest funding for physical education and its weak position within curriculum arrangements. That said Thorburn, while recognising that physical education careers may well be more complex to navigate than previously, argued that meeting new governance requirements need not automatically be bad news for physical education. Thorburn argued for a perspective that appreciates that tomorrow's physical education teachers need for their own benefit to continually review: their subject values and professional identity; their role in policy enactment; their involvement in greater networking; their contribution to realising wider societal goals as well as grappling with the multiple odds and ends of neoliberalism.

Chapter 2 by Steven Stolz and Malcolm Thorburn reviewed 'Aims and values in physical education' and specifically whether opposing traditions in physical education can ever be reconciled. The axiological debate in physical education is complex, but essentially revolves around an understanding of instrumental and non-instrumental goods and where to draw and demarcate these. The chapter then tried to answer a self-imposed question: Can rival traditions of physical education ever be resolved? This led to the development of an argument that, for physical education to be transformative, the subject needs to be synthesised into a new tradition based around embodied learning and physical culture. In so doing, the chapter adds to the conceptual vibrancy associated with the historic traditions of physical education through providing a brief outline of how the embodied learning claims of physical education as part of whole-school physical culture might constructively be advanced.

Theoretical perspective: The two chapters in this section presented an historical and contemporary-informed overview of the varied ways in which physical education can plausibly be conceptualised and supported. Chapter 3 by Mike Jess and Matthew Atencio considered how 'The transformational wind of theoretical change' might take place and draws upon studies associated with the Developmental Physical Education Group (DPEG) at the University of Edinburgh over the last 15 years. The chapter discussed from a complexity thinking perspective how new curriculum approaches can help learners negotiate their learning experiences across the lifespan with a clear positioning of physical education as a subject area of educational value. Thereafter, the chapter discussed how efforts are being made to create overarching curriculum frameworks that are more holistic, robust and flexible, and of how the integration of the models-based practice and 'connective specialism' approaches could act as a catalyst to support future overarching curriculum developments.

Thereafter, Chapter 4 by Mike Jess, Nicola Carse and Jeanne Keay focused specifically on primary school teachers' perspectives on physical education through deploying an 'ecological framework and complexity principles as the basis for analysing teachers' professionalism'. This is an important matter, as evidence suggests that traditional professional learning does little to support primary teachers' confidence and competence to teach physical education. Informed by principles from ecological perspectives and complexity thinking, the chapter proposed that professional learning should seek to support teachers' capacity to self-organise their practices in ways that more effectively support children's learning. The chapter continued by exploring key lessons learnt by DPEG as it transitioned from delivering more traditional professional learning programmes towards a more transformative complexity-informed approach. In conclusion, the chapter called for more strategic, long-term and situated approaches to primary physical education developments: approaches that support teachers and builds the capacity to create physical education learning experiences that are developmentally appropriate for all children across their primary school years.

School perspective: The three chapters in this section identified and reviewed many of the diverse ways in which physical education can be a key component in realising whole-school aims. Chapter 5 by Mike Jess considered the 'developmental possibilities for Physical Education' and argued that there is a need for a transformative agenda in primary physical education that operates at three inter-related levels: as a subject area; integrated across the primary school curriculum; and as a catalyst for engagement in a physically active life. Reorienting the curriculum, pedagogy and teacher's professional learning, alongside a 'shifting perspectives' agenda were presented as ways forward for the subject area.

Similarly, Chapter 6 by Justine MacLean was concerned by the factors that enable teachers to initiate curriculum development and enact policy in a context where 'Teachers are agents of policy and curriculum change'. The chapter examined discourses on policy and curriculum change and analysed the complexities involved in enabling teachers to enact new policy in schools that are utilising a flexible curriculum framework. In these contexts, teachers play a central role as 'agents of change'. This requires teachers to translate, mould and recreate policy to fit in with the opportunities and constraints of the cultural, social and material structure in the schools they teach in. In connecting more widely with international knowledge in the field of policy formation as a perspective for analysing teachers' capacity to embrace, translate and transform practice in physical education, the chapter also reviewed the potential for teachers' working environment to enable educational transformation.

Chapter 7 by Andrew Horrell and Rosie Mulholland analysed how 'Supporting professional communities' can take place. The chapter presented findings from an interpretive study that revealed the role professional learning communities played in supporting teachers to reimagine and recast physical education. The role local (unitary) authorities played in the formation of a professional learning community was also highlighted as were the tensions between concepts of professional learning and regimes of accountability. The findings presented lend support to research methodologies that seek to uncover the professional learning teachers engage in during a process of curriculum change, as analysis of data indicated that, although government policy and curriculum frameworks produced organisational effects, these were subject to a complex process of reinterpretation when mapped onto local conditions.

Practice perspective: The four chapters in this section critically analysed how teachers' pedagogical practices can enhance learning in physical education. Chapter 8 by Shirley Gray, Fiona Mitchell and John Wang considered how to 'Create supportive learning environments' and began by reviewing the strategies many governments have taken to promote physical education as part of health and wellbeing within the school and wider social context. In this light, the purpose of the chapter was to highlight the ways in which teachers of physical education might approach this remit and described how success in doing so could be facilitated by a greater awareness of the relationship between the psychological needs of learners and their pedagogical practice. Self-Determination Theory was presented as a framework for understanding how the learning environment created by teachers can support learners' basic psychological needs, which, in turn, impacts positively on learners' intrinsic motivation, personal development and learning and wellbeing in physical education. On this basis, the authors argued that transformation comes from understanding learners and the ways in which they contribute and shape the learning process. From this perspective, teaching is a developmental process that nurtures the inner resources of the learner so that they become independent, motivated, and self-directed learners.

Chapter 9 by Shirley Gray, Kevin Morgan and John Sproule considered further how teachers' pedagogical practices might benefit learners 'Motivation, Learning and Development in Physical Education.' The chapter began by noting that teachers of physical education have often adopted teaching strategies that are both teacher-led and performance-focused. Consequently, the authors outlined three alternative teaching approaches that offer a much broader view of learning in physical education, namely: learner-centred games teaching; a mastery motivational climate; and self-regulated learning. The authors described how each has the potential to facilitate the development of the learner's personal, social and cognitive skills, thus providing learners with a platform for effective and self-regulated learning now and in the future. The authors also argued that for learners to become self-regulating they require a teacher who is also a leader; one who inspires challenges and empowers.

Chapter 10 by Paul McMillan aimed to 'Understand teachers' day-to-day practice' and began by noting similar limitations to those highlighted in Chapter 9 about teachers' practices being over-reliant on forms of 'direct' teaching. However, this chapter argued that these accounts present an unfair picture of the practices of many teachers. The chapter, through reporting on findings from a qualitative research study with six teachers, presented a 'fresh' interpretation of physical education practices in secondary schools. Analysis of observation and interview data confirmed that while direct teaching was evident there were also instances of teacher-guided practice, learner-led practice, teacher–learner-negotiated practice, and learner-initiated practice. Given there was a degree of variation in all the teachers' practices, this empirical evidence contrasted markedly with many strands of existing physical education research. As such, investigating teachers' practice in this way was found to transcend a number of the top-down and taken-for-granted ways in which teaching has previously been conceptualised in physical education.

Chapter 11 by Ben Williamson considered 'the digitised future of physical education' as there is an increased expectation of using digital technology in learning and teaching, especially as recent technological advancements in mobile technologies means that appliances and software can better benefit physical education. The chapter provided an analysis of the emergence of wearable and mobile activity trackers, biosensors and personal analytics apps in physical education, and argued that the algorithmic processes embedded in these devices and software has an increasingly powerful part to play in how people learn about their own bodies and health. These activity-tracking and biosensor technologies rely on algorithmic processes that can analyse data about learners' physical activity and then recommend activities to improve their health and fitness. The algorithmic biopedagogies of activity tracking and biosensing aim to produce 'socially fit biocitizens' who will comport their bodies according to the norms associated with expert medical knowledge, governmental health agendas and commercial ambitions that are combined and enacted by algorithmic processes. The chapter challenged readers to question taken-for-granted assumptions about the role of digital devices and platforms in the quantification of bodies and health during physical education; and concludes by arguing that future research in digitised physical education will need to engage with the biosocial dynamics of physical and digitised environments and the moral, medical and computer codes that connect them with embodied biological and behavioural processes involved in learning.

Taking all of the above chapters into consideration the final chapter (Chapter 12) by Steven Stolz considered 'Past, present and possible futures in physical education' and revisited the *past*, critically discussed the *present*, and offered some thoughts on *possible futures* for physical education. Stolz argued that if progress is to be made in the discipline area of physical education, then dialectical engagement between rival traditions needs to be fostered in such a way that there is a willingness and openness by adherents of each tradition to learn the language of the other in the hope of coming to understand what exactly it is they disagree about. Only when agreement about matters of disagreement has been reached is dialectical engagement between rival traditions possible. If this is not possible, then past historic problems will recur. As a result, how physical education overcomes related challenges will in a major way determine its future.

And, a final associated point . . .

The intention by this stage is that engaging with chapters in *Transformative Learning and Teaching in Physical Education* has provided readers with various perspectives on learning and teaching that motivate them towards building a successful career in physical education and perhaps in education more widely. And, as noted earlier, this involves not only an enhanced knowledge and understanding of learning and teaching in physical education but a connection with readers' own capabilities, thoughts and feelings. Added to this there is a place as well for mentioning *personal commitment*; for, if nothing else, teaching is a giving profession. At the outset of my own career in the late 1970s I read a mountaineering book of the 'against the odds' type about four Scottish mountaineers who tackled for the first time a clutch of remote and unclimbed Himalayan peaks over four months. The expedition was a great success, both in terms of how the four climbers got on with each other and in terms of the achievements realised. In planning for the expedition, the leader, W.H. Murray, stated that:

> Concerning all acts of initiative, there is one elementary truth, the ignorance of which kills countless ideas and splendid plans: that the moment one definitely commits oneself, then Providence moves too. All sorts of things occur to help one that would never otherwise have occurred.
>
> (Murray, 1951, pp. 6–7)

On the basis of my many years in physical education, the notion that timely preparation can lead to successful future eventualities (providence) remains a strong one. The many outstanding teachers of physical education I have had the chance to work alongside and discuss ideas with and observe have all possessed definite commitment. This benefited immensely the quality of learners' learning experience, even though teaching often took place in less than ideal circumstances – modest facilities, relatively small amounts of curriculum time and large class sizes. In short, very good things, sometimes inspirational things, occurred, as definite commitment was part of teachers' professional curiosity, part of their ability to take calculated pedagogical risks, part of their capacity to seek out further knowledge and reflect upon how it might benefit and transform their learning and teaching. So the book concludes with the quiet hope that the various chapters in the book can play a constructive part in developing readers' professional curiosity about learning and teaching in physical education and also in sustaining readers' professional commitment towards making transformative learning and teaching gains.

References

English, A. (2010). Transformation and education: The voice of the learner in Peters' concept of teaching, *Journal of Philosophy of Education, 43*(1), 75–95.

Murray, W.H. (1951). *The Scottish Himalayan Expedition*. London: Dent.

Index